D0723005

CITIZENSHIP EXCESS

CRITICAL CULTURAL COMMUNICATION
General Editors: Sarah Banet-Weiser and Kent A. Ono

Citizenship Excess

Latinas/os, Media, and the Nation

Hector Amaya

NEW YORK UNIVERSITY PRESS
New York and London

NEW YORK UNIVERSITY PRESS
New York and London
www.nyupress.org

References to Internet websites (URLs) were accurate at the time of writing.
Neither the author nor New York University Press is responsible for URLs
that may have expired or changed since the manuscript was prepared.

Library of Congress Cataloging-in-Publication Data
Amaya, Hector.
Citizenship excess : Latinas/os, media, and the nation / Hector Amaya.
p.   cm. — (Critical cultural communication)
Includes bibliographical references and index.
ISBN 978-0-8147-0845-3 (cl : alk. paper) — ISBN 978-0-8147-2413-2
(pb : alk. paper) — ISBN 978-0-8147-2383-8 (e-book) —
ISBN 978-0-8147-2417-0 (e-book)
1. Hispanic Americans. 2. Latin Americans—United States. 3. Citizenship—
United States. 4. Hispanic Americans and mass media—Political aspects.
5. Mass media and immigrants—Political aspects. 6. Racism—United States.
7. United States—Emigration and immigration—Government policy.   I. Title.
E184.S75A43 2013
305.868'073—dc23   2012036851

New York University Press books are printed on acid-free paper,
and their binding materials are chosen for strength and durability.
We strive to use environmentally responsible suppliers and materials
to the greatest extent possible in publishing our books.

Manufactured in the United States of America

c 10 9 8 7 6 5 4 3 2 1
p 10 9 8 7 6 5 4 3 2 1

CONTENTS

And then all good things come to those who have the one best thing. Possess that one, and the others come in train. Or, to change the metaphor, a dominant good is converted into another good, into many others, in accordance with what often appears to be a natural process but is in fact magical, a kind of social alchemy.

—Michael Walzer, *Spheres of Justice*

I have not had a usable citizenship for the past couple of decades. I have been living in the United States with a Mexican passport. I moved away from Mexico, my country of birth, in 1992 and have lived a life that I did not plan. I could not have planned it. In Navojoa, the small Mexican northern city where I was born, I had few contacts with immigrants, and immigrant narratives were relatively rare, unless they came from Hollywood films. Who can forget Chaplin on the move? Several uncles, aunts, and even my sister eventually migrated to either Los Angeles or Calgary before me, but I now recognize that the years when they were immigrants and I was not, they spoke about their experiences too enthusiastically, even when describing the penuries of loneliness in countries not theirs. It was not their fault. I know that as an immigrant I have never fully talked about the strangeness of my experiences to people back in Mexico, not because I am trying to hide it but more because I am a bit ashamed of complaining while stubbornly holding on to a life-project that I chose and has given me some grief. There is also some guilt about complaining about emotional things while my wallet is full. I am a professor, after all: do I really have the right to complain?

My life is relatively good, but not having a usable citizenship has become a constant issue and the inspiration for my scholarship. I live in a political world in which I cannot fully participate. But I would be lying if I claimed to feel always victimized. That is not how it works. For the most part, there is simply a strong sense of otherness that marks my affective relations to social and political systems. Once in a while I do feel outraged or moved to commiseration. A few other times, I actually take pleasure in my difference and relish being able to step back and simply watch, like an anthropologist, the world unfold with the strange logic of an alien civilization. In all of these issues, I am not the standard but the exception. Most residents of the United States who walk around without citizenship have more reasons than I to be outraged. The majority of immigrants from Latin American must fight against poverty, biased law enforcement, educational systems that refuse to treat them as equals, and, increasingly, a lack of political rights and basic access to basic goods and social benefits. To make matters worse, Latino culture and Latino media seem marginal. What is the value of Univision or Telemundo if you cannot talk about telenovelas around the cooler with others? Latino social networks seem overdetermined, socially engineered by a masterful mind set on ghettoizing immigrant life. The incentives seem sweet enough: the Mexican store around the corner; the international-food aisle at the supermarket; the American Express card; every four years, the World Cup of soccer (Go Costa Rica! Go Mexico! Go El Salvador!); politicians trying to talk in Spanish (often a bit funny); and Spanish-language media reminding you that you belong to a large community of nonbelongers.

I have thought enough about citizenship that I could come up with dozens of silly similes to try to explain how it feels not having it (for instance, "Not having citizenship is like walking without shoes"). I will spare you. Neither will I place in front of you a tragic narrative exploring our postcoloniality, our loss, becoming undone. I will also try to avoid constructing a romance that lionizes a fight against all odds. Instead, in this book, I explore a simple metaphor from another scholar. In the epigraph, Walzer talks about dominant goods, and throughout the book, he discusses citizenship and wealth as two such goods. Compellingly, he describes how dominant goods have currency in many social fields, and thus they assure the bearer a trading advantage. Over time, this trading advantage in multiple social spheres accumulates and exponentially multiplies, allowing the possessor of the one good to be at the top of many hierarchies. Echoing Walzer, this book shows the centrality of citizenship. But unlike Walzer, I am invested in querying liberalism and the public sphere, two central theoretical constructs that explain and reconstitute the centrality of citizenship. My hope is to provide a theoretical framework and vocabulary that explains the state of marginalization of Latinas/os in the United States.

I need to thank an array of people, organizations, and institutions that were essential for the completion of this project. I first have to mention Southwestern University, the place where I began writing on the subject of citizenship and Latinas/os seven years ago. There, I received expert and kind advice from Mary Grace Neville, Jay Baglia, Teena Gabrielson, Erika Berroth, and Katy Ross, who lent me their editing and theoretical skills. However, the book itself was written at the University of Virginia, a place where Jeffersonian ideals seep deeply into the ground. It is perhaps natural that it is in these buildings and gardens, full of hope for the political, that my own reflections on citizenship, discourse, justice, and equality happened.

At University of Virginia, I received the sustained support of the College of Arts and Sciences, Dean Meredith Woo, Associate Dean Karen Parshall, and Vice President for Research Dr. Thomas Skalak. Last, I have to thank the Department of Media Studies at the University of Virginia, Chair Andrea Press, and the Verklin Program on Media Ethics for energizing my research financially and emotionally.

My writing group at the University of Virginia must be singled out for providing me with their expertise and insights every step of the way. This book could not have happened without them. Sylvia Chong, Daniel Chavez, and Jennifer Petersen have left a deep imprint in my work, and their knowledge on ethnicity, race, film, media, and the juridical are now central to the project. I cannot thank them enough for their patience, their theoretical views, and the unwavering commitment to excellence that pushed me forward. Last, I need to thank New York University Press for providing such a rigorous set of reviewers.

Biography is also origins. I wish to thank my parents, Mita and Hector, who are the real origin of the book and to whom this work is dedicated. They are the structure in my thought, my moral fiber, and my perseverance; whatever wisdom I may possess I have only borrowed from them.

Introduction: Latinas/os and Citizenship Excess

In April 2010, Arizona governor Jan Brewer signed what at the time many observers considered the toughest immigration bill in the nation at a state level (Archibold 2010). The law ordered immigrants to carry their alien registration documents at all times and required police to question any detainees that they believed might be in the United States illegally. Opponents of the law argued that it would inevitably lead to racial profiling against the Latino population. In the weeks that followed, a mediated national debate about the merits of the law pitted Latino groups, human rights and social justice activists, nativist organizations, politicians, city councils, members of state and federal congresses, and an ever-polarizing media against each other. President Obama criticized the law but also explicitly agreed with some of the rationale used by Governor Brewer; he allocated an additional twelve hundred National Guard troops and half a billion dollars for increased border security. In the weeks that followed, politicians in other states began contemplating copying Arizona's law. On May 2010, the Quinnipiac University Polling Institute released data showing that a majority of voters wanted similar laws passed in their states (48 percent versus 35 percent). The support for this type of legislation came despite the fact that the majority of voters also believed (45 percent versus 40 percent) that it would lead to discrimination against Hispanics (Quinnipiac's terminology). Tellingly, according to Quinnipiac, the majority of blacks and Latinas/os opposed the legislation. As in other times in history, state discrimination and mistreatment of minorities was accepted as reasonable, a sacrifice the majority was willing to make for the well-being of the nation-state. Here, a majority defined the nation-state decisively and undisputedly in ethno-racial terms and embraced political and legal excess as the proper privilege of ethno-racially white citizenship.[1]

Inspired by events such as those in Arizona, this book introduces *citizenship excess* to investigate the convergence of legal and political excess with ethno-racial privilege. Citizenship excess theorizes that citizenship is inherently a process of uneven political capital accumulation and that the unevenness follows ethno-racial lines. As important, the term *excess* signals that citizenship cannot be rehabilitated within the nation-state. This theory helps us see that excess happens when those who are in power can organize political markets in such a way that political transactions yield a surplus value that they accumulate. The accumulation of such surplus political value, over time, becomes the basis for more and for easier accumulation.

Citizenship excess is a political and media theory that explains ethno-racial inequality as the product of the nation-state and the political, cultural, and legal systems that sustain it. In particular, citizenship excess explains why Latinas/os in general and immigrant Latinas/os in particular are the target of so much ethnic resentment and hate by a large portion of the citizenry and by mainstream politicians, media, and law. I find the problem very complex and traditional racial explanations of why this is happening rather unsatisfactory. Traditional U.S. explanations of race, such as those put forward by Michael Omi and Howard Winant (1994), emphasize vertical racial hierarchies within nations. Their theory of racial formations would explain anti-Latino and anti-immigrant sentiment as a sort of pushing down of these communities with the goal of reproducing a vertical racial hierarchy with whites on top and the rest fighting for political crumbs. As in Omi and Winant's explanation, citizenship excess starts with empirically verifiable vertical racial hierarchies in the United States, but it historicizes and theorizes these hierarchies in transnational terms, as hierarchies that are not strictly vertical: they are also about geography, about the difference between the here and there, about borders, about us-versus-them and the protection of the nation-state. Citizenship excess hence explains anti-Latino and anti-immigrant sentiment as both a pushing down (racism) and a pushing away (xenophobia) that accomplishes the goal of preserving the ethno-racial character of the nation-state. That is, citizenship excess is concerned with the ability of whites to claim a legitimate monopoly over the state. This ability is based in ideas of race that not only work internally (as vertical hierarchies) but are always embedded in transnational relations and politics *because* they originated in transnational relations and were used to justify internal and external colonialism (D. Gutiérrez 1999; Molina-Guzmán 2010, 14; Pérez 2004, 6, 95; Ana Rodríguez 2002; Romero and Habell-Pallán 2002, 4; Valdivia 2008). I call this theory *citizenship excess* because it is the citizen who is the political actor within the nation-state, because citizenship is how we articulate the relationship of individuals to states, and therefore citizenship and its excess is how we express ethno-racial supremacy.

To construct political legitimacy in today's society requires media, and therefore citizenship excess is also a media theory that explains how media structures participate in the pushing down and the pushing away of Latinas/os. The pushing down is done by discriminating against Latino participation in mainstream media (discussed in chapter 5) and by foreclosing Latino participation in media narratives that problematize Latino life in the United States (discussed in chapters 3 and 6). As in politics, the pushing down secures the preservation of vertical ethno-racial hierarchies.[2] The pushing away is accomplished in media through processes of ethnic and linguistic balkanization that separate Spanish-language media (SLM), the only segment of U.S. media that consistently serves Latinas/os, from mainstream media, which most Americans define in linguistic terms (discussed in chapters 2 and 4). The pushing away reconstructs the walls that stop access of Latinas/os to traditional ethno-racially white media, hence making it practically impossible for Latinas/os to participate in the majority's public sphere. Both the discrimination (pushing down) and balkanization (pushing away) of Latinas/os secure the supremacy of ethno-racially white interests in political cultures and over the state.

The theory of citizenship excess is rooted in history, and it relies on a set of political and cultural theories that explain political capital accumulation and its impact on Latinas/os. This introductory chapter elaborates on these roots by showing that uneven ethno-racial political capital accumulation is an intrinsic and foundational characteristic of the United States that relates to its political roots and that is crucial to the way political majorities have debated and treated Latinas/os. As importantly, this unevenness is a political and legal foundation of the nation-state and not only the contingent manifestation of deep-seated racism and xenophobia that surfaces in times of political and economic crisis. I support this claim with scholarship on race, gender, and globalization coming from political theory, critical legal studies, citizenship studies, critical race theory, and Latino studies.[3] So I do not make this claim alone, but I bring to the table the language of excess and do so for a very tactical reason. Excess signals that this theory of citizenship is filtered through a Marxian understanding of politics based on one axiom: political and judicial systems can be described as interrelated social fields that follow economic rules. Just as excess of economic wealth is a social problem, I argue that excess of political capital is a political and legal problem. The political and legal fields, which define the nation-state, organize the production and distribution of political goods and give political and legal ground to the racism and xenophobia that give meaning and texture to the lives of Latinas/os in the United States.

In the following sections, I bridge the gap between citizenship excess and a Marxian view of politics and critical race theory, the two most immediate theoretical contexts for citizenship excess. The link to Marx explains the reason for choosing the word *excess*, and the link to critical race theory explains why I approach the problem of ethno-racial inequality from the perspective of citizenship and not centrally from the perspective of race. These sections should prepare us to tackle the basic question of why I use citizenship excess and not simply citizenship or, if you wish, what is the difference between citizenship and citizenship excess and what are the advantages of using the term *citizenship excess*. My goal is that by the end of the introduction, I will have shown that there is something intrinsically poisonous in citizenship, a quality that cannot fully be contained, an excess that feeds the power hungry and that convinces otherwise good people that oppression is just.

The Marxist Roots of Citizenship Excess

Today, Arizona is not the exception but the rule. The first decade of the new century has been very difficult for Latinas/os in general and Latino immigrants in particular.[4] A decade that began with the recognition that the number of Latinas/os was growing at a remarkable pace became a decade of anti-Latino and anti-immigrant politics. Our media environment reflected this duality, with SLM extolling the national benefits of Latino growth, and, increasingly, large portions of English-language media (ELM) crying foul. What began as fringe politics and extreme ELM by decade's end had become relatively mainstream nativism and ethnonationalism mostly against Latina/o immigrants. By *nativism* I mean the "opposition to a minority on the basis of their 'foreignness'" (Jacobson 2008, xxi). With *ethnonationalism* I refer to a strong affective investment in a nation that is defined in terms of ethnicity (Connor 1994, xi). Both nativism and ethnonationalism are the pushing away, the xenophobia, I referenced earlier. They share the political view that the United States ought to remain an ethno-racially white nation with ethno-racially white values and socio-cultural characteristics. Unlike nativism, ethnonationalism may welcome immigrants, but only after they radically assimilate.[5] Arguably, ethnonationalism is a milder form of nativism. For brevity's sake, I will refer to both groups of people who espouse these views as nativists but will specify when needed as to whether the nativism I refer to is radical or mild. In this book, I am concerned with political, social, and media events that have pitted Latinas/os against vocal and powerful nativist forces. I am concerned with social, cultural, and political battles that will undoubtedly shape the future of Latinas/os and the type of liberal democracy the United States will have in the twenty-first century. I am referring to battles such as immigration and securitization, which are broad sites of conflict in which Latinas/os and nativists play important but different roles as social agents. Nativists try to harness the power of the state to discipline, control, and shape the political potential, and future, of Latinas/os. Latinas/os try to appeal to broader definitions of belonging and liberalism to claim the complex rights of citizenship. In a post-9/11 world, these battles have been won by nativists who have used the issues of immigration and securitization to produce anti-Latino legal and political structures, as in recent events in Arizona. For me, the issue is how to make sense of these very complex phenomena without losing sight of the key moving pieces and their histories. So applying some Marxian and economic ideas helped me organize these moving pieces and allowed me to see a predictable pattern in the way discourses and practices were woven through time.[6] This pattern has three types of effects, which produce three types of citizenship excess: institutional effects, which I discuss first; specific forms of consciousness; and political and cultural effects, which I discuss in the following sections and in the rest of the book. So let me start by quickly describing this Marxian perspective. I will do so, first, by describing how this perspective organizes four of the key moving pieces. The next sections will deepen these propositions.

Citizenship Excess at Institutions

The four moving pieces are tightly interwoven in a dramatic structure, a battle over social positions and political power between (1) nativists and (2) Latinas/os that is brokered by (3) the state and (4) the media. (1) There is broad anti-Latino hate among the political right deeply influenced by nativism and a general anti-Latino sentiment among the majority of the U.S. population. Nativists concentrate their hate and political efforts on attacking undocumented immigrants, but nativists also have broad concerns about the willingness of immigrant Latinas/os to assimilate, to learn English, and to play by the political and economic rules by which everybody else plays. (2) Latinas/os are becoming more powerful, and they showed their political might in the pro-immigration reform marches. Latino civic organizing has succeeded at making visible the might of the Latino electorate, and that has influenced local and state politics, but in 2006, Latinas/os failed to push for immigration reform at the federal level. (3) Although ideally the state should broker between groups, that has not been the case. Under Republican control from 2000 to 2008, the state, as represented by the political and legal systems, seemed co-opted by nativists, and it produced, through legal or political systems, anti-Latino law. Although Democrats took control of the federal government in 2008, the influence of nativism did not subside. In 2010, Republicans, energized by a Tea Party that includes many nativist voices, took control of the House of Representatives, and, with that, the power of nativists to set the political agenda was cemented.[7] Simply, the power of the state to broker between nativists and Latinas/os is practically gone. (4) Ideally, media, in its capacity as public sphere, should be a space where different groups can come together and present their points of view, debate them, and influence general public opinion. That is the way the Founding Fathers imagined it; it is the way most Americans think of it today. So, has media played the role of a public sphere? In the United States, we have an incredibly dynamic and diverse media system that, regardless of its dynamism and variety, has failed to provide a general platform for Latino voices. Simply put, it has gone nativist. This is not only because of Fox and Rupert Murdoch but also because of CNN (Lou Dobbs), talk radio, and the general unwillingness of mainstream fictional media to include Latino narratives. Ironically, SLM, which serves the majority of Latinas/ os, has been thriving, but it is isolated and incapable of shaping general public opinion because of linguistic differences. So, like the state, the power of the media to broker seems negligible, and the fight between Latinas/os and nativists appears absolutely rigged. How do we explain these complex and important phenomena, particularly as this type of national scenario seems to echo events in Europe, where nativism also seems to be on the rise?

We can start by noting that we are witnessing a battle of Marxian proportions between the haves and the have-nots. Nativists are economically wealthier, and they have sizable political capital because they claimed legal and cultural ownership of the U.S. territory. Nativists then transform this political capital into legal and cultural capital (Bourdieu 1986).[8] For instance, nativists characterize undocumented immigration in terms of sovereignty under threat. This narrative has played wonderfully in political cultures and media, and it has provided the narrative energy for news that framed Latino immigrants as an invading horde, the barbarians knocking at the walls, and the nativists as defenders of the motherland. Latinas/os, on the other hand, are poorer; they have weak territorial claims; and the legal and political frameworks that, since the 1960s, have given them a foothold in the state have become increasingly unpopular since Reagan.[9] Yes, Latino numbers have been growing, but this also means that the Latino population seems more like a threat to a majority that, after 9/11, is too concerned with security of the physical and economic kind. So nativists have accumulated political capital that they have used both to accumulate even more political, legal, and cultural capital and to make their political messages seem more mainstream. In contrast, Latinas/os' political capital has dwindled, and the losses have been in direct proportion to the gains of nativists.

The Marxian analogy does not end here. Witnessing the past couple of decades of political battles between nativists and Latinas/os, it is impossible not to notice a certain economic logic to the way political and legal losses and gains have been allocated. Pierre Bourdieu's work on political and cultural capital is useful here to help us understand that society works as a giant political market, a field of power if you wish, where different communities bring their wares and trade with the goal of surviving or moving up the political and cultural ladder.[10] Following Bourdieu, I propose that the political market follows a few basic rules of trade that are easily observable and worth mentioning right here:

- The first thing that is striking about this field of power is that in order to participate, you must be a citizen. Noncitizens have practically no say, and undocumented immigrants are simply the worst off of the have-nots.
- Although all citizens are allowed to participate in the field of power, the most politically wealthy class is ethno-racially defined. They tend to be white and economically wealthy; they often attend the same universities; and they are frequently members of the same clubs. They also have the habit of speaking on behalf of everybody else and succeed at doing so because they often own or control media. It is not a monolithic class. Others may become part of it, but they must adopt the "ethnic" part of the ethno-racial. Those who wish to join the ranks of the political elite must speak with their accent, eat their food, go to the same universities, and succeed at accumulating something that can be traded for political wares, for example, money, cultural capital, or votes.
- This giant field of power allows for trade in several fine currencies including votes and civic behavior. But there is no finer currency than law, and many citizens would gladly trade their political wares for having their views become law.[11] So communities with quick access to legal systems have the power to trade that access in exchange for the votes and energetic civic behavior of other communities.
- Although a great deal of political capital is the accumulation of political currencies, such as votes and civic behavior ("I will vote for your proposal if you vote for mine"; "I will march for your cause if you march for mine"), political capital is also the result of currency accumulated in other social markets including wealth, prestige, and, as Bourdieu (1986) would note, cultural capital.
- Because law not only applies to the political market but shapes every other social market including the financial, cultural, educational, labor, health, housing, and media markets, the accumulation of political capital typically translates well into accumulation in other markets (Dudziak and Volpp 2005; Oliver and Shapiro 2006). Bourdieu calls this principle "interconvertibility," or the ability of one type of capital to be converted into other types.[12] In Arizona, for instance, shortly after the draconian immigration bill I mentioned earlier, the government produced a law prohibiting the teaching of Ethnic Studies in public schools. Ethnic Studies is the only area of the public school curriculum that places the history of

ethno-racial minorities at its center, and as a result, it is a type of cultural capital for ethnic minorities.

- Similarly, decreased political capital can easily translate into decreased capital in other markets. A lack of political capital is quickly converted into a lack of prestige or cultural capital, and this is typically the case for ethno-racial minorities and immigrant populations. Forbidding Ethnic Studies in public schools in Arizona decreases the prestige and cultural capital of ethno-racial minorities in the state.

What these rules tell me about the field of power is that, left to its own devices, it tends to produce excessive accumulation of political capital, and this tends to end up in the hands of citizens who are ethno-racially defined. Although these communities are not racially monolithic (e.g., President Obama or Governor Bill Richardson), they tend to welcome those who are white and those who are willing to assimilate by taking on white ethnic markers.

Of course, the field of power was never left to its own devices, and there have been plenty of legal, administrative, and discursive tools meant to provide checks and balances. We have always had administrative walls separating politics from other social fields, and none were more essential than the walls separating wealth from politics, those two most important social fields. But new laws allowing corporations almost unrestricted access to the political system by giving them free rein to fund election campaigns are increasingly eroding these walls.[13] The ability to convert economic capital into political capital has become a grotesque part of our political present, and the results are in: the advertising cost of the 2010 elections (which was not a presidential election) was upward of $3.7 billion. Who can compete? Not many. Our media system is rich and has the potential to be prolific and diverse, but after the 1996 Telecommunications Act, our media has consolidated so that only a few corporations dominate most of the public sphere. Powerful political classes have used extraordinary events such as 9/11 to transform the institutional character of important government agencies and to reframe their activities in terms of security. Significantly, the creation of the Department of Homeland Security (DHS) and the move of the Immigration and Naturalization Service to the DHS have permanently transformed both the discourse around immigration and state practices toward immigrants into state practices against immigration. And, perhaps most importantly, we have drastically redefined liberalism and republicanism,[14] two political

platforms that were meant to remind us that the role of the state is to provide the ground for all sorts of equality and that all people should have a
right to participate in government. What happened to this definition of
liberalism and republicanism? There are two types of answer that can help
us here. One would propose that liberalism and republicanism are under
siege and have been perverted by capitalism (neoliberalism) and racist
xenophobia. The second view argues that liberalism and republicanism
were never that pure. Thanks to critical legal scholars, political scientists,
critical race theorists, and theorists of globalization, we know that liberalism and republicanism share too much genetic material with colonialism, racism, and imperialism to be so pure, and I show this throughout
the book. Liberalism and republicanism appear alongside the formation
of nation-states and alongside a world economy that depends on colonial
expansion and uses theories of race and racist theories of law to justify
human exploitation and land robbery. I expand on these points in the following section, but now I want to mention one last lesson from Marx that
is worth remembering.

Citizenship Excess, Forms of Consciousness and Culture

Besides inspiring us to see the nation-state as a field of power where political capital is accumulated in complex but predictable ways, Marx is
useful for helping us think about the long-term effects of social systems
on forms of consciousness and culture. When Marx investigated the capitalism he encountered in the nineteenth century, he used the figure of the
bourgeoisie to criticize a class of people capable of controlling the narrative frames that reconstituted their privilege. These frames centered on
the values of profit, entrepreneurship, and efficiency in everyday life. They
worked because all classes shared them, albeit as different elements of the
narrative of wealth. I believe the long-term effects of citizenship excess
impact consciousness in complex ways, producing an array of platforms
for subjectivities and identities that allow for this relatively rigid political
system to be legitimated by the majority. Not all of these effects translate
into racism and xenophobia, but some do. Other effects simply help the
majority rationalize the current system, even while recognizing its imperfections. With Marx and Michel Foucault, I believe one of the most
common and deepest effects on consciousness is interiorizing the law,
or what Foucault calls the production of "juridical subjectivities." When
I mention these juridical subjectivities, I have in mind the now-famous

"Letter from Birmingham Jail," written by Dr. Martin Luther King Jr. in 1963 during one of the harshest moments of his political career. In this letter, Dr. King responded to clergymen who complained about the timing of the marches and who, Dr. King believed, would have preferred the embrace of slow reform instead of the push for speedy resolutions to the racist law that African Americans were facing. These clergymen seem the perfect example of complicit majorities that would rather endure the racial oppression of others than challenge racist law. These majorities are similar to the majorities today that would rather tolerate racial discrimination against Latinas/os than oppose legal frameworks such as the one passed in Arizona in 2010. These majorities have interiorized the law in such a way that it is easier for them to imagine that state harmony is more important than opposing the state in the name of justice. While political capital accumulation speaks to institutionalized citizenship excess, modern forms of consciousness that reproduce internal and external colonialisms are also evidence of citizenship excess that shape contemporary political cultures. These forms of consciousness include harsh forms of excess as in nativism, racism, and xenophobia but also more ambiguous forms of consciousness that are often complicit or implicitly supportive of uneven political capital accumulation. These latter forms include ethnonationalism and the coward liberalism exemplified by the clergymen and most of the respondents to Quinnipiac's polls who would tolerate racial profiling of Latinas/os. According to citizenship excess, both harsh and ambiguous forms of consciousness contribute to ethno-racial injustice.

Inspired by Marx, a term such as *political capital accumulation* is meant to suggest that the distribution of rights and duties is unequal and that this inequality is patterned. This book, like most citizenship studies, shows that this pattern is partly based on ascription, that is, on birth characteristics such as race, ethnicity, gender, and nationality. Just as wealth attracts wealth, political capital seems to attract more political capital, making the pathways to social and political relevance of some people much easier to navigate than the paths of others. The point of accumulating political capital is to allow easier access to positions within the political field, as Bourdieu shows in other contexts with other types of capital. Just as ascription is not destiny, some bearers of the wrong ascription(s) can negotiate the difficult paths to social and political relevance. But a few success stories are not likely to change the basic pattern of resource distribution that the excesses of citizenship produces. Nor are they likely to challenge the basic political values that give control of a nation-state to a relatively small political class whose tenure in power is maintained by accumulated political capital and by political cultures that reproduce narrow definitions of political action and political agency.

Citizenship Excess and Critical Race Theory

Citizenship excess follows contemporary understandings of race and is directly indebted to the theories of racialization by Omi and Winant (1986, 1994), including the latest theories by Winant (2004), which recast the problem of race as a global problem. Omi and Winant's theory of racial formation "refers to the process by which social, economic, and political forces determine the content and importance of racial categories" (1986, 61). Racial formations change over time, as do the meanings of race, racial etiquettes, and the aspects of life that are understood as racial. Citizenship excess theorizes the contemporary racial formation in the United States that is determining Latinas/os' lived experiences. So, in one sense, citizenship excess is an application of the theory of racial formation that accounts for the growing importance of immigration, nativism, and linguistically differentiated media in the lives of Latinas/os. In another sense, citizenship excess reframes Omi and Winant's ideas on race by proposing that the hierarchical power of race, the ability race has to naturalize and produce power differences, has been its ability to speak to ethno-territoriality, the link between a people and a territory (N. Rose 1999, 113).[15] Ethno-territoriality has helped establish legal or illegal sovereignty over land. When mixed with race, ethno-territoriality provides the legal framework for imperialism, as when European colonizers of the New World defined it as *terra nullius*, empty land. As noted by Omi and Winant, theories of race, from the conquest of the Americas to the present, were created and have been consistently used to justify, explain, and promote territorial expansion and the plundering of other geographies (1986, 58–59). European in origin, ethno-territorial theories of race were part of the political, cultural, and legal arsenal that the British, French, and Spanish used in North America to destroy local Native American cultures, to uproot Africans and subject them as slaves in the British colonies, to colonize Mexican territory and force subjection on Mexicans, and to foster the importation and exploitation of labor from Asia. As important for this book, ethno-territorial theories of race later became nationalized in nativism, which discriminates against the foreigner; in ethnonationalism, which equates the values of the white ethnicity with the state;

and in legal theories of citizenship. Because of this, I believe that Omi and Winant's ideas about race must work in concert with theories that account for ethno-territoriality in order to explain the U.S. racial formation from a Latino perspective. Citizenship excess is one such theory.

Citizenship excess illustrates a particular racial formation and gives contingent meaning to the relation of race in a state and society increasingly attentive to racialized language (Oliver and Shapiro 2006, 37). So the issue becomes, how do we manage to sustain racial difference within legal and political systems increasingly aware that racism is bad? Here, I am not saying that our law is not racist. What I am saying is that in order to have racial effects, the meaning of race had to be dramatically changed, and it changed in two significant ways. It generated what Eduardo Bonilla-Silva (2001, 193), Herman Gray (2010), and Carter Wilson (1996, 219), among others, call the new racism, a type of racism that is institutionally hidden and that has the effect of stratifying without using openly racially prejudicial language. This new racism appears in the way racial language has been excised from law and much policy. In legal decisions such as those that have eroded affirmative action in the past fifteen years, the decision is often posed in terms of ending racism by ending racial discrimination against whites. This new racism has also generated a puzzling new form of racial consciousness. Today, everyone seems to be engaged in the project of ending racism, and yet the effects of racism do not end. One finds this commitment to ending racism among the Minutemen, the vigilante organization monitoring the U.S.-Mexico border, or among skinheads (see http://skinheads.net), who nonetheless rant about all sorts of racial others. I recognize that both issues can be answered by pointing out that neither the legal system nor the ultraright are honest when they say they reject racism. Perhaps deep down they remain equally committed to racial hierarchies. Perhaps. But my point is that in today's racial formation, nobody can be openly racist, not even the state: how is it, then, that the effects of racism persist?

The answer to this important question is partly the new racism, an answer that fits with Omi and Winant, but also partly the evolution of citizenship. The meaning of race has been changing since the abstracting language of the law made citizenship the foundation of the state (Hong 2006, 11, 32). Although for most of U.S. history race and sex have determined citizenship, the process of making citizenship a more abstract category continues moving forward, as noted by Omi and Winant and any legal historian of the nineteenth and twentieth centuries. Today, as Melvin

Oliver and Thomas Shapiro (2006) have argued in their work on wealth inequality in the United States, the push-down effects of racism are made possible by insidious law and political policies that never mention race but that seem to be calculated to have long-lasting racial outcomes, such as housing policy, lending practices, public-education funding policies and laws, health care policy, and, I would add, media policy. In other words, if legal language in the eighteenth, the nineteenth, and part of the twentieth century could explicitly discriminate based on race, today the state cannot use that language, even if the goal of politicians and lawmakers is to produce law and policy that stratifies racially.[16] This old-style racism is out of political fashion as a public performance of political selfhood.[17]

The modern state, however, remains deeply ethno-territorial, and the pushing-away effects of xenophobia continue to be quite central to the law. With fear and sadness, we have witnessed the rise of nativism and ethnonationalism as accepted political and legal platforms in the United States, France, Germany, Italy, Spain, Japan, and even Denmark, Sweden, and Holland, which are often treated as the socialist-democratic exceptions where things are simply better. In the United States, it is quite okay to speak against immigrants, Spanish speakers, Islam, and other nations without being excommunicated from the mainstream political community. It is worth mentioning that the effects of this pushing away are, like racism, hierarchical and have the long-term effect of debilitating the political strength of ethno-racial minorities, of foreclosing avenues to political power centers, of producing injurious stereotypes that make prestige impossible, and of devaluating ethnic cultural markers. In what political market can speaking two languages become a political deficit? Bilingualism is a political and cultural deficit in the political markets of many advanced nation-states: in the United States, if your first language is Spanish and your second language is English; in Germany, if your first language is Turkish and your second language is German; in France, if your first language is Arabic and your second language is French. Ethno-territoriality shapes the field of power and efficiently overvaluates and devaluates political and cultural goods on the basis of national, ethnic, and racial origin.

In the current racial formation, Latinas/os suffer the double damage of highly abstract forms of state citizenship excess, the new racism, that have racial effects (in, for instance, the unequal funding of public schooling) and direct forms of state citizenship excess that have xenophobic roots (as in the adoption of English as the official language of twenty-eight states and hundreds of English-only initiatives across the nation).

I have begun assembling the theoretical scaffolding that will allow me to engage the large claim mentioned at the beginning of this introductory chapter: citizenship excess proposes that uneven ethno-racial political capital accumulation is a political and legal foundation of the nation-state. The following section has the goal of explaining how citizenship excess differs from common uses of citizenship in contemporary citizenship studies, and it argues that this difference is important because it is the grounds for a particular type of analysis of the nation-state, one that is more attentive to the ethno-territorial, to the nation-state in the world system, and to the evolution of racist and xenophobic culture and law. To illustrate the type of critical analysis that results from citizenship excess, I use the case of Latinas/os and their complex relationship to U.S. political, cultural, and legal systems.

From Citizenship to Citizenship Excess

There is something intrinsically confusing about the term *citizenship*. It is used in so many different and interrelated ways that it is hard, in one glance, to envision the spectrum of things and practices referred to by it. This book may add to the complexity by introducing yet another term and definition for citizenship, albeit with the modifier *excess*, but this section explains why this addition is necessary. Moreover, here I narrow down the spectrum of things and practices that I understand as citizenship and explain the difference between citizenship and citizenship excess. To do this, I will first briefly reflect on the definitions of citizenship that I find more inspiring. I will then explain how citizenship excess relates to these definitions and describe the types of historiographies of the nation and of Latinas/os that are engendered by citizenship excess. I will never claim that citizenship excess engenders a fully unique type of historiography of the nation or Latinas/os. What I will argue is that citizenship excess will always remind us of the most troublesome roots of citizenship and of the modern nation-state.

The better uses of *citizenship*, in my view, define it as political, legal, and cultural processes that give shape to the nation-state, the citizen, and the national political community. So citizenship is more than the ability to have a passport or to be a national. Citizenship is technology of power that has productive capabilities at the level of institutions (the nation-state), forms of consciousness (the citizen), and political and cultural practices (the national political community). In this spirit, Engin Isin and

Patricia Wood write, "We conceive of citizenship broadly—not only as a set of legal obligations and entitlements which individuals possess by virtue of their membership in a state, but also as the practices through which individuals and groups formulate and claim new rights or struggle to expand or maintain existing rights" (1999, 4). Echoing this complex political weaving, Suzanne Oboler notes that "to speak of citizenship in any meaningful way is, thus, to speak of the specific historically constituted, politically verified, and socially conditioned and differentiated relations within and across sovereign communities" (2006, 4). While also emphasizing political practices and relations, others such as Toby Miller (1993, xvii), Lauren Berlant (2002, 107–108) and Anthony Elliott (2001, 51) conceive of citizenship as a technology of power by which nation-states constitute modern political forms of consciousness, including political agents and political subjectivities. Through political practices, the political agent structures the political world and gives fluidity to the nation-state. Modern political subjectivities, these scholars would note, are not individual; they are determined by history, discourse, and social and racial formations.[18] Otherwise stated, the very large institution that we call the nation-state has some flexibility and can be changed by political agents engaged in political activism. But the nation-state is also quite resilient and very hard to change, and this is partly because our political subjectivities, which are determined often by discourse, histories, and practices that legitimize the state, reduce the likeliness of massive and effective activism.

As a technology of power, citizenship has both positive and negative historical effects on Latinas/os.[19] Some Latinas/os have benefited from curious racializations that allowed them to claim a Latinidad rooted in Europe; for instance, significant groups of wealthy Mexicans in New Mexico and California have enjoyed relatively robust versions of citizenship since the nineteenth century. The Treaty of Guadalupe Hidalgo, the document that in 1848 legally formalized the annexation of half of Mexico by the United States, included the provision that Mexican citizenship should be respected and converted into U.S. citizenship. U.S. citizenship, hence, was collectively and automatically granted to the roughly 120,000 Mexican citizens in the southwest territories, but at the time, U.S. citizenship was restricted to whites; so, of necessity, Mexicans were classified as whites (Carbado 2005, 637).[20] Nevertheless, the great majority of Mexicans did not enjoy the social and legal benefits of whiteness and instead suffered from the systematic erosion of all rights, including property rights, originally drawn in Mexican law, as well as political and linguistic rights. Some

Mexican elites, however, were able to exploit the legal descriptor of whiteness and became incorporated into the process of colonization, acting as mediators between U.S. white interests and the rest of the newly annexed residents, which included poor Mexicans, Native Americans (who were a large part of the population in such as places as New Mexico), and African Americans (Glenn 2002, 146; Gómez 2007, 81–115; see also Montejano 1987). More recently, the majority of Latinas/os have benefited from the expansion of citizenship rights that happened as a result of civil rights struggles and that include a legacy of vibrant egalitarian legal and policy frameworks. Significant outcomes of this era include the Bilingual Education Act of 1968, the Voting Rights Act of 1965, and the 1982 Supreme Court ruling in *Plyler v. Doe*, which guaranteed the right of undocumented children to attend public schools.

The benefits to Latinas/os because of citizenship are, however, dwarfed by the significant damages this technology of power has brought to Latinas/os. For instance, citizenship law has been part of the imperial arsenal used to subject Latinas/os, and the two clearest examples of this are the subjection of Puerto Ricans and of Mexicans in the Southwest. Colonized in 1898, Puerto Rico became a territory of the United Status with different types of official designations such as U.S. territory, protectorate, and, from 1950, commonwealth. From 1898 to 1917, the legal status of Puerto Ricans vis-à-vis the United States was extremely ambiguous. After much deliberation and internal conflict, partly due to racist views about the islanders, the U.S. federal government agreed to give citizenship to Puerto Ricans through the Jones Act in 1917, passed on the eve of World War I. Twenty thousand Puerto Ricans were quickly drafted, and sixty thousand eventually served in the war (Nieto-Phillips 1999, 58–64; De Genova and Ramos-Zayas 2003, 8).[21] In addition to this example of abusive use of citizenship law, Ediberto Román (2006, 58–66) and Rogers Smith (1997) have noted that the U.S. federal government created specific citizenship legal provisions for Puerto Ricans, which included a citizenship without self-determination and one that provided only a limited set of legal, political, and social rights. As Smith writes, Puerto Rican citizenship "carried no implications of political" or legal "equality" (1997, 437).[22] The reasons for this were the profound racisms of Washington politicians who typically characterized Puerto Ricans as unfit for self-government, worth a second-rate citizenship but no more. Puerto Ricans in Puerto Rico, for instance, did not have the right to a trial by jury (ibid., 439) (Cabranes 1979, 29; Pérez 2004, 16; Valdivia 2010, 9).

Prior to Puerto Rico's colonization, the annexation of the Southwest, including Texas, brought with it a racist legal system and political cultures that were used to taking away citizenship rights, thereby creating legally sedimented lower and laborer classes that could be systematically exploited. This began with the Treaty of Guadalupe Hidalgo, a document mostly drafted by U.S. legislators that included the one provision the Mexican legislature was able to negotiate, the granting of U.S. citizenship to Mexican residents. What the Mexican legislature did not know was that in the United States, state law was more powerful than federal law and federal citizenship did not grant political rights. These were granted by states, and when states were formed out of the former Mexican territories, state laws were written to legally disenfranchise Mexicans (Acuña 1988; Glenn 2002, 149; Gómez 2007, 43; Montejano 1987). When paired with immigration law and labor practices, citizenship has been a tool of ethno-racial oppression against all immigrants who had to endure legally structured underclass status because of racist laws and periodic hate, violence, and en masse deportation (Haney-López 1996). Examples abound, but two have been extremely damaging to Latinas/os of Mexican origin. During the Great Depression of the 1930s, after decades of using Mexican immigrants to remedy labor shortages and to support nascent industries, the United States turned the political and immigration system against Mexican workers, deporting them en masse regardless of legal status. Roughly 415,000 immigrants, including citizens, were deported, and another 85,000 were "voluntarily" repatriated (Acuña 1988; De Genova and Ramos-Zayas 2003, 5; Navarro 2005, 185). Later, during World War II, the U.S. federal government used the initiative known as the Bracero Program to address labor shortages, a program that produced a huge upswing in undocumented migrants, lured by employers' invitation. In 1954–1955, when the labor shortage ended, the United States used militarized tactics, often referred to as "Operation Wetback," to expel 2.9 million undocumented Mexican/migrant workers (Acuña 1988; García 1980; Navarro 2005, 254; Ngai 2004, 156). In these and other cases, mainstream political and legal cultures secured the economic and political power of ethno-racial whites over Chinese, Mexicans, Filipinos, Japanese, and other immigrants whose ability to accumulate social, political, and economic capital was weakened by labor and property laws and who had to endure the loss of valuable members of their communities to deportation because of nativist upsurges.

Without a doubt, from a Latino standpoint, the technology of power that is citizenship has produced more negative outcomes than positive benefits. This is why a theory of citizenship excess is necessary. Citizenship's proclivity to produce negative outcomes relates to the key political practices of citizenship mentioned earlier. Citizenship legitimizes and functions within political markets that tend to concentrate political capital in the same groups. While citizenship excess references endemic political inequality, the term *citizenship* by itself implies some intrinsic positive political outcomes such as the possibility of equality, the powerful feelings of national membership and togetherness, the wonderful sense of duty and responsibility that is part of civics, and the optimistic view that we can change citizenship, expand it to include the have-nots, and open our borders as if they were the open arms of a welcoming nation. When we simply theorize citizenship as a neutral technology of power, we are being generous to a concept that citizenship excess defines as intrinsically polluted. Citizenship excess acknowledges that citizenship is a technology of power, but it also theorizes that excess has always been part of citizenship and that citizenship also means the willingness to coerce and to remain ethically pure while coercing. Citizenship excess reframes citizenship as inclusive of the desire to conquer, to build empire, and to profess ethical cleanliness by clinging to the notion of legality. In sum, I believe citizenship excess is more useful to Latinas/os who need a more robust theoretical framework to explain why 160 years after joining the Union they continue to be unwelcome. And yet the practices just listed are not the only reasons for theorizing citizenship excess. I believe that excess has always been part of citizenship, and the sooner we come to terms with this, the sooner we can imagine radical transformations.

The Nation-State and Citizenship Excess

We can see how excess and injustice are built into the category of citizenship by tracing the genesis and development of citizenship through three significant stages, all of which are part of today's legal systems and political cultures and all of which are central to the shape of the political market. The first stage is the political/legal move of equating citizenship to political currency, an equivalence that links today's citizenship with quite old political practices including those found in Athens and Rome (see also chapter 3). This stage explains who gets to participate in the political market. The second stage coincides with the development of modern nation-states, which harness increasingly complex legal systems in the project of governing quite large territories that are multiracial and multiethnic (see also chapter 2). In this stage, we speak of citizenship as a portfolio of rights and duties, and citizenship becomes textured and multiple. It is at this point that the sciences of race, which were originally ethno-territorial legal and political frameworks for imperial conquest, become embedded in the complex practices of government, which will use ideas of race, ethnicity, and sex to texture citizenship and to produce its multiplicity. In this stage, slavery becomes legal and women can be labeled citizens but cannot vote. This stage explains how ascription becomes the base for political capital accumulation. We are now in the third stage, where racial language is increasingly falling out of favor and the portfolio of rights and duties is morphing into a highly abstracted set of rules and prescriptions. In this stage, racism is differentiated from nativism and ethnonationalism, which continues to be accepted in political and legal frameworks (see also chapter 4). I use this stage to explain how rates of trade between political goods are established. Citizenship excess in contemporary liberal democracy is the result of the convergence of these three stages into a political moment in which both the texture of citizenship and political practices are made possible through myriad laws and policies that secure differentiated forms of citizenship and accepted forms of political excommunication.

The following subsections expand on these stages. The first two subsections provide arguments that speak to institutional effects of citizenship excess based on arguments about how citizenship became political and legal capital. These subsections help explain how political capital accumulation is the result of the structuring of the political market. The third subsection deepens the analysis of the political market by examining a central mechanism for establishing rates of trade. That is, some cultural and political currencies are worth more than others, and this worth is dependent on the elevation of the value of these currencies at the expense of others. In this subsection, I analyze how processes of symbolic erasure facilitate the devaluation of Latino political and cultural capital to the benefit of ethno-racially white majorities.

Citizenship as Political Currency

Citizenship became political currency when it became a symbol of, and a legal trope for, political agency. The French Constitution of 1791, for instance, grants upon the citizen all natural and civil rights, including the right of assembly, juridical equality, and freedom of expression. Similarly, the U.S. Constitution reserves for citizens the rights to vote and to be elected. From the Greeks to the Enlightenment, the communities that put forward these definitions of citizenship always defined themselves as citizens and hence proper political agents. In a sort of circular form, citizens constituted the state, and the state, through its legal apparatus, built the political worth of citizenship. Closing the circle, the legal system, in deciding who can vote and be elected, structured the field of power from which the state, as a community of elected officials and appointed legal voices, emanated. This characteristic of citizenship is not new, but in this section I argue that the citizen–political agent equivalence has taken new meanings and forms in modernity. In the era of the nation-state, the equivalence of citizenship with political agency meant constructing the citizen as a legal and administrative category proper to an age of legal compliance and precise administration: however, many of the modern juridical and administrative structures, from the economy to education, relied on the legal racial paradigms of empire. If in the previous section I showed that citizenship excess has been used in the U.S. project of securing the marginalization and control of Latinas/os and other ethno-racial others, this section shows that citizenship excess is a constant feature of the nation-state in modernity and that historicizing Latinas/os in the United States should mean facing up to the almost constant coercive force of citizenship excess on Latino experience.

The equivalence of citizenship and political agency is old. Some elements of this political system have been at play since the Greeks, who began the tradition of granting the citizen "the right to being political" (Isin 2002, 1). Since the Greeks, an almost constant flurry of political systems, including republics, empires, and city-states, have used the equivalence of citizen with political agency as the most basic political equation. Because it helps distinguish between political actors and nonactors, members of the polity and nonmembers, this equivalence is the basic structure of politics and most political systems. From the origins of citizenship to the present, Isin (2002) argues, the citizen has been created in relation to others: those who do not belong to the city, such as foreigners, slaves, and travelers; those who live outside the city walls, which in Athens included workers and craftspeople whom the city depended on but who were not protected by the city's infrastructure; and those who do not have the personal characteristics, regardless of ancestry, to be citizens, a large group that in Athens included women and the offspring of slaves (slaves themselves were often imagined as foreigners). Most people in the so-cial world we now know as Ancient Greece were not citizens. Yet, by and large, citizens wrote the political history of Athens; as Isin notes,

> While our received view of the origins of citizenship comes from how dominant groups defined themselves against distant others, aliens, and barbarians, the dominant groups have never been inclined to give an account of their dominance. Rather, the dominant groups have always been inclined to naturalize their "superiority" and the "inferiority" of the dominated, interpreting the struggles that resulted in their domi-nation as epic struggles against transitive and distant aliens and bar-barians. As a result, their dominated others appear as the distant and transitive (barbarians), rather than the near and immanent (strangers, outsiders, and aliens) (2002, 5).

Isin's way of interrogating the origins of citizenship helps us see the politi-cal pursuits of nativists and ethnonationalists as continuations of quite old political traditions, rather than a purely modern phenomenon.

Indeed, those wonderful Athenians were firm believers in what today we recognize as nativist principles espoused by figures such as Tom Tan-credo, the former Republican representative from Colorado and notori-ous anti-Latino bigot. Like Plato before him, Tancredo believes that the right to govern should be given to the educated elites as long as they are citizens by birth. Tancredo argued the point, stating that "President Obama was elected because we do not have civics, literacy tests before people can vote in this country. . . . People who could not spell the word vote or say it in English put a committed socialist ideology in the White House—name is Barack Hussein Obama" (interview, *CBS News*, Febru-ary 5, 2010). Perhaps Plato would not have remarked negatively about socialism, but in *The Republic*, Plato is committed to the idea of rule by privileged elites, the citizens also known as "the Guardians," who are bur-dened with governing and forced to embody civic virtues as part of their task as rulers. Tancredo, like many other extreme right-wing nativists, is convinced that the character of America is at stake when undeserving individuals are allowed to participate and shape politics. He is a repub-lican not because of party affiliation but because, like Plato, he stresses specific definitions of civic virtue as necessary for government. The vir-tues that Tancredo has stressed over his political career include being law-abiding, speaking English, having American values, and, in general, conforming to ethno-racially white socio-cultural parameters. Always a conservative, Tancredo's views on foreigners were exacerbated after 9/11, and since then, he has been on record many times linking immigration to terrorism. In 2003, he introduced a House initiative called the Mass Immigration Reduction Act (H.T. 946), in which he proposed drastic reductions in immigration and refugee admissions. In 2008, he ran in the presidential Republican primary on basically an anti-immigration and antiterrorism platform. He dropped out once he realized he was going to lose and was invited by then-governor Mitt Romney to support his candidacy. Only Senator John McCain got in-between Romney and the Republican nomination. Tancredo is not your typical conservative. Moderate conservatives and financial conservatives dislike him. But Tancredo is a voice that continues to have resonance. The speech I referenced was given at the 2010 Tea Party convention, and Tancredo has since been part of the political arsenal of the Tea Party, consistently using the nativist card to rally support for it.[23]

Similarities between Tancredo and Plato are important reminders of unflattering political equivalences that can help us demystify the past and recontextualize the present, but the similarities are also a bit misleading. Citizenship in modernity has become much more than what the Greeks envisioned or required. In the Classical period, Athens was a city-state with 40,000 citizens ruling over roughly 120,000 resident aliens and slaves. The legal and social separation between citizens and noncitizens was rigid. Plato did not have to reflect extensively on the morality of this rigid separation, and his writings on ethics were always already centered on the citizen. The privilege of citizenship made citizenship somewhat invisible. Contemporary politicians such as Tancredo do not enjoy that privilege. Although citizenship in Athens was necessary to participate in politics, the modern state has expanded the uses of citizenship at a rate similar to the rate that the nation-state has expanded the political technologies of government. Practically every contemporary nation-state is larger than Athens, and with regard to population, ethno-racial variety, and geographical size, most nation-states are more similar to old empires, which were ruled by a combination of brutal coercion and judicial systems often organized around the principle that monarchies were divinely ordained (Anderson 1991). If one is to leave aside systematic brutal coercion or political-religious principles, the problem of legitimizing the state becomes a central political problem (Foucault 2007, 116; Burchell, Gordon, and Miller 1991; Bennett 1998; Gordon 1991, 3).

Citizenship Excess in the Nation-State

Historians and theorists of the nation-state have provided several explanations as to how modern nation-states manage to appear legitimate to majorities. Benedict Anderson (1991) notes that monarchic and religious ways of organizing the political were substituted by new sets of secular ideas about politics and kinship and new ways of experiencing the social. Some of these secular ideas about politics we now recognize as nationalism, and some of the new ways of experiencing the social included new kinship structures, which Anderson calls "imagined communities," made possible by modern ways of experiencing time and space that were the result of new media technologies and capitalism. Anderson is great at explaining how the political technologies central to the nation-state have grown in complexity due to Enlightenment ideas of liberalism, capitalism, and the need to reimagine government as democratic. His arguments can be productively used to explain how nation-states today, in spite of their complexity and size, are perceived as legitimate. They provide a way of understanding how common liberal ideas of equality and justice become affective structures that may lead to self-sacrifice, as in war times, and how national histories are told as worthwhile teleological projects that seek to produce the most just and equal society, as when we use the phrase "a perfect union." However, Anderson fails to reconcile the horizontal camaraderie that nations seem to engender with the hierarchical organization of life and systems of inequality inherent to all nations. Others are better at explaining de facto national vertical arrangements.

Prior to Anderson, Etienne Balibar and Immanuel Wallerstein (1991) had proposed similar links between the rise of the nation-state, capitalism, and culture. But they went beyond these links to argue that the emergence of the nation-state is linked not simply to the rise of the bourgeois class, central in capitalist societies, but to the fact that capitalism is rooted in what Wallerstein has been calling—since 1974—the "world-economy." Balibar and Wallerstein believe that this world-economy "is always already hierarchically organized into a 'core' and a 'periphery,' each of which have different methods of accumulation and exploitation of labour power, and between which relations of unequal exchange and domination are established. . . . Beginning from the core, national unities form out of the overall structure of the world-economy, as a function of the role they play in the structure of a given period. More exactly, they form against one another as competing instruments in the service of the core's domination of the periphery." This means that "every modern nation is a product of colonization: it has always been to some degree colonized or colonizing, and sometimes both at the same time" (Balibar 1991, 89). The core-periphery basis of capitalism helps Balibar and Wallerstein place racial and ethnic difference as seminal to nation-states, for it is the core-periphery ethno-territorial hierarchies that culturally legitimize and give legal form to racial and ethnic hierarchies (ibid., 95). Others such as Enrique Dussel (1995, 2002), Anibal Quijano (2000, 2007), and Walter Mignolo (2000, 2005) have expanded on the role the Wallersteinian "world-economy" has had on the Americas and have used the term "coloniality" to reference the way colonial domination between the European core and the American periphery was concretized through law and administrative processes. As relevant, these Latin American thinkers also argue that racialized colonial law and administrative processes survived independence movements and became part of the legal and policy frameworks of nation-states.[24] Hence, according to scholars of coloniality, racialized law has been as important a legal base for the U.S. nation-state as had, for instance, Jeffersonian liberal ideals of equality or Madisonian republican ideas of civics.

Giving credence to theories of coloniality, critical legal scholars such as Ian Haney-López (2006), Cheryl Harris (1997), Grace Hong (2006), George Martinez (1994, 2000), Michael Olivas (2006), Rogers Smith (1997), and Patricia Williams (1991), among others, have shown that U.S. law and policy are partly built on hierarchical ideas about race and ethnicity. Prior to independence, the political relevance of citizenship was minimal, and the American colonies organized themselves around the more ambiguous categories of whiteness, masculinity, and property, which complemented the notion of the British subject and helped allocate judicial privileges (Hong 2006, 4). As predicted by theories of coloniality, with independence came the need to construct a new location of legal privilege—citizenship—and this new location largely reconstructed colonial legal traditions of privilege minus the subjection to the British monarchy. For instance, U.S. prohibitions against miscegenation were preceded by laws such as the 1667 law of the House of Burgesses, which set rules regarding the inheritance of slave status in Virginia. This law stipulated that a newborn would be held "bond or free only according to the condition of the mother" (qtd. in Hickman 2003, 105). The logic here was threefold: to protect white men from legal issues when having a child with an enslaved black woman, to assure the racial deficit of blackness, and to protect the racial solidity of the economy of slavery in which "pure" whites could hold property rights over slaves. Laws against miscegenation after independence basically followed this 1667 primer. I use this example to illustrate the following: after independence, citizenship did become a dominant political/legal construct, but the ability of this juridical location of privilege to dominate, for instance, the slave economy is a continuation of old, colonial, racist, legal traditions of adjudicating legal privileges to white propertied males (K. Johnson 2003; G. Martinez 2000, 42; Nelson 1998; R. Smith 1997, 40–69). Arguably, what allowed citizenship to become dominant in law and all legally regulated social fields (education, the military, the economy) is partly the continuation of colonial racist and classist rules of political and legal privilege. This is not to deny that the U.S. independence movement was partly rooted in egalitarian Enlightenment ideas, but it never was a full departure from the legal and social principles that allowed the British monarchy to expand its empire in the Americas. Citizenship had to be codified in law in such way as to simultaneously acknowledge the promise of legal equality and the justification for inequality. These very principles of juridical ambivalence and juridical indeterminacy were later used in the colonization of the Southwest and determined the complex ways in which Latinas/os came to the Union and have remained since (Dudziak and Volpp 2005).

Citizenship excess is indebted to theories of coloniality and critical legal scholarship that acknowledge the ethno-racial roots of the U.S. political system (Carbado 2005, 651). Rogers Smith (1997), in the latter tradition, argues that ascription is the third column of the U.S. legal and political system and is as important as egalitarian ideas of liberalism and republican ideas of civics. Ascription, the sense that individuals' hierarchical location in society corresponds to birth characteristics such as race, sex, and nationality, is taken on in law by providing the basis for legal inequality. That is, while liberal understandings of law assume that all subjects of law occupy similar locations in relationship to the law, ascriptivism in law constructs different legal locations on the basis of birth characteristics and assures different legal treatment of different peoples. Some are closer to the law; some are farther. Smith presents hundreds of legal cases that have secured the legal deficit of propertyless individuals in early U.S. history, African Americans all throughout history, Latinas/os after the imperial annexation of the Southwest and Puerto Rico, and women of all races all throughout U.S. history. The organizing principle of Smith's argument is the notion of citizenship, which marks legal membership. In his bleak argument about American legal and political history, citizenship refers to multiple legal locations from which individuals' ascriptive identities have been used to constitute legal and political deficits and privileges. Examples abound. Written law was subject to interpretation, and it was often through interpretation that privileged communities of citizens constructed hierarchical legal scaffoldings. The Constitution did not mention women but used male pronouns dozens of times, and these pronouns were "used to argue on the floor of Congress and in state courts that the Constitution denied federal office-holding to women" (Smith 1997, 131). Either as written law or as interpretive practices, the juridical world became a nexus where citizenship as political agency would be transformed into the basic legal embroidery that would regulate most spheres of life. The economic and the political became complexly linked and ascription became ambiguous, but, regardless of ambiguity, ascriptivism rarely became the ground for political egalitarianism. Some Native Americans were considered part of the political community and some were not, and the difference often rested on their role in the economy. Broadly, Native Americans were not counted for political representation, nor did they pay taxes. However, many Native Americans worked under conditions of indentured servitude, and as such they paid taxes but could not vote, hence benefiting state coffers and securing the economic privileges of their masters.[25]

Smith shows how complex views of political and legal membership affected most state and federal institutions, including immigration, education, the armed forces, the economy, gender, and the broad field of crime and punishment. He provides extensive evidence that law and administrative policies in citizenship law, immigration law, educational law and policies, judicial procedures, imperial law and administration, policies in the armed forces, and labor law were systematically used to construct a citizenship deficit among ethno-racial communities and women and that these same legal and administrative policies created citizenship excess among white, propertied communities of men.

In the nation-state, law and policy are the most relevant political technologies because they inscribe and legitimate, on a semipermanent basis, the social and political values of those who write them. Critical legal scholars show that the U.S. legal and administrative framework has been organized from its national beginnings to produce and reproduce citizenship excess, legal inequality based on ascriptivism, the judicial deficit of nonwhites and women, and the legal privileges of white, propertied men. This is consistent with theories of coloniality, which are useful for placing these very facts into the longer history of colonialism and the administrative and legal practices that were colonialism's political ground. Finally, world-system theories help us see ascriptivism as a transnational political strategy that was meant to legitimate unethical behavior and to govern those unfortunate others caught in the middle. Hence, citizenship excess recasts the genesis of the nation-state in terms of the political and legal processes that gave credibility to nations and that simultaneously concretized imperialism and the domination of ethnic and racial others.

Citizenship Excess and Ethno-Territoriality

In this third stage, which began after the Civil War and accelerated after the 1960s, racial language falls out of favor and law becomes more abstracted. This movement away from ascriptivism is the result of political and civic movements (from the suffragettes to the civil rights movements) that targeted law and juridical practices. Although racial stratification does not disappear—on the contrary, several markers of racial stratification have been exacerbated since the 1960s—stratification is achieved through law and policies that are more difficult to track, such as bank lending practices that on paper look "color-blind" but are carried on in racially differentiated ways, hiring practices that seem fair but always result in ethno-racially white leadership and power, or legal and police systems that are set to increase everybody's security but treat racialized populations radically differently than white ones (Oliver and Shapiro 2006, 144–145; Inda 2006, 52–58). This is the era of the new racism, mentioned earlier. Yet not all ascriptivism is gone; ethno-territorial ascriptivism based on national and ethnic origin remains central to political and legal systems. The worst examples are nativist laws, such as Arizona's. But more common than nativism are myriad ethno-territorial ascriptivist laws and policies that marginalize languages, histories, and political traditions important to ethno-racial minorities in general and Latinas/os in particular. Altogether, these laws, policies, and political practices produce the political capital accumulation of ethno-racially white majorities by symbolically erasing Latinas/os from the U.S. national consciousness. These laws, policies, and political practices are the basis of U.S. ethnonationalism, a common political view that proposes that the United States has been and should remain ethno-racially white. By devaluing Spanish, Latina/o history, or markers of Latino cultural prestige, the white ethnic majority increases the political capital of English, Eurocentric history and values. Citizenship excess proposes that in this stage of citizenship, political capital accumulation depends on the systematic erasure of the cultural and political capital of ethno-racial minorities. Erasure works alongside the new racism and the mainstreaming of color-blindness to normalize the hegemony of the ethno-racial majority (Roque Ramirez 2008, 167; Valdivia 2010, 81–83; Viego 2007, 7, 105). These symbolic erasures are more patent in the tendentious ways in which preferred memories and histories become the basis for educational curricula, mediated forms of nationalistic imagery, and commonsense notions of belonging.

Historically, education has been part of processes of erasure, either because curricula disregard histories important to ethnic and racial minorities or because curricula are understood as tools for the assimilation of immigrants and marginal peoples. Let me introduce two brief examples. George Sanchez (1993) narrates how in the California of the 1920s, the progressive movement translated its goals of using K–12 school curricula to make better citizens into the goal of Americanizing immigrants. In these cases, Americanizing meant the systematic disregard for Mexican and Mexican American culture and the embrace of civic, historical, and political lessons that gave credence to the second-class citizenship status of Mexican Americans (104–107). Although full erasure never succeeded and Mexican and Mexican American aspects of culture and history continued being taught in many California schools, the progressive movement did succeed at further establishing the racialized and ethnicized meaning of being American (their term), at fostering the political value of education, and at using educational policy and law to further the racialized goals of the nation-state.

Erasure is present in contemporary educational settings. For instance, in postsecondary educational curricula, as Frances Aparicio (1994) has argued, a soft multiculturalism has become a way of defanging the critical potential of Latina/o critical theory. This soft multiculturalism is the result of critical efforts by scholars of all ethnicities and races trying to reshape universities into egalitarian cultural and epistemological spaces, but the way multiculturalism has been institutionalized is quite imperfect and the imperfections reconstruct old marginalizations. Examples of new erasures common in university settings are curricular segregation and a type of racial ventriloquism by which white scholars speak on behalf of racial and ethnic others (and are given more credence than the very Latina/o or African American scholars they are meant to represent). Curricular segregation categorizes work such as Aparicio's in the subfield of "Ethnic

Studies," while work engaged with whiteness is always already central to disciplinary concerns. Through these neocolonial practices, as Aparicio terms them, white privilege is repositioned at the center of academic curricula, and Latinas/os are gently erased from the canonical bibliographies that define academic disciplines and from the structures of racial power that these disciplines embody.

Mediated forms of nationalistic imagery are constructed through racial paradigms that erase Latina/o participation in the building of the United States. Traditionally represented as economically marginal, educationally challenged, politically troubled, and ruled by emotion and not reason, Latinas/os are erased from nationalistic media narratives such as the war genre film or the historical film. As far as film and television, the only historical event in which Latinas/os are central is, ironically, the Alamo. This event, typically depicted in a truly distorted and racist fashion, has been represented in film and television dozens of times, starting with D. W. Griffith's *The Martyrs of the Alamo* (1915) and ending with John Lee Hancock's *The Alamo* (2004) (R. Flores 2000). Outside the Alamo, Latinas/os are often absent from war or military narratives of nation, as when Ken Burns presented a finished seven-part documentary (fifteen hours) about World War II without mentioning Latino participation (*The War*, 2007). Due to protests about the lack of Latino and Native American recognition, Burns had to scrap parts of his film and dedicate some twenty-five minutes of extra interviews and footage to these groups. He was able to do this thanks to the quick and expert work of documentarian Hector Galan. However, Burns refused to reedit the film, leaving this new material as addendums at the end of the central narrative. Considering that Burns is the main documentarian engaged in producing official PBS histories of the United States, his lack of historical knowledge and sensitivity becomes a significant example of institutional disavowal and marginalization, one enabled by PBS's acquiescence.

Given Latina/o lack of representation in educational curricula and media narratives, it is not surprising that Latinas/os fail to appear in commonsense narratives of citizenship belonging. All too often, Latinas/os do not figure in descriptions of the national community. Although Latino belonging can be traced back to the origins of the United States as a nation, Latinas/os continue to be coded as immigrants, foreign populations whose arrival either enriches the cultural diversity of the nation or, more commonly, threatens to undermine the values of the national community. Because of their supposed foreign status, Latinas/os are the common target of nativist ideology today, but also throughout our history. Consider this: already in 1855, only six years after California had become part of the United States, English was made the official language of instruction, and the systematic marginalization of Spanish began full force (see chapter 3). Erasure is a general process of symbolic discrimination found in citizenship excess and is one of the preferred ways in which to generate value in political markets for ethno-racial majorities. Hence, as I show throughout this book, erasure is central to ethnonationalism and, its most extreme variant, nativism. Beyond this, in the following chapters, I show that Latina/o erasure is so common in mainstream ways of imagining the nation, the state, and the national community that it is possible to argue that ethnonationalism is the basis of most U.S. ways of imagining politics and citizenship.

I began this section noting that citizenship is becoming an increasingly abstract category, partly because ascriptivism is out of favor (Hong 2006, 11). The racial effects of law, I also noted, are achieved through legal and administrative mechanisms that are harder to pinpoint (e.g., lending practices) and in harmony with the new racism. Instead of racial language, current political cultures value color-blindness and race-neutral language. Ironically, this movement away from racial language gives credibility to processes of erasure. This is so because, as Wendy Brown (1993) has noted, identity politics, a modern form of political consciousness that includes Latina/o politics and history, necessitates an emphasis on particulars, but this emphasis cannot be delivered within the increasingly abstract logic of liberal political membership. Liberal regimes, she continues, rely on abstracting one's life and depoliticizing one's particulars. In the process of becoming "we," the "I" is effaced (391–392). Identity politics, hence, invariably leads to a perception of injury, to a self-definition that marks identity through symbolic wounds. Identity politics is always about erasure of particulars and stands in contrast to the liberal tendency to construct a universal "we." Although Brown's argument stands as a classical nonhegemonic theorization of liberalism and identity politics, it has intractable weaknesses worth mentioning. The worst is Brown's failure to recognize that liberal regimes do not equally erase the particulars of all. Erasure, as Brown would note, signals a state of injury, but the reason for this injury is not the impossibility of liberalism to behave as a utopian system of government but the very reality of the political and discursive practices that characterize liberalism as a way of government with definite historical and social roots. Liberalism does not erase the particulars of

ethno-racial majorities. Through law and institutions, liberal regimes record, embrace, and sediment the particulars of a small number of people,
and these particulars become the natural, normal ground for governance.
Contrarily, ethno-racial neutral language and color-blindness simply
recenter ethno-racially white political and cultural values and erase the
particulars of ethno-racial others. In citizenship excess, this aspect of liberalism is the ground for excess because it positions some people to easily
take advantage of a universalism that in practical terms embraces white
ethnonationalism.

Erasure links to political capital accumulation because erasure always
signals a political capital deficit. So the problems with erasure are multiple. They include the very injustice of constructing a discriminating political, legal, and cultural world that is inattentive to the particular histories and experiences of sexual, racial, and national minorities. But this
injustice is compounded by the fact that erasure from memory, history,
and narratives of belonging weaken the political ground from which these
minorities can issue claims for justice and equality. Lastly, the weakening
of minorities' political ground occurs while the political and legal capital
of the hegemonic community strengthens, making citizenship excess its
predictable outcome. In sum, there is net political capital accumulation
for hegemonic communities when they normalize Latino erasure.

In a society such as ours, where political cultures and discourse exist
largely in and because of media, reflecting on political capital accumulation and erasure means also reflecting on the way media is part of these
important processes. Media shape, constitute, and behave as relevant
mechanisms for political capital accumulation, and they participate in the
erasure of Latinas/os from mainstream life. Media thus present complex
issues and problems that require closer examination, particularly in regard to citizenship and citizenship excess. The rest of the book is dedicated to these very issues.

Objectives and Chapters

This book deals with citizenship excess against Latinas/os and the role
of media in constituting, reproducing, and challenging this excess. Because of the book's concern with types of social/legal membership that
directly affect Latinas/os' social standing (in particular media and citizenship), it situates itself at the intersection of Latino media studies and
citizenship studies. Together, the following chapters articulate citizenship

excess in media and conclude with a transnational theory of Latino cultural citizenship.

Exceptions illustrate the rule, and my cases have been selected to help me consider Latinidad, citizenship excess, media, and politics through the figure of the undocumented and documented Latino immigrant (Molina-Guzmán 2010, 3). I do not propose that all Latinas/os are immigrants or that Latinas/os are systematically excluded from political or legal cultures. Yet the cases I have selected show that the contemporary treatment of undocumented and documented Latino immigrants belongs to broad and lasting traditions of citizenship excess. Hence, the cultural and legal treatment of these Latinas/os brings to relevance the histories that give shape to Latino social, political, and cultural standing. Moreover, these traditions are constitutive of the way we think and we do citizenship excess. Because citizenship excess is a type of process that legalizes inclusion and exclusion, alienage constitutes citizenship excess (Isin 2002; Honig 2001).

The following chapters are organized in two parts meant to signal two processes involved in the reproduction of citizenship excess. Part 1, "Defending the Walls," investigates political processes involving Latinas/os that required the participation of the media field and that reinstituted nativist or ethnonational political agendas. Each chapter in this part elaborates on one of the stages of citizenship excess presented earlier, albeit in a different order. Chapter 1 engages citizenship excess in the public sphere; chapter 2 engages citizenship excess in the articulation of social movement and nation; chapter 3 explores citizenship excess in the citizen–political agency equivalence; chapter 4 examines citizenship excess and ethno-territoriality.

These chapters use the working assumption that the political health of Latinas/os is related to participation in the public sphere, but in exploring this participation, these chapters force us to reflect on a sort of Catch-22: the Latino public sphere is vital and energetic, but it is also mostly in Spanish; and this linguistic separation from the majoritarian public sphere limits Latinas/os' mainstream political participation.

Chapter 1 explores linguistic separation in the public sphere. It starts with the observation that the issue of multilinguistic public spheres is not simply a technical one. It is also an issue of political theory and, in the United States, an issue that ought to be evaluated against the egalitarian goals of liberal democratic theory. I carry on this evaluation of liberalism by reference to Foucault's theory of liberal governmentality, a framework particularly apt to engage with questions of governmental technologies.

This chapter introduces coloniality, a theoretical framework from Latin America that corrects some of Foucault's weaknesses and helps us re-imagine public sphere theory with the colonial subject in mind.

Moving from theory to ground, chapter 2 investigates the implications of having a public sphere in a language different from the majority's. The case is the Latino social advertising campaign that helped organize the 2006 pro-immigration reform rallies. This case illustrates how citizenship, nation, justice, and law are integral parts of the national regime and work as a closed self-referential social and discursive universe. Mediating be-tween people and government is a civil society that has to access media to participate in the formation of consensus. The rallies were a classic example of civil society using the Latino public sphere, mostly SLM, to produce a spectacular set of events that should have worked to make the case for pro-immigration reform. Attesting to coloniality, the results were the opposite.

To further illustrate the limits of liberal governmentality and the ben-efits of coloniality, chapter 3 analyzes the problem of equating the citizen with the political agent. The case is the T. Don Hutto Detention Center in Taylor, Texas. Starting in 2006, immigration authorities used Hutto to detain undocumented immigrant families, including children. Fram-ing this as part of the post-9/11 state of exception that saw the creation of legal tools such as "enemy combatant" and "extraordinary rendition," this chapter argues that the practice of claiming anything political as part of the universe of the nation is an example of the political capital accumula-tion that assumes all politics are the purview of the nation. When taken to the extreme, as in Hutto, this political capital accumulation becomes tyr-anny, a nefarious but common manifestation of citizenship excess. To ex-plain Hutto, however, one must go beyond the political and examine how consent was achieved and explore the relationship of consent to erasure. Hence, the chapter analyzes mainstream news coverage of the issue and finds that the coverage of Hutto was scant and too attentive to a national legal political framework in which the mistreatment of children was bal-anced against the needs of the nation for security.

Chapter 4 explores ethno-territoriality and erasure in relation to the linguistic marginalization of SLM. This instantiation of erasure, however, is framed by the discourses of media deregulation and technological con-vergence. Deregulation and convergence have long been predicated on the utopian neoliberal principles of market competition and openness. Given these phenomena and their popular utopian connotations, it is tempting to imagine that our media industries obey the principle of radical open-ness. However, a highly restrictive notion of the national is at work when we talk about language. In this chapter, I draw attention to this linguistic marginalization and treat it as a disavowal and as a naturalized violation of Spanish speakers' language rights that is echoed by media regulatory bodies. To make these arguments, I locate the omissions of Spanish in the United States' systems of legal and cultural definitions of American citi-zenship and argue that the omissions are examples of ethnonationalism. Because of this, the omission of Spanish-language television becomes a political act: the omission naturalizes English as the state language, and it thus supports the claim that white ethnicity and the U.S. state are synony-mous. This deceptive political act fits within neoliberalism, which claims that its power is color-blind and ethnically neutral.

"Defending the Walls" showcases examples of political, legal, and media practices that resulted in the exclusion of Latino political goals (pro-immigration rallies), media (SLM), and political value (Hutto). They historicize Bush-era nativism and the legal and media processes that na-tivists were able to harness to keep Latinas/os at bay. Together the chap-ters theorize liberal governmentality and criticize this framework for its inability to accommodate transnational populations and media systems, and they suggest that theorizing the liberal state must account for the way legal, political, and administrative frameworks continue to manifest the realities of our colonial past (Valdivia 2010, 14). Hence, theories of nation-states and citizenship must always transcend the nation, for the roots of its discursive and legal organization are as transnational as the nation's present.

Although a significant number of social and discursive processes are used to reconstitute a majoritarian political field that can also be de-scribed as a racial patriarchy, there are also a number of social and discur-sive tactics that allow for the political field to have flexible membership. The egalitarian promises of liberalism and capitalism so allow it. In part 2, "Conditions of Inclusion," I explore two cases that illustrate comple-mentary processes of inclusion. One engages contemporary conditions of inclusion of Latinas/os in mainstream English-language media vis-à-vis political capital accumulation. The other explores conditions of inclusion in national mythologies and in the mainstream institution of the armed forces and their relationship to biographical erasure. Together these chap-ters illustrate the narrow path that Latinas/os must follow to be part of mainstream cultures of politics as well as political cultures.

Chapter 5 uses the media example of the popular television dramedy *Ugly Betty* to explore how political capital accumulation is manifested under the guise of media corporate ethics and liberal politics of accommodation. I argue that this television show forces us to face political capital accumulation for two key reasons: (1) The show brings to relevance the convention of having the discourse of citizenship produced and disseminated from the subject/legal position of the citizen. Although *Ugly Betty* stands as an exception to this norm (it is the only one-hour show in English-language broadcast television with Latinas/os at its center), the show is authorized to speak about citizenship because, in doing so, it helps to reproduce notions of labor equity that are ultimately harmful to Latinas/os; in particular, the show reproduces dangerous notions of diversity. (2) Most uses of citizenship in media studies leave to the side what De Genova calls "the legal *production* of citizenship" (2005, 2): how law effectively generates the category of the citizen and its companion, the "illegal" noncitizen. Simply put, citizenship and law are mutually constituted. Going further, I see the legal production of citizenship linked to the management of diversity in today's media structures, which have translated the goals of the civil rights era into managerial techniques and a discourse that lauds diversity because it is marketable.

If Latinas/os must represent profitable diversity in order to participate in our culture of politics, the rules for participating in our political cultures are different. In chapter 6, I explore how some Latinas/os have had the rare honor of being called heroes by our politicians and newscasters and how the actions of these Latinas/os fostered positive change to U.S. immigration laws. In this case, mediation is central. The case centers on some of the first coalition soldiers to die in Iraq in 2003; they were noncitizen Latinas/os who were later given posthumous citizenship, a right that became instituted in our immigration laws. This chapter places the mediation of these events against the backdrop of liberalism, particularly the notions of consent and voluntarism. The central argument is that giving posthumous citizenship to the soldiers was an illiberal practice made possible by mediated ethnocentric fantasies that justified imposing citizenship on these deceased Latinas/os. This mediation relied on the erasure of these Latinas/os' personal biographies, which were substituted with fantastic narratives of what Lauren Berlant calls the "infantile citizen" (1997, 27). Beyond this disavowal, public mediation of the issues obscured the illiberal ways in which the armed forces in America are staffed. These two types of erasure were supported by ethnocentric discourses of citizenship and nationalism that assumed the soldiers desired naturalization and that reproduced the idea that the volunteer army equally targets all Americans as potential conscripts.

Political capital accumulation and disavowal happen in processes of both exclusion and inclusion. I conclude the book by reengaging with some of the issues raised in the cases and supported by the findings of these chapters. My goal is to summarize findings and to more formally introduce the need to engage with transnational theories in order to further accommodate Latino reality.

I want to end this introduction with a final remark on the relation of citizenship to history. It is tempting to think that theorizing and historicizing citizenship excess with post-9/11 cases and with political practices carried on by two Bush administrations is itself dealing with a sort of historical exception. Post-9/11 citizenship practices against immigrants, some people may add, were exceptional in the way that they relied on nativism. But I do not share this position, for the bulk of my arguments are constituted through the social reordering of our political world in neoliberal and ethno-territorial terms, and this process is not slowing down. On the contrary, I see a neoliberalism bound to nativism as the most important recent shift in citizenship practices, one which will give shape to the way we do law and politics in the future and which will further affect the rules of social and political membership and stratification. This is true in the United States, but neoliberalism is by now a global phenomenon. In fact, I see the U.S. era of liberal citizenship rights as a historical period that reached its peak somewhere in the 1960s. Since then, the liberalism of rights has been eroded by neoliberalism and nativism, which we love to call Reaganism but we may as well call Clintonism. I fear that if we stay in this trajectory, the U.S. experiment that gave the world the liberalism of rights will come to an end. A neoliberal and nativist future, though not without charms and without freedoms, will be unrecognizable to those who fought (and died) for the expansion of citizenship rights.

PART I

Defending the Walls

1

Toward a Latino Critique of Public Sphere Theory

There is a paradox that defines Latino political and cultural power. No other ethno-racial minority group has as much access to the mediated public sphere as Latinas/os, and yet Latino underrepresentation in the field of power is substantive. Paul Taylor, the director of the Pew Hispanic Center, offers the metaphor, "Latinas/os have so far punched below their weight in American politics, in contrast to blacks, who have punched above theirs" (Power in numbers 2010). Kim Geron (2005) places this metaphor in perspective when she notes that in 2004 Latinas/os accounted for less than 1 percent of the elected officials in the nation, significantly lower than their 10 percent share of the electable population (see also L. Daniels 2011). (By the way, in 2004 blacks were 13 percent of the electable population and only accounted for 2 percent of elected officials.) Judging from the underrepresentation of Latinas/os in politics, one may assume that the Latino public sphere is extremely weak, but this is simply not true. Latinas/os struggle to get access to English-language media

(ELM) but have significant access to Spanish-language media (SLM). The sheer economic and cultural power of SLM, which includes Univision, the fifth-largest television network in the nation; half a dozen other TV networks; hundreds of radio stations; hundreds of newspapers; and significant presence on the Web, speaks of a vital cultural resource that behaves as a mediated public sphere.[1] If we consider SLM, we are forced to question the very axiom stating that access to media correlates to a healthy public sphere and that access to the public sphere somehow correlates to access to political power. With Latinas/os, more access to a public sphere equals less political power.

Clearly, access to a public sphere alone cannot solve inequality. As Eduardo Mendieta (2003) has noted in his discussion of Latino publicity, for Latinas/os, things are more complicated than having or not having access. He argues that, at least ideally, conditions of publicity should match conditions of oppression, and thus Latino publicity should "denationalize and delocalize, globalizing and postcolonializing processes of social transformation and critical self-reflection" (220). Latino publicity, in other words, is not simply about being able to participate in current power structures, but it should also do the strenuous work of changing the political paradigms that constitute Latino subjection. As Mendieta also notes, this is a significantly high bar for publicity that, nonetheless, presupposes and problematizes access.[2] Access alone can hardly guarantee that Latino publicity will be understood, respected, perceived as reasonable, agreed on, or even politically useful, yet access remains an a priori to publicity. Thus, in this chapter I query the relevance of access and its political efficacy. So profiting from Mendieta's insights and arguments by others who question the public sphere from the perspective of feminism (e.g., Benhabib 1992), ethics (e.g., McCarthy 2004), rhetoric (Garnham 1992), and political theory (e.g., Fraser 1990, 2007), in this chapter, following Peter Dahlgren (1995) and W. Lance Bennet et al. (2004), I investigate access as a structural precondition for publicity.

The issue of access to publicity has two significant foundations: liberalism and political economy. Public sphere theory is based on liberal political theory, a particular subset of political thought that assumes that liberalism and its pursuit of legally defined individual freedoms can only exist in societies in which citizens can actively participate in the structuring of government and society. The public sphere is an essential part of this beneficent liberal structure.

Just as the public sphere is based on liberalism, the notion of access is rooted in political economy. Access is meant to denote the ability of someone to participate, enter, reach, and/or influence a social structure. Access also connotes the capacity of a social structure to have some flexibility, to accept new members, and, potentially, to change. Yet the Latino paradox reminds us of the limits of both publicity and access. I believe that the Latino public sphere paradox (more access has equaled less power) is a call for understanding access and publicity from ethno-racial and political perspectives that match, following Mendieta (2003), the patterns of Latino oppression. These patterns include oppressions rooted in transnationalism, colonialism, immigration, and multilingualism.

So, in tension with public sphere scholarship that takes liberalism and political economy as truisms, I question both. I do this by reference to Michel Foucault's theory of governmentality and, later, coloniality, a Latin American theory of power. Because governmentality historicizes basic political ideas found in liberalism and capitalism, governmentality is useful for explaining how contemporary ways of thinking about politics and the economy give way to specific technologies of governance, including, I show, the public sphere. In addition to a theory of politics and the economy, governmentality is also a theory of the modern subject, a characteristic that makes it a great tool for theorizing the links between politics, the public sphere, the economy, and citizenship. These links are, often, processes of mediation that participate in the mutual constitution of political and personal practices. Because of governmentality's sophisticated use of history, power, and discourse, as well as its ability to link macro and micro levels of analysis, some of the most exciting work connecting media to political theory uses governmentality (Amaya 2010; Miller 1993, 1998; Ouellette and Hay 2008).

Governmentality, however, is not a perfect analytic tool. Its weaknesses can be theorized by reference to nation-centrism. In the spirit of criticizing and complementing governmentality, in the last section of the chapter, I propose a way of reassembling the different concerns, from public sphere theory to Latinas/os, by referencing coloniality, a political theory developed by Latino and Latin American scholars that properly theorizes the deficiencies of liberal governmentality. Coloniality places the colonial past at the center of the U.S. national project, hence allowing us to properly evaluate the role of ethno-racialization in U.S. liberalism.

From the Public Sphere to the Nation and Back

Public sphere theory marks the most significant intersection between media and normative political theory. As Nancy Fraser notes, public sphere theory proposes that, at least in liberalism, citizens need spaces for de-liberation, a public sphere where they can come together and positively influence the nation-state (1990, 57). I focus on Fraser because her theo-ries of subalterns, which I detail in the following sections, offer the most robust theorization of power and the public sphere for a multicultural society. She proposes that the public sphere, in its ideal form, is not the economy or the private realm or spaces inserted in the apparatus of the state. It is a discursive realm that allows for making the state accountable to the citizenry (59). These ideal conditions are rare, particularly when we reflect on access and its political economy. If political economy re-fers to the influence of capitalism in politics and law, then the way media structures in the United States connect to regulation (law and policy) and capitalism is one the biggest predictors of a healthy public sphere, at least from the perspective of access.

Yet it would seem that the political economy of access to the public sphere does not fully explain the political and media world in which Lati-nas/os exist, particularly if immigration, Spanish, and linguistic difference enter the equation. This is so because transnationalism and multilingual-ism force us to retheorize the economy, particularly media economy, be-cause media is substantively fragmented in terms of language. A political economy of media must start with the recognition that languages make markets plural, not national. In addition, transnationalism and multi-lingualism force us to retheorize the state, the other side of the political economy equation, from a transnational perspective. As noted by Fraser, public sphere theory must be redrawn for transnational and multilin-gual conditions:

> In general, then, the task is clear: if public sphere theory is to function today as a *critical* theory, it must revise its account of the normative legitimacy and political efficacy of public opinion. No longer content to leave half the picture in the shadows, it must treat each of those notions as comprising two analytically distinct but practically entwined critical requirements. Thus, the legitimacy critique of existing publicity must now interrogate not only the "how" but also the "who" of existing pub-licity. Or rather, it must interrogate parity and inclusiveness together, by asking: *participatory parity among whom*? Likewise, the efficacy cri-tique must now be expanded to encompass both the translation and ca-pacity conditions of existing publicity. Putting those two requirements together, it must envision new transnational public powers, which can

be made accountable to new democratic transnational circuits of public opinion.

But only if public sphere theory rises to the occasion can it serve as
a critical theory in a post-Westphalian world. For that purpose, it is not
enough for cultural studies and media studies scholars to map existing
communications flows. Rather, critical social and political theorists will
need to rethink the theory's core premises concerning the legitimacy
and efficacy of public opinion. Only then will the theory recover its
critical edge and its political point. Only then will public sphere theory keep faith with its original promise to contribute to struggles for
emancipation. (2007)

Here, Fraser notes that the goal of public sphere theory is to have normative legitimacy and political efficacy. Normative legitimacy is partly
achieved with participatory parity, that is, by assuring that different
groups will have equal access and equal deliberative powers. However,
Fraser notes that transnationalism is a condition of marginalization that
constitutes groups beyond the reach of politics. Otherwise stated, the
"who" of publicity is typically the citizen. Noncitizens are not the typical
concern of public sphere theories, which assume political agency. Transnational communities hence are a challenge to the normative legitimacy
standard. In addition, transnational communities and diasporas, particularly those marked by linguistic difference, force us to query the political efficacy standard. By political efficacy, Fraser understands the ability
of publicity to be translated into arguments that can shape politics. Yet
transnationalism and multilingualism produce marginalities particularly
difficult to translate into traditional political language because, as Fraser (1990) noted, they often originate at the border of the polis. Because
publicity typically assumes citizenship or translational efficiencies, public
sphere theory is fundamentally political and relates to the type of government that public sphere theory legitimizes: the liberal state.

The challenges to the normative legitimacy and the political efficacy
standards can be traced back to what Anthony Smith (1983), Daniel
Chernilo (2007), and Andreas Wimmer and Nina Glick Schiller (2002),
among others, have called "methodological nationalism."[3] Methodological nationalism refers to the conflation of the concept of society and the
nation-state and, as Wimmer and Schiller put it, to the methodological
assumption that the "natural social and political form of the modern
world" is the nation-state (2002, 302). As these scholars have noted, one of

the key problems with methodological nationalism is that it precludes us from properly understanding the nation-state and, as Wimmer and Schiller highlight, from properly studying immigration processes and populations. Because public sphere theory starts with the state, it inherits the weaknesses of methodological nationalism, including the central weakness of the political imaginary of citizenship excess: the notion that political agency is equal to citizenship (see the introduction). Because this basic assumption about political agency has such profound consequences for public sphere theory, an examination of public sphere theory must start prior to arguments about good government, publicity, deliberation, or equality. It must start with an examination of the nation and the modern liberal state at its core and then move forward to examine the role of publicity in the liberal nation-state.

The Political Economy of the Public Sphere

Because citizenship is so central to the processes we associate with the public sphere, a political economy analysis of culture and media attentive to the public sphere cannot rely on economic arguments alone. It should be anchored on the political. Yet the centrality of citizenship to political economy is not the place where theories of culture start. Instead, citizenship and the nation are often taken-for-granted categories of analysis. This weakness starts with Marx, a seminal thinker in political economy and culture, and continues with Foucault and his theories of liberalism. By reflecting on political economy and liberalism, this section moves citizenship to the surface of public sphere theory.

Political economy is fundamentally a theory of power that emphasizes the role capitalism has in shaping politics. Yet Marxian political economy may have been different if Marx had reflected more on his own citizenship status. Much of Marx's work was carried on while he was stateless, either in Paris, Brussels, or London. But, speaking at a historical moment when nations were just becoming normal, Marx's concerns were not statelessness or the socio-political problems of immigrants. His interests, state capitalism and labor, had originated back in Prussia. There Marx learned that his training in law and philosophy was insufficient to make sense of the political maneuverings that had depicted his journalistic practice at the *Rheinische Zeitung* in Cologne as unsavory to the Prussian state. These same maneuverings had allowed Frederick William IV to tightly control political opposition. Friedrich Engels notes that it was at this point that

Marx abandoned a Hegelian philosophy of law, which was concerned with the power emanating from the state, for a philosophy of law that privileged the study of civil society and political economy. From 1842 onward, Marx dedicated his life to producing a theory of civil society that could explain material interest and power. So what culminated in 1867 with the history-changing theories of labor found in *Capital: A Critique of Political Economy* began as a reflection on the relationship of media censorship, law, political control, civil society, and the state.

Although Marx's economic theories have come to tower over all his others, his cultural theories and his concern with civil society continue to be central to Marxian thought and can be found in work seminal to media studies from Antonio Gramsci to Louis Althusser. The central continuity found in these thinkers is that state power depends for its stability on the management of civil society and that conditions of hegemony rely on cultural control that, in a liberal democracy, as Michel Foucault suggests, can only be achieved through citizen participation and the interiorization of the law. But law is not only inside people: it is also outside, and it governs. It is this law as exteriority that censored and exiled Marx, imprisoned Gramsci, and spurred contemporary theories of legal subjectivity including Althusser's and Foucault's. So law poses two interrelated problems to political economy approaches to culture and media theory. In its exteriority, law organizes, maintains, and legitimizes material allocation (as in public and private media infrastructure), social structures (as in membership, labor pools, and so on), and discourses (by giving primacy to some voices over others). As an interiority, which is partly produced through popular culture, law produces, reproduces, and maintains docile subjectivities. As both interiority and exteriority, law is a political technology that poses a third additional problem to a political economy concerned with transnationalism and Latinas/os, a problem Marx could not have predicted, even if his own juridical identity was similar to an immigrant's. Law, as a political technology, naturalizes the national as the preeminent social sphere, monopolizing the discourses with which we talk about justice, equity, and freedom.[4]

Marx's notion of power distribution is concerned with culture but emphasizes economics. Other scholars have recentered the cultural in political economy, notably, the work of Bourdieu and his vision of power in society (1984, 1990, 1991, 1993, 1996). Bourdieu's work recenters culture in political economy by highlighting the ways in which culture is a product of forms of social domination and competition and by remarking on the way culture also functions as a type of capital that individuals and groups use to compete for social positions. In his work on literature, aesthetics, photography, art museums, and academics, Bourdieu reveals how the cultural product and the cultural producer are linked not only because of the dynamics of product and producer but also through the social character of product and producer. That is, cultural producers endow culture with more than material, economic, or monetary value. They endow it with social meanings that help cultural consumers construct identities of distinction. Product and producer, hence, lend social value to consumption, and this value can be exchanged for social positioning. Eminently concerned with fluid and complex class definitions, Bourdieu's sociology explains stability by noting that the value of any given stock is typically determined prior to the moment of exchange, and the moment of exchange works as a confirmation of the stock's value. Cultural capital, thus, becomes necessary to enter specific social markets, which are hierarchically positioned.

In addition to culture, Bourdieu theorizes different types of symbolic capital and their relationships to fields of social organization, including the political field. Political capital accumulation is concerned with Bourdieu's sense that contemporary forms of governance rely heavily on the acquisition of cultural, social, and political markers that individuals can use to naturally occupy positions of power. Bourdieu arrives at this insight by updating Marx's notion of capital. According to Bourdieu, capital has several "guises" including economic capital (money and tradable commodities, as in property), cultural capital (cultural markers and credentials such as educational titles and certifications), social capital (acquaintances and social networks), and symbolic capital (which secures legitimization) (Bourdieu 1986, 242). Accumulation can happen in all of these guises, and, as importantly, accumulation in one type of capital can be converted into a different type of capital. As Marx would note, economic capital easily translates into social and cultural capital (as in the superstructure). Bourdieu notes that cultural capital can become economic and social capital (the term he uses is "interconvertibility"), as in the acquisition of distinction that becomes symbolic capital legitimizing access to wealthier social networks and so on.

Although political capital is not one of Bourdieu's central guises or concerns, he defines the term, albeit succinctly. For Bourdieu, political capital governs the field of politics and corresponds to the types of symbolic capital that members of the field compete for. Although others after Bourdieu, including Niilo Kauppi (2003) and Kimberly Casey (2008), have tried to expand on the term, their definition of the field of politics and, of necessity, their definition of political capital are skewed toward electoral processes. That is, for Bourdieu, Kauppi, and Casey, the type of symbolic capital used in the field of politics is one that can bring a person or a party electoral victory.

Public sphere theory can be seen as essentially a theory of interconvertibility that assumes that under the right circumstances, cultural capital can be converted into political capital. What Fraser calls normative legitimacy and political efficacy are in fact two of the fundamental rules that convert the cultural milieu that is the public sphere into electoral power. Yet, from the perspective of Latinas/os, the difficulties of this conversion point to a factor beyond the scope of the rules of capitalization of either the cultural or political fields. Both fields are organized around the figure of the citizen: the citizen is both the foundational element of both social systems and the ultimate target of their existence.

In Bourdieu's recognition that political economic principles are applicable beyond economics, he adds to Marx. But in Bourdieu, as in Marx, the centrality of citizenship remains hidden. Hence, neither approach is sufficient to theorize the public sphere from a Latino perspective. Yet, together, they point us in the right direction. Bourdieu is better than Marx at painting a social system that is ruled by communities with access to different types of capital. Yet more traditional Marxist approaches to power, such as those found in Gramsci or Althusser, have a substantial advantage over Bourdieu. Gramsci, Althusser, and, later, Foucault understand that not all social markets are equal: those markets that are closer to the law will have substantively more power. Interconvertibility, including normative legitimacy and political efficacy, is not random. Citizenship excess theorizes that the juridical holds the rules of capital conversion and effectively shapes the allocation of immediate and lasting capital. Both the centrality of the juridical and the relevance of different types of capital are necessary for a theory of the public sphere. As I show next, public sphere theory depends on the fundamental liberal idea that consensus can always be expressed in law.

Governmentality and Political Economy

The dynamic process of political capital accumulation that characterizes citizenship excess does not exist independent from the theories that legitimize and normalize politics, including liberalism and democracy.

According to Foucault, these theories generate the discourses, knowl-edges, and descriptions of reality that serve as bases of action for govern-ments and populations. I would add, they also produce the conditions of citizenship excess, for, as I argued in the introduction, these theories fran-chise a citizen who is ethno-racially constituted. Typically discussed under the rubric of governmentality, Foucault's vision recaptures Marx's concern with political economy in contemporary states, but contrary to economi-cist interpretations of Marx's work, Foucault refuses to believe that profit is always the answer to questions of government and power. In other words, his governmentality invigorates the political in political economy.

Like Marx, Foucault could have broken with methodological national-ism, but he did not. Biographers acknowledge that French colonialism, especially in Algeria, influenced Foucault's scholarship to the point of changing its direction in the late 1960s (Miller 2000, 185). But the turning point was caused not by a concern with colonialism alone but also by a general concern with the state of French politics at a time when Marxisms were popular political cultures in French universities but not popular enough to become winning political propositions. The 1968 violent de-feat and subsequent political retreat of French communisms forced Fou-cault to reevaluate politics and power, and the results were expressed in his theories of governmentality. His main concerns remained the nation-state and the politics it engendered, and his highly influential theories of power did not consider the French immigration problem of the time or the systems of racialization that were giving way to a highly stratified and nativist social reality. Predictably, Foucault's post-1968 work is better for theorizing the resilience of liberal nation-states controlled by a single breed of ethnonationalism. Although Foucault's work did not address im-migration as such, his ideas help outline the reasons why nativism is so apt at sustaining hegemonic arrangements that remarginalize immigrant populations such as Latinas/os. Governmentality helps us understand how this marginalization is partly engendered by legal and political sys-tems and can shed light on the political complexity of the nation-state. Governmentality, in short, is particularly good at theorizing the nativism and legalism described in the introduction.[5] As influential as Foucault's work on governmentality has been, it is also a theoretical framework ill suited for making sense of ethnic minorities and immigrants within the project of liberalism. In fact, Jonathan Inda argues that theories of gov-ernmentality limit the types of questions we ask about ethnic minorities and immigrants (2006, 24).

Governmentality refers to a series of theoretical questions introduced by Foucault in lectures aimed at exploring the relationships between governance, power, and conduct. He was interested in illuminating both governmental and individual practices of governance, discipline, and self-construction (Foucault 1991, 87). In bringing to the same arena issues of government and self, Foucault recast questions about politics and furthered his theories of power. Governmentality, understood as the arts of government, is thus essential to everyone and central to questions of ethics and justice (Foucault 2007, 116; Burchell, Gordon, and Miller 1991; Bennett 1998; Gordon 1991, 3). Foucault's concerns are partly historical (e.g., he explores East Asian pastoral forms of governance), but his historical explorations are meant to highlight aspects of governmentality found in modern state arrangements and in contemporary liberal nation-states such as the United States (e.g., liberalism is a governmentality that uses the pastoral) (Foucault 2007, 123). Liberal governmentality assumes that the modern state gathers and uses historically particular techniques to create technologies of power that can bring the population under control without breaking the delicate balance between social consensus and hegemony. In modernity, governmentality consists, among other things, of a variety of epistemic and institutional techniques that define individuals in highly measurable ways, befitting of an epoch that overemphasizes productivity, commodification, and planning (Inda 2006, 3–23). To make populations knowable and manageable is partly the role of policy and law.

This type of governmentality enacted through law is found in the United States from its beginnings to the present. Already the founding documents are invested in producing governmental techniques that will allow government to know the population so that government can apply this knowledge for administration and management. The very first article of the U.S. Constitution accomplishes this when it institutes the census, which would be used to number and classify citizens but also to calculate taxation, revenue, and political representation. It states,

> Representatives and direct Taxes shall be apportioned among the several States which may be included within this Union, according to their respective Numbers, which shall be determined by adding to the whole Number of free Persons, including those bound to Service for a Term of Years, and excluding Indians not taxed, three fifths of all other persons. The actual Enumeration shall be made within three Years after the first Meeting of the Congress of the United States, and within every

subsequent Term of ten Years, in such Manner as they shall by Law direct. (U.S. Constitution, art. 1, sec. 2, cl. 3)

Although it is quite remarkable that the very first article institutes the census, it is equally significant that it does this in language that today we recognize as proto-nativist. That is, in addition to instituting the census, this article is the basis for the logic of citizenship inclusion and exclusion. First, the Indian exclusion reformulates the basis for political exclusion of colonial others. Second, the citizen, defined as a "free Person," stands opposite to the "three fifths." The "three fifths" rule is euphemistic language referring to the counting of slaves, who are not, it should be noted, counted because slaves are thought to be superior to Indians. Rather, states with large slave populations negotiated this provision to secure a larger portion of direct taxes and representatives, not because of the welfare or political rights of slaves.

These governmental techniques, such as the census and the loaded notion of "free Persons," anticipated an ethno-racial capitalism and liberalism (N. Rose 1999, 215). Together, the techniques suggested that politics ought to behave and be understood primarily through the economic logics of efficiency and progress and that the political world ought to be populated by ethno-racialized individuals (Mezey 2003; C. Harris 1997). More importantly, what I call *ethno-racial liberal governmental* techniques continue to have a huge impact on contemporary racializations, and Latinas/os are often victims of their logic. Census data today dictate the allocation of more than $100 billion of federal funds, and to be counted becomes economically significant. To be counted is also central to political access for minorities. For instance, "Voting rights laws explicitly link census data with political access for minorities. . . . [Voting] rights enforcement depends on the racial make-up of Congressional districts as determined by census numbers" (Mezey 2003, 1745). Public funding money depends on census data. Labor discrimination cases are often solved by comparing labor statistics with census statistics. In a Foucauldian tone, Naomi Mezey argues that "where the census is one of the primary vehicles for the distribution of certain group protections and entitlements based on race, one sees the strategic investment in the politics of enumeration for many groups in the modern welfare state" (2003, 1746). The census as a technique of governance is invested not simply in knowing the real but in producing a political reality that will serve the basis for the enfranchisement of citizens. It is thus among the processes franchising citizenship excess. The U.S. census did not have an official category for Hispanics, Mexicans, or Latinas/os (or for Native Americans) for the longest time; in 1930, Latinas/os were briefly quantified by the census as a race, but they disappeared from the following census (Almaguer 1994, 46). Only in 1970 did the census include the category of Hispanic, and despite the great controversy over the term *Hispanic*, this census marked a new era for governmentality and Latinidad (Gibson and Jung 2006, 9–10). Governmental techniques, here, are the root causes of the political and legal practices molding a national polity in racialized ways (Aparicio 2003, 93).

In liberalism, the political and economic fields are closely entwined, and hence, political economy is truly about the coming together of economics and politics. Foucault argues that law is at the center of this convergence, which I illustrate in the figure of the citizen. Yet, as discussed earlier, there is more to political economy than politics and economics. In the U.S. Constitution, the citizen ("free Person") becomes the depository of political and economic rights that are outlined by reference to ethno-racial characteristics. Hence, in liberalism, the citizen has always already existed in several different and substantive fields: in politics, in economics, and, through ethno-racialization, in the fields of social membership and culture. Because it is legally and simultaneously coded in these four fields, *the figure of citizen is the technical innovation that liberalism brought to governmentality.*

Interconvertibility depends on one element of a system having identity and import in another one. Because the figure of the citizen exists centrally in the economic, political, social, and cultural fields, it allows for the interconvertibility between them. Thanks to the citizen, what originates in the social may shape the cultural, the political, or the economic. Public sphere theory, of necessity, cannot be divorced from the fantastic potentialities of the citizen figure or from its dreadful foundations in ethno-racialization.

The Public Sphere and Pastoralism

The citizen may be the anchor that allows for conversion between the cultural, political, social, and economic fields, but interconvertibility itself relies on the concretion of a space of conversion where faculties inherent to the citizen can be put to use. In the contemporary world, this space is the mediated public sphere. In Gramscian parlance, culture and media become central to governmentality as a public sphere for the transaction of ideas, the formation of consensus, and modern citizenship. On this, Tony Bennett notes, "the relations of culture and power which most typically characterize modern societies are best understood in the light of the respects in which the field of culture is now increasingly governmentally organized and constructed" (1998, 61). In the United States, the field of culture exists in such close proximity to politics and economics that both partner to give discursive and social shape to ethno-racial liberal governmentality. And because the field of culture, and particularly media, is the most important element of the public sphere, the potential for the public sphere to function as a space for political deliberation is always already limited.

Ethno-racial liberal governmentality improperly shapes the public sphere through the juridical and economic fields. Foucault anticipates this political effect. Foucault's ideas on governmentality explain the formation of the political field through the juridical-legal constitution of subjects in liberal states and the relationship of the juridical-legal to the economic realm, which I detail later. Because of this link between the juridical-legal and economic realms, governmentality is useful for exploring the particular brand of capitalism that Latinas/os must engage as a condition to participate in majoritarian political systems, legal fields, and the public sphere.

In Foucault's work, as in Marx's, the link between the juridical constitution of the subject, the central form of consciousness in the nation-state, and liberal governmentality lies in the notion of security (Marx 1975, 230). While in other types of governance political power is relatively centralized —thus guaranteeing the state's stability through the monopoly of political authority—in liberalism political power is diffused through, among other things, the political franchise of citizenship. Hence, in liberalism power is potentially unstable because the question of "how to stay in power" cannot be answered without referencing the will of the people (Anderson 1991, 16; Brown 1993, 391). This will is, in capitalist societies, correlated to the people's physical safety and economic interest, and consequently social prosperity becomes a matter of state security. The U.S. Constitution, again, serves to support Foucault's views on the matter when it states, "We the people of the United States, in order to form a more perfect union, establish justice, insure domestic tranquility, provide for the common defense, promote the general welfare, and secure the blessing of liberty to ourselves and our posterity, do ordain and establish this Constitution for the United States of America" (U.S. Constitution, Preamble). Security, both physical and economic, is bound to the establishment of law and justice. Although the "We the people" sounds inclusive, Article I, which orders the establishment of the census, is not. Hence, the establishment of a U.S. juridical subjectivity must also be seen as an ethno-racial practice, and so must the notion of physical and economic security.

Caring for the people's interests and security is not a general requirement of governance, but it is a common characteristic of liberal governmentality. Foucault believes that this very characteristic, which he relates to the pastoral, is emblematic of liberalism and modern political cultures. The pastoral is a type of governance discursively constructed around the figure of the shepherd, whose goal is to lead his or her flock to safety and to take care of the flock's subsistence. "[Pastoral] power is fundamentally a beneficent power" (Foucault 2007, 125). Liberalism continues this discourse of beneficent power and constructs its raison d'être in doing good ("a more perfect union"). This ethical self-justification is, however, part of its governmentality. To stay in power the liberal state must fulfill the economic interests of the population or, at the very least, of the population with political franchise (Burchell 1991, 120). And, in the pursuit of this goal of imparting security through prosperity, the state becomes also the shepherd of the economy, which is led through policy and law. On this, Foucault is at odds with neo-Marxian theorizations of liberalism and law, which see the importance of law in relation to law's ability to legitimize government (e.g., liberalism is a contract between government and subject). In neo-Marxian conceptions, Colin Gordon (1991) argues, law is in ideological harmony with government. For Foucault, the centrality of law has more to do with law's ability to incorporate exceptional measures (changing doctrine), "because the participation of the governed in the elaboration of such law through parliament constitutes the most effective system for a governed economy" (Foucault, qtd. in Gordon 1991, 19). In his emphasis on security and interest, Foucault aims to bring together the legal and economic logics central to liberal governmentality in a sort of field (Bourdieu) dialectics. As Gordon writes, "Prosperity is the necessary condition of the state's own security, and prosperity in itself is nothing if not the capacity to preserve and hold on to, and where possible even to enhance, a certain global level of existence" (1991, 19).

In Foucauldian theory in particular and political theory in general, the social instrument that enables the government and society to adapt to the changing understanding of security, prosperity, and popular interest is civil society, a space closely related to the public sphere. In civil society, groups, clans, or classes come together to redress issues of distributive justice and economics at a political-juridical level (Gordon 1991, 22–23; Lipschutz and Rowe 2005, 21). Civil society is thus a space of transaction and the space for the alchemic transformation of the economic (interest) into the political (solidarity). This transaction or alchemic transformation is not only across groups or classes; it is also discursive and is energized by media cultures that separate speakers, marginalizing some and giving others the cultural relevance to produce the metaphors and literary tropes linking the economic and political socio-discursive realms. Critical race scholars working in media and communication studies have made this point clear. More specifically, regarding Latinas/os, stereotypes (Keller 1985; Ramírez Berg 2002; C. Rodríguez 1997; C. Rodríguez 2004; Noriega 1992), metaphors (Santa Ana 2002), and discourses of success and failure (Beltrán 2009) are the semantic ground on which the meaning of a Latina/o politics is built. So Latinas/os, like other groups, have to enter the space of civil society not only as political actors but as discursively constructed groups with more or less defined political meanings attached to them and to their political goals. This discursive platform guides political transactions and fosters and limits solidarities. Transactional outcomes in civil society are not solely or even primarily about "politics"; the outcomes of civil society are manifested in formal politics and law but are largely the result of discursive transactions. This is the point of public sphere theorists who correctly calculate the importance of deliberation, discursive wars, publicity, and media to the political field and civil society. Although these discursive transactions already imply access, they are at the core of public sphere theory. Arguing for access makes no sense without believing in the power of discourse. I believe that exploring this further will shed light on Foucault's weaknesses and the potential ways in which theories of the public sphere can be modified to better theorize Latinas/os.

The public sphere serves at least two roles in liberal governmentality: it is a mechanism for consensus building, and it legitimizes liberalism. Just as culture is central to the production of consensus, the public sphere is the mechanism of this consensus. If liberal governmentality is centered around beneficent processes of consensus, the public sphere is the instrument that makes such consensus possible. According to Jürgen Habermas (1989), the public sphere is a space for deliberation where citizens come together independent of state pressures to discuss issues, to form opinions, and to coalesce as publics. As Fraser has noted, the usefulness of the public sphere has to do with the specificity that Habermas brought to the concept; ideally, it is a discursive space independent from the economy or the state that citizens can use to engage with the state (1990, 59). Although Habermas understands that the public sphere is an ideal that has rarely been met in modern states, it is an ideal worth pursuing (Mendieta 2003, 228). Since Habermas's original propositions, Fraser and others have perfected, criticized, and modified the notion of the public sphere on theoretical and historical grounds. Habermas's ideas have been criticized for overemphasizing "rational norms of communication" and, in so doing, "[excluding] certain speakers and modes of communication" (Petersen 2011, 8). This includes women and nonwhites, whose communication styles have discursively been understood as emotional as opposed to rational, embodied as opposed to cerebral, and particular as opposed to universal (ibid., 10–14). As Jennifer Petersen and others argue, expanding notions of deliberation, argumentation, rhetoric, and publicity are thus necessary steps toward better theorizing the public sphere.

Historically, as Fraser (1990) notes, the liberal public sphere sketched by Habermas never quite existed, and in fact, as history, Habermas's account is faulty. His argument's greatest fault was, according to Fraser, its lack of recognition that vibrant counterpublics, with different modalities of discourse and political goals, have always existed but were often marginalized by a masculinist class in control of power. Once public sphere theory has been rewritten to accommodate these complex histories and theoretical corrections, Fraser proposes that it should abandon the idealistic notions that people can bracket off their difference from others when they enter the public sphere. As Fraser notes, people's speech in the public sphere is "marked" by differences in power that are effects of material inequalities (1990, 61). In a stratified society, not all speech will be considered equal in the majoritarian public sphere. To better account for specificity and difference, Fraser proposes that a plurality of public spheres is required to meet the needs of our complex societies. Some will correspond to subordinated social groups, which Fraser calls subaltern counterpublics. This term signals "parallel discursive arenas where members of subordinated social groups invent and circulate counterdiscourses, which in turn permit them to formulate oppositional interpretations of their identities, interests, and needs" (ibid., 67). For these subaltern counterpublics to have an impact in wider publics, they need to share enough protocols of communication to be able to bridge cultural differences and participate in processes of deliberation and contestation (63–70).

In these theories of the public sphere, the structural role is roughly similar. The public sphere (or public spheres or subaltern counterpublics) makes possible some citizen participation in processes of government. There is a second structural role of the public sphere that relates to Foucault's concerns. The public sphere legitimates liberalism because these spheres of transaction play the role of constructing the aura of beneficence central to liberal governmentality. This aura is a discursive production through which the existence or appearance of public spheres signifies that government is adaptable, open, and responsive. Because of the meanings attached to public spheres, they legitimize government, the nation-state, and the political processes that define them. Unsurprisingly, the terminology we use to evaluate the public sphere implies juridical subjectivities and political processes that replicate our national creed and, in the case of the United States, legitimize this bizarre bipartisan democratic system and ethno-racial liberal governmentality. So we call good citizens ("the" juridical subject of the nation-state) those who participate in a public sphere; and we call democratic consensus the outcomes of the deliberative processes that justify the existence of multiple public spheres. We call deliberative processes the relationship of media coverage and public opinion that can be polled by legitimized research organizations. In all of these cases, the structural functions of the public sphere serve as evidence of the shepherd's care.

If ideas of the public sphere also serve to legitimize liberalism, then even subaltern public spheres help constitute liberal governmentality, for they are instruments of consensus and political adaptability. While this is a general critique of the construction of consensus, Fraser reminds us that subaltern public spheres are quite different from each other. As importantly, she helps us update a theory of the public sphere that can accommodate cultural and ethnic difference, as in the case of Latinas/os. But as Fraser would note, a subaltern public sphere requires preconstituted spaces for expression. Minorities, in particular, need spaces where *their* ways of being and their political concerns can be expressed as if they were majoritarian, outside the brutal market of the public sphere, where minoritarian ways of being and minorities' political concerns may be dismissed and even ridiculed (Noriega 2000; Fraser 1990, 69).[6] While this makes sense, I began this chapter noting that, for Latinas/os, having such a separate, subaltern public sphere has not improved their political power. This paradox is a meaningful reminder that while concerns about the public sphere are key to understanding citizenship's relationship to media and politics, we need to return to Foucault's understanding of

governmentality, security, and the juridical. This is so because though political struggles are often decided in the public sphere, the public sphere
is itself constituted by law, particularly as law relates to the economic and
political fields. Just as the citizen is the node that allows for interconvertibility between fields, the space of publicity where the citizen operates is
juridically constituted.

Like Habermas and Fraser, research on the public sphere often incor-
porates political economy concerns and approaches. Ideally, this political
economy should specify the commonalities between public sphere, media
cultures, and media industries, but it should also clarify their differences.
For broad political projects, the public sphere largely overlaps with media
cultures and media industries. In regard to broad political issues, the public sphere cannot exist without media. But a political economy of media
culture and media industries is not enough to comprehend the way media
connects, shapes, and is shaped by governmentality or the way different
media participate in processes of deliberation and confrontation between
public spheres. Political economy approaches may overemphasize capital
and ratings and put too little emphasis on the ability of small publics to
have a huge impact if they are embraced by majoritarian media.

Let me illustrate this point with a glimpse of a case that will be thor-
oughly argued in following chapters. In 2006, Latinas/os and sympathizers used Spanish-language radio, television, and print to organize the
largest marches the United States has seen involving Latinas/os. Millions
participated. The goal was to produce immigration law that would provide a path to citizenship for millions of undocumented immigrants. La-
tinas/os lost. Nativists won because, though in the minority, they used
English-language media to launch a successful counteroffensive. In the
months that followed, city, state, and federal governments passed hundreds of changes to law and policy that secured the power of nativists. Significantly, nativist discourses gave the impression that a larger percentage
of U.S. citizens opposed pro-immigrant legal reform than the percentage
that actually did, indeed proving that the power of mediated rhetoric was
to unduly amplify the commonality of nativist views.

I find no comfort in Fraser's discussion of the political work of subaltern public spheres when I look at this example, because public sphere
theory is at its weakest when analyzing subalterns that are marked by
language. However, my criticisms of Fraser and Foucault should not be
read as invitations to abandon theories of the public sphere or liberal governmentality. I believe these have much to offer, for they are theories of

politics that, while giving a central role to the juridical, make the juridical amenable to cultural analysis. This is why Miller and Ouellette and Hay are so wonderful. However, I believe that in order to use liberal governmentality productively, we ought to understand it as a process of ethnoracialization. Hence, government beneficence can be seen as a technology of power with the role of securing the prosperity of specific citizen populations at the expense of others. Linguistic and ethno-racial markers can help us understand this processes of securitization, for they structure civil society and public spheres in ethno-racial ways.

Coloniality as an Answer to Governmentality

Foucault dedicated his intellectual energy to explaining national homeostasis and, in the process, produced immanent theories of national stability that can be interpreted as Eurocentric. Foucault's historical vision took him from the roots of Judeo-Christian political and philosophical thought to a present in which monarchic arrangements have given way to liberal and democratic forms of government. These modern political arrangements have political stability because of the ongoing balance between disciplinary forms of governance (e.g., political coercion) and pastoralism.

I argue that Foucault's is not the only way of historicizing European forms of liberal governmentality and likely not the best. For one, he does not consider the role that colonialism and racial hierarchies played in the constitution of European modernity. Several Latin American scholars have made this their point of departure and have produced theorizations more suited for explaining the pastoralist paradox. For instance, Enrique Dussel, Anibal Quijano, Walter Mignolo, and Mendieta try to denaturalize the epistemic cage of modernity and Eurocentrism from the standpoint of the colonialized other. In their views, modernism, capitalism, racism, Eurocentrism, and the nation-state share a common origin: the invasion of the Americas (e.g., Quijano 2000, 534; Dussel 2002, 234). These sixteenth-century events, which Immanuel Wallerstein placed at the roots of the first world-system (the first manifestation of a global rationality), allowed, as Marx points out, for the wealth accumulation and the expansion of markets that are required for the flourishing of capitalism.[7] Ideologically, these processes were in relative harmony with a new vision of history and of the world that defined racial hierarchies among peoples as natural, thus legitimizing the obscene human exploitation of the new colonialism and capitalism (Ruskola 2005, 862–865). With racism, slavery (the naturalized economic position of the African), and serfdom (the position given to the Amerindian) came the basis for a new way of seeing society, history, and knowledge production.

Quijano uses the phrase "coloniality of power" to refer to the extension and expansion of administrative logic born out of colonialism to administration practices after colonialism (Quijano 2000, 2007). Centrally concerned with explaining contemporary social inequalities, Quijano reflects back on the conquest of the Americas to understand the contemporary centrality of race, capitalist exploitation, and modern epistemology to the constitution and reproduction of inequality. In his historical-sociological thesis, the first modernity brought about by the discovery and conquest of the Americas set in motion the ways of thinking, justifying, and administering societies that still exist today. So, instead of locating contemporary governmentality in the Greco-Roman and Judeo-Christian traditions, as Foucault does, Quijano locates it in the first modernity and the systems of ethno-racial domination that became lodged in the West's political and legal traditions.

With coloniality in mind, I argue the following: *The very juridical center of the nation-state, which is the notion that rights are given life by (*politics*) and for (*law*) the citizen, is a juridical-subjectivity born out of colonialism and slavery.* Engin Isin (2002) notes that the equivalence of citizenship with political agency is as old as the Greeks. The tradition has continued, and as I showed regarding Article I of the U.S. Constitution, it is the central tenet of the U.S. legal system. From Athens to modernity, the citizen has always been defined in contrast with the colonial other, the slave, or, in more contemporary political imaginaries, the undocumented immigrant. Hence, the citizen's political agency is constructed in contrast to the lack of agency of the other. It is always the quality of "free person" that defines the citizen. And it is the lack of freedom of the colonial other, slave, or undocumented immigrant that defines its abject personhood (Inda 2006, 53).

Liberal governmentality understood through the prism of coloniality is simply a different system of governance than the one Foucault imagines. Internal administration logics that govern the citizenry coexist with tyrannical forms of governance designed to control population at the nation's political and racial borders. The legitimacy of these tyrannical forms of governance, which include provisions to assure the appropriation of the labor of noncitizens, dates back to the age of colonialism, when imperial powers constituted international legal systems that gave juridical basis to, for instance, land usurpation, as in the reactivation by the British and Spanish of the Roman notion of *terra nullius* (empty land) to "legally" take possession of the Americas. Slavery, international war, and copyright frameworks are but three different manifestations of a coloniality that reaches deep into our past and present legal traditions. These traditions include issues of law but also the cultures of impunity that allow social arrangements to blatantly subvert legal provisions. Examples abound that illustrate citizenship excess. For instance, the history of public schooling in places such as Mississippi clearly illustrates the legal and political function of impunity. Only for seven years (1868–1875) after the Civil War did Mississippi provide competitive funds to black schools, a legal requirement grafted onto federal and state law. After these seven years, impunity cultures and legal chicanery reconstituted pre–Civil War stratifications. The combination of impunity and legal chicanery enabled blatant cases of stealing money earmarked for black schools to go unprosecuted, but such cases were also the product of a system of law carefully crafted to dispossess black schools (Jackson State University 2010).

In immigration, coloniality is not the exception but the rule. Cultures of impunity allow for the importation of labor from other nations and working conditions well below legal standards, while legal cultures harness state power to enact arrest, detention, and deportation procedures en masse when economically and/or politically convenient (Akers Chacón and Davis 2006; Bacon 2008; De Genova 2005; Ngai 2004; Ono and Sloop 2002). Contemporary legal requirements of arrest, detention, trial, and deportation are shocking in their incompatibility with legal traditions in other contexts. As Daniel Kanstroom argues, compared to criminals, non-citizens—documented or undocumented—have minimal rights:

> Suppression of evidence that may have been seized in violation of the Fourth Amendment will be impossible in most cases. The noncitizen will not be read "Miranda" rights. Indeed, he [*sic*] may not even be advised that he has the right to obtain a lawyer (at his own expense) until after a government agent has interrogated him. He will never have the right to appointed counsel. If he believes he has been singled out due to race, religion, or political opinion, he will generally not be able to raise a "selective prosecution" defense. He will never have the right to a jury trial. If he has a formal hearing before an immigration judge, he will have certain due process rights: to be heard, to examine evidence, and to receive a written decision. He may, however, find that the burden of proof will be shifted to him once the government has made a showing

of "alienage." If he wants to appeal the immigration judge's decision, he may face incarceration during the length of that appeal—which could easily be years. He may then receive a summary decision made by a single member of the understaffed and overwhelmed Board of Immigration Appeals produced after a ten-minute review of his case. If he seeks a further appeal to a federal court, he may well find that the court declines review of "discretionary" questions, such as his potential eligibility for "relief" from removal. (2007, 4)

If noncitizens are detained under fast-track deportation procedures, which are used for nonresidents with criminal convictions, they have "no right to in-person hearings—their cases are adjudicated on paper. They are given only ten days to respond, in English, to charges against them. They do not even have the right to be provided with a copy of the evidence against them" (ibid., 11–12). Fast-track applies to documented and undocumented aliens, tourists, foreign students, and others accused of crimes as minimal as carrying small amounts of marijuana or shoplifting. The Sensenbrenner Act would have placed all undocumented immigrants under fast-track. Today, most Mexicans detained without proper documentation face versions of fast-track, regardless of whether the state can provide proof of criminal convictions and regardless of whether they are legal residents or, in some cases, U.S. citizens.

Through the lens of coloniality, law converts the social into a political field created by and for the citizen. Moreover, law expands and, I would argue, hides the logic of colonial administration, producing the suppleness that Foucault notes is central to liberal governmentality. Coloniality also facilitates the epistemological and social rationales at the base of the reproduction of law and legal structures, furnishing the social scripts that make unsustainable the justice claims of Latinas/os in general and immigrants in particular. Coloniality, in short, explains citizenship excess and locates its most nefarious manifestations in the ethno-racialization of politics and the economy.

Coloniality and the Public Sphere: The Beginning of a Conclusion

When I say that methodological nationalism is at the root of the shortcomings of public sphere theory, I am referring here to something so fundamental that is practically invisible even to the most astute scholars.

Fraser, in her highly celebrated critique of Habermas, introduced public sphere as follows: "[The public sphere] designates a theater in modern societies in which political participation is enacted through the medium of talk" (1990, 57). Just as Marx missed the chance of theorizing a political economy from the standpoint of the stateless, or Foucault failed to see how French colonialism was at the root of liberal power in the modern state, Fraser started with "talk" and did not address the problem of the public sphere from a multilingual and transnational perspective until much later. She lucidly examines how talk is differentiated by cultural and economic position and power yet fails to examine the power differentials between talk in different languages. For each of these seminal thinkers, not to mention Habermas, the problem of politics begins and ends with the nation-state, imagined in ethno-racial terms. This is coloniality at work. Methodological nationalism hence connects to coloniality, and the work of these thinkers of liberalism and the public sphere is evidence of this connection. Beyond coloniality's role in administration, it reaches deep into our modernist ways of thinking and knowing. Reviewing Marx, Foucault, and Fraser helps us see that coloniality is hidden too in theory. Because so much academic work has been done under the shadow of methodological nationalism, it is difficult to theorize disenfranchised populations who, like Latinas/os, exist in substantively different legal, cultural, and linguistic contexts.

Talk. The public sphere paradox begins here. The Latino public sphere, which relies heavily on SLM, does not reach the linguistic majority and thus remains isolated. Fraser states this problematic as follows:

> Consider, too, the presupposition of a single national language, which was supposed to constitute the linguistic medium of public sphere communication. As a result of the population mixing already noted, national languages do not map onto states. The problem is not simply that official state languages were consolidated at the expense of local and regional dialects, although they were. It is also that existing states are de facto multilingual, while language groups are territorially dispersed, and many more speakers are multilingual. Meanwhile, English has been consolidated as the lingua franca of global business, mass entertainment and academia. Yet language remains a political fault line, threatening to explode countries like Belgium, if no longer Canada, while complicating efforts to democratize countries like South Africa and to erect transnational formations like the European Union. (2007)

The United States, which has more Spanish speakers than all the minority-language speakers of Belgium, Canada, and South Africa combined, does not make the list. Under the spell of the colonial, Fraser is unable to see the United States as a site of linguistic turmoil. That said, the spirit of Fraser's ideas animates my own. The Spanish-language public sphere can create consensus internal to Spanish-speaking Latino communities, as the pro-immigration marches showed in 2006, but it cannot create consensus beyond (see the next chapter). Yet Latino talk is more complex than this. We Spanish-speaking Latinas/os become isolated from the majority not simply because we are not speaking in English but also because we speak in Spanish, a language that is systematically and semiotically marginalized. As I show in chapter 5, Spanish is a linguistic insult to many people in the United States, and this nativist perspective gives meaning to our speech. Spanish, according to many, pollutes the public sphere. The great majority of us Latinas/os, of course, are bilingual and can speak English, but when we do it, our accents convey stereotypical visions of ignorance, poverty, and foreignness. Unlike French, German, or Italian accents in the United States, which are interpreted as evidence of sophistication and cosmopolitanism, having a Spanish accent in the United States is interpreted as having a cultural deficit. Such is the ethno-racial world that nationalism constructs. Is it then surprising that SLM is isolated?

Translation does not fully solve this problem. If the Latino public sphere is mostly in Spanish, bilingual Latinas/os could translate the concerns of Spanish-speaking Latinas/os. But this simply places the problem of talk in a different arena (J. Martinez 2003, 255). In the media system we inhabit, public credibility is the result of media stardom. News anchors such as Katie Couric, famous journalists such as Charlie Rose, media-enfranchised political commentators such as Glenn Beck and Wolf Blitzer, media stars such as Sean Penn, public intellectuals such as Larry Sabbato, and politicians monopolize the majoritarian public sphere. In this "theater," to use Fraser fortuitous term, the speaking parts are all taken. Univision news anchors such as María Elena Salinas or Jorge Ramos do not have the recognition and credibility in the English-speaking news world. Latino public intellectuals such as José David Saldívar, Richard Rodriguez, Jorge Gracia, and Linda Chavez are able to speak broadly to political and cultural issues, but they are a small cohort. The Latinas/os who do get to speak regularly in both Spanish- and English-language media and, hence, in the minoritarian and majoritarian public spheres are media celebrities such as Salma Hayek and politicians such as Bill Richardson.

Translation implies authority in at least two spheres. Predictably, the situation for Latino translators, as commented by Mendieta (2003), Jacqueline Martinez (2003), Jane Juffer (2003), and Paula Moya (2003), is dire. When Mendieta reflects on the relative lack of Latino public intellectuals, he is taking a cue from the role Cornel West plays in American political and intellectual life in general and his significant role among African Americans. West, without a question, is recognized and respected as an intellectual who speaks critically about race to a particular broad brand of American liberalism. Arguably, no Latino public intellectual has similar standing, and this is not because Latinas/os lack a public sphere, as Mendieta suggests, but rather because the sphere we bilingual Latinas/os do have is isolated from majoritarian politics and culture. As striking as it is to notice the way Marx, Foucault, and Fraser miss significant opportunities to theorize the social from a non-Eurocentric perspective, neither Mendieta, Martinez, Juffer, nor Moya, scholars deeply engaged in Latino studies, mention Spanish or SLM in their otherwise insightful reflections on the Latino public sphere. The situation, indeed, is dire.

Attentive to coloniality, the following chapters show how SLM and ELM are organized and given political value through administration, law, and policy. I show that a substantive number of these administrative and legal traditions originate in colonial schemas, including the way ethno-racialization allowed for nativist minorities to occupy prominent cultural roles at the expense of Latinas/os and the way SLM has been treated by media policies in the United States.

The core premises that Fraser is challenging us to question are more complex than publicity. Publicity implies speech, listening, visibility, and understanding. In short, publicity implies a shared language. Unsurprisingly, because language is the a priori condition of isolation, access to a public sphere is not enough for Latinas/os. The majoritarian political markets do not recognize the importance of Latino public opinion if this opinion is stated in Spanish. Hence, the issue of "participatory parity" that Fraser mentions becomes irrelevant in conditions of coloniality. Participating in a section or segment of the public sphere, such as SLM, does not guarantee the ability to engage in discursive transactions, particularly if this language is systematically and semiotically marginalized.

Can Latinas/os use the public sphere to emancipate themselves? Not without first transforming the ethno-racial character of the U.S. State and the manner in which current political culture isolates SLM. Can Latinas/os access the majoritarian public sphere? Minimally. Can Latinas/os transform the ethno-racial character of the U.S. State without access to the majoritarian public sphere? No. Can the majority transform itself to allow access to Latinas/os to the majoritarian public sphere? Maybe, but not while nativists occupy so many prominent cultural and political positions. The conditions of coloniality cannot be undone without a radical rewriting of our political imaginaries.

2

Nativism and the 2006 Pro-Immigration Reform Rallies

The GOP won't be a majority party if it cedes the young or Hispanics to Democrats. Republicans must find a way to support
secure borders, a guest-worker program and comprehensive immigration reform that strengthens citizenship, grows our economy and keeps America a welcoming nation. An anti-Hispanic
attitude is suicidal.
—Karl Rove, "A Way Out of the Wilderness," *Newsweek*,
November 15, 2008

In 2006, millions of Latinas/os and supporters took to the streets de-
manding reforms to immigration law that would create a path to citizenship for millions of undocumented residents. Although the marches were
extremely successful, the pro-immigration reform movement (PRM) did
not succeed. Instead of producing an opening for the legalization of millions, state and federal governments enacted harsher immigration measures, bringing increased suffering to documented and undocumented
immigrants. Armando Navarro (2009), a political scientist at the University of California–Riverside, gives several reasons for the PRM's relative
defeat, including the lack of a sustainable activist effort, lack of national
leadership, and a coalitional effort that became hard to organize around
issues other than immigration reform. He also documents how nativists,
without huge marches or the sophisticated political mobilization apparatus used by pro-immigration reform leaders, counted on the support of
the political field, mainstream hegemonic media, and legal structures.

While Navarro's approach is quite apt at explaining the convergence of different contexts that produced the PRM's struggles, he historicizes the rise of nativism as a sort of anomalous civic manifestation in an otherwise promising liberal democracy where hope is possible and reasonable. Implied in his conclusion is that the PRM may have succeeded with better organization, leaders, long-term political platforms, and coalitions. Perhaps. But lost in his analysis are two issues that offer alternative hypotheses to explain the challenges encountered by the PRM. The first is the issue of whether to characterize nativism as anomalous civic behavior or whether to think of it as traditional. I explore the latter possibility. The second is whether the PRM's successes and failures should be explained mostly in terms of civil society, as Navarro does, or whether to explain them in terms of the public sphere. I concentrate on both elements while emphasizing the latter. My goal is to complement Navarro's work by suggesting that the PRM's lack of success at the federal level was partly the result of nativists' ability to tap into traditional legal and political discourses of xenophobia and their ability to dominate the majoritarian public sphere. At stake here is a view of politics that understands that discourse is central to political processes legitimized by consensus and that to successfully participate in civil society, social movements (and their opponents) need media. A political group may be able to change leadership, may be able to change and refine political programs, but it cannot change the need for media, nor can it, by itself, change media structures. In addition to relying on theorists of the public sphere such as Nancy Fraser (1990) and Jürgen Habermas (1989), I carry on this analysis using Michel Foucault's (1991, 2007) work on liberal governmentality, a theoretical approach that places discourse at the center of the political while recognizing the liberal reliance on civil society (see chapter 1).

It is not difficult to argue that nativism is citizenship excess, evidence of coloniality, and that nativists tend to abuse their political and legal privileges to enact xenophobia. It is harder to think of nativism as normal political and legal behavior that is constitutive of nation-states, as proposed by coloniality. But I believe this hypothesis can be sustained if we reflect on the ease with which nativists came to occupy key locations in the political and media world, without much struggle or fanfare. The ease with which nativists managed to shape the public sphere and actual government speak to the fact that these were not xenophobic exceptions. Attentive to coloniality's propositions regarding administration, law, and policy, I argue that our traditional political culture of liberalism is organized around dispositions that legitimize the legal and discursive grounds that nativists used against the PRM and that citizenship excess is one predictable outcome of the U.S. political system.[1]

As a social movement, the PRM succeeded at making Congress aware of the need to oppose some of the most draconian legislations against undocumented immigrants, such as the Sensenbrenner Bill (I expand on this later). It also succeeded at energizing Latinas/os as a political group, following the PRM marches with naturalization drives (to increase the number of people capable of voting) and voting drives. These drives are responsible for increasing the number of Latino voters in the 2008 presidential election by more than 27 percent from 2004 (Taylor and Fry 2007; Félix, Gonzalez, and Ramírez 2008). But on the issue of immigration reform, the PRM did not succeed. This chapter analyzes this failure.

In this chapter, I examine the battle between the PRM and nativists and start contextualizing the environment of nativism out of which PRM came into being. First, I reflect on civil society and, in particular, on how Latinas/os organized themselves to carry out the giant pro-immigration reform marches of 2006 and the role played by the Latino public sphere in shaping these marches. I detail the defeat of the PRM and argue that ethno-racial and linguistic differences between the Latino public sphere and the majoritarian public sphere are partly to blame for this defeat. Then I show that the majoritarian public sphere is given shape by traditional political, economic, and legal frameworks that marginalize ethno-racial and linguistic minorities, foreclosing the possibility of state adaptability to political pressures coming form ethno-racial and linguistic minorities. Using the examples of the pro-immigration rallies of 2006, I show that the U.S. public sphere, as it is represented by the broadcasting system, is already fragmented along ethno-racial and linguistic lines and thus incapable of providing platforms for what W. Lance Bennett et al. (2004, 438) call recognition (who is formally identified as a source by name, status, or social membership?) and responsiveness (is there "mutual responsiveness between sources with different claims"?). I also show that this particular fragmentation forecloses the justice claims of undocumented immigrants, regardless of their political worth or consensus-building potential.

Contextualizing Nativism

In March and April 2006, millions of Latinas/os and sympathizers took to the streets in different U.S. cities to demand positive reforms in immigration law from the U.S. Congress. Republican President George W. Bush, a Texan and arguably the most Latino-friendly president ever, had proposed early in his presidency a set of bills that would give millions of undocumented immigrants a path toward citizenship. Together with Mexico's President Vicente Fox, Bush had drafted an immigration reform bill by 2001 that would have allowed a path to citizenship for undocumented immigrants. But 9/11 changed the president's priorities, moving the agenda away from Bush's hopes for Latino immigrant workers to his fears for mainstream U.S. citizens. For the next few years, the executive office and Congress embraced these fears with almost a pathological gusto, giving shape to a legal framework that effectively accomplished two things. Government legislated more legal ways of enacting xenophobia (e.g., the so-called Patriot Act, extraordinary rendition, and wiretapping) while legally weakening the extraordinary promise of egalitarianism through adjudication of rights represented in the U.S. Constitution and the Bill of Rights. If citizenship is understood, echoing T. H. Marshall, as "full membership in a community" (1973, 70), everybody's citizenship suffered. But not everyone suffered to the same degree. Adding ground to the claim that citizenship excess is an active process of ethno-racial political capital accumulation, the post-9/11 United States became a social and cultural landscape fertile for general expressions of ethno-territorial xenophobia ("this is our land"), paralleling the speech acts of a troubling and troubled administration. The United States of Bill O'Reilly (Fox), Lou Dobbs (CNN), Pat Buchanan (Clear Channel), and Colorado congressman Tom Tancredo (U.S. House of Representatives) went mainstream. This post-9/11 political culture, which was nurtured by mainstream media (especially Fox, CNN, and talk radio), rearticulated U.S. ideas about citizenship in terms of nativism and ethnocentrism, negatively affecting Arab Americans, Muslims anywhere, South Asian American communities, and by some strange chain of events, Latino residents.

With political maneuverings that marked the betrayal of the 9/11 victims, nativist politicians used the attacks on the Twin Towers and the Pentagon to engage in a political and legal war against undocumented immigrants in general and Latin American immigrants in particular. Citing border-security concerns, these politicians pushed for the further militarization of the border with Mexico. The four-thousand-mile Canadian border, huge and porous and patrolled by less than 7 percent of the Border Patrol personnel, never became the issue. It was always the border with Mexico, already militarized thanks to the successive presidencies of Reagan, Bush, and Clinton, which would receive the bulk of the new discursive and economic resources to stop all crossings. The Bush administration militarized the very institutions in charge of immigration, refranchising the Immigration and Naturalization Service (INS) into the Immigration, Customs, and Enforcement (ICE) under the securitizing umbrella of the Department of Homeland Security (DHS).

Nativist groups, acting on media already energized by citizenship excess, succeeded at publicizing hugely exaggerated numbers of undocumented crossings, and news organizations participated in this publicity (Navarro 2009, 283).[2] Nativist claims came from diverse sources including political leaders—in a publicized letter to a constituent, Republican senator John McCain declared that 4 million undocumented immigrants crossed the border annually (February 10, 2004)—and small activist organizations: the American Resistance group, a Web-based organization invested in publicizing these calculations, estimated 4.4 million undocumented crossings per year. According to the DHS, the number was around 700,000 per year. The census calculated between 350,000 and 500,000 per year, closer to 1990s rates (Navarro 2009, 283). Newspapers such as the *Washington Post* (on March 20, 2005) acknowledged from 500,000 to 2.5 million. There was a general sense that the exaggerated numbers represented reality, particularly because they were at times supported by the DHS, mouthed by political leaders (McCain), and repeated on CNN (Lou Dobbs). Nativists seemed to control the public sphere, and this translated into political reality as state legislations produced the first wave of legal measures targeting undocumented residents. Arizona's 2004 Proposition 200 echoed California's Proposition 187 limiting all social services for undocumented immigrants. It passed. Arizona's Proposition 300, which denied undocumented university students access to in-state tuition, also passed. Virginia, Colorado, and Georgia quickly passed similar legislation. New Mexico and Arizona, seeking federal funding for increased Border Patrol, declared a state of emergency in several counties. Anti-immigrant legislation went mainstream, with new laws passed in Hawaii, Colorado, California, Utah, Washington, Idaho, Wisconsin, Kansas, Nebraska, Missouri, Oklahoma, Arkansas, Alabama, Tennessee, Ohio, North Carolina, New Jersey, Wyoming, Louisiana, and Maryland. According to the *Nation*, in January 2008 alone, forty-six states passed roughly 250 immigration laws, making it easy to believe that on the issue of immigration reform, the United States had consensus. Consensus, however, was a mirage, a magic trick requiring smoke and mirrors, on the one hand, to occlude the power of a politically connected minority and, on the other hand, to magnify and multiply anti-immigrant rhetoric.

The nativist offensive at the federal level followed. On December 16, 2005, the Republican-led House of Representatives passed H.R. 4437, otherwise known as the Border Protection, Antiterrorism, and Illegal Immigration Control Act of 2005. Introduced by Wisconsin's Republican representative F. James Sensenbrenner, Jr., the bill called for a fence along the southern border of the United States, made it a felony to be undocumented, and called for the criminalization of organizations invested in helping undocumented immigrants cope with the new nation (such as churches and civic organizations). The bill passed in the House, with a vote of 239 to 182, and though it failed in the Senate, it became the footprint for other bills criminalizing the otherwise civil offense of residing in the United States without a proper visa. Latino immigrants and U.S. citizens who cared for new immigrants became the enemy, and the border with Mexico became a forward trench in the war on terror, a line separating friend from foe.[3] In the epigraph to this chapter, Karl Rove wisely advises that accommodating immigration is key to the future of the Republican Party; it is important to note that in 2005, Rove was in the minority.

This brief context to the PRM provides the key elements needed to historicize nativism in the contemporary United States. Nativists, unfazed by the contradictions of excess, relied on the discourse of national security to justify legal frameworks that would make the social and economic lives of undocumented immigrants intolerable. But even before nativists had this platform, the federal government was reorganizing institutions to make immigration a matter of state security (the DHS). Both government and nativist voices made use of the public sphere to craft consensus around the anti-immigrant legal measures that have characterized the post-9/11 United States. How does this combination of national security, xenophobia, law, and the public sphere fit within citizenship excess?

Nativism and Liberalism

Although power is everywhere in society, it is useful to recognize that specific social fields generate distinct types of power and specific social currencies. The economic field uses the currency of wealth. Politics organizes itself around votes. The academic field trades on published research and educational credentials. Pierre Bourdieu (1986) has noted that, sometimes, power within one field can be converted into power in another field, and he calls this process "interconvertibility" (see chapter 1). Money becomes votes. Educational credentials become money.

Yet not all currencies can be converted into other currencies. Texting speed or yodeling virtuosity rarely become anything else than that. Conversion is not random, and this is not lost to social theorists. In fact, one may argue that a significant number of social theories try to predict or explain the ease with which a social currency can become another. Marxian economic theories predict that money will too easily become votes and law. Feminism predicts the ease with which sex and gender become valued or devalued currencies in the field of power. Critical race scholarship predicts that whiteness too easily becomes money, educational credentials, and/or votes. Coloniality explains how past practices of exploitation have been converted into modern administration techniques. Indebted to these theories, citizenship excess predicts that ethnicity, nationality, and race will easily become social currencies in economics and politics that will legitimize exploitation. Nativism is the most glaring manifestation of this phenomenon. Under the spell of nativism, a powerful minority of white ethno-racial communities uses the discourses of liberalism and capitalism to legitimize anti-Latino laws. Under the powerful influence of liberalism and capitalism, the majority of Americans condone it, even if by condoning it they contradict their views against xenophobia and racism.

The reason a majority condones anti-Latino laws is central to the functioning of liberalism. Consider these two interrelated points. What fosters certain types of interconvertibility and not others is discourse. For instance, one may be forbidden from buying votes, but it is discourse that legitimizes the type of economic excess that rules our electoral processes. Thanks to the discourses of capital, personhood, and speech in juridical cases such as *Citizens United v. Federal Election Commission* (2010), the U.S. electoral system allows for an almost unfiltered participation of corporations into political campaigning. Money does buy votes. In this and other cases, discourse normalizes transactions between fields, creating the rates of exchange of currency and the possibility of conversion. However, as in *Citizens United*, discourse becomes formalized in law, and law survives even if the discourses have ceased to be proper parlance. This is clearly exemplified by noting how the discourse of racism, which is no longer popular, survives in the laws and policies that create radically different educational, economic, and political experiences for people of different races. Discourse normalizes interconvertibility. Law assures relative permanence.

Now let us consider that liberalism is a political system based on a so-called social contract between the state and its citizens that establishes, as Jean-Jacques Rousseau noted more than two centuries ago, that citizens will obey laws in exchange for state protection against harm and violence. In liberalism, law abidance becomes the most important political value, particularly if laws are indeed protecting a franchised majority. Seen in this way, liberalism becomes a political system that proposes that it is better to accept some negative outcomes that are legal than to overthrow legality (Benjamin [1921] 1996, 239). Citizenship excess predicts that the bulk of legal negative outcomes will affect the lives of ethno-racial minorities and other disenfranchised communities such as women, sexual minorities, and the disabled. And, connecting back to Foucault's governmentality, citizenship excess helps us theorize that the central cultural force normalizing legal negative outcomes is the discourses of the pastoral, which include safety, security, and prosperity. Unsurprisingly, these are the discourses mobilized by nativists.

Nativists have used the discourses of the pastoral to make their political and juridical views central to the nation-state. As Jonathan Inda (2006) and Aristide Zolberg (2006) have noted, the nativists' influence on the United States has relied on the continuous use of the discourses of safety, security, and prosperity to justify social and legal techniques for monitoring membership through, among other things, immigration law. Simply, nativism has been a constant feature of U.S. politics, as Zolberg contends, acting always as an invisible instrument of nation-building (2006, 1–24). Nativism, in interaction with labor and corporations, has given shape to immigration law, accounting for the limited, and often contradictory, ways immigration is defined in our political cultures. Often fostering vigilantism, as in the late 1870s against the Chinese in California, the violence against Filipinos in the 1920s, the zoot suit wars against Latinas/os in 1942, all the way to today's Minuteman Project, nativism rarely stays on the sidelines, instead actively and at times violently participating in the agonistics of membership and ethno-racial purity (Akers Chacón and Davis 2006; Navarro 2009; L. Flores 2003).

Although contemporary understandings of U.S. national identity often rely on the mythology of immigration, as when U.S. citizens state, "we are an immigrant nation," our political culture makes use of this myth to iron out the contradictions of a U.S. identity that has institutionalized nativism and capitalism to regulate citizenship (R. Smith 1997, 13–39). Because citizenship law and immigration policy give shape to the national community and because nativisms, corporatisms, and other capitalist organizations hugely influence these types of legal frameworks, national membership can be seen as the material manifestation of ethno-racial capitalism and liberalism. As demonstrated by legal slavery, indentured servitude, the open European migration from 1880 to 1920, the 1882 Chinese Exclusion Act that lasted sixty-one years, the Alien Labor Law of 1931, the Mexican Bracero and Caribbean guest-worker programs from 1937 to 1965, the Cactus Curtain initiated by President Bill Clinton, and the Sensenbrenner Act, formal political and legal systems have always been attentive to the demands of corporations, other large capitalist enterprises, labor, and nativists (R. Daniels 2004, 7–26; Navarro 2009; Ness 2007, 429–432; Ngai 2004; Sanchez 1993, 211; Santa Ana 2002, 66–68).

The concerns of nativists, labor, and corporations have often taken the popular form of a commonsense economics that uses national prosperity as the basis for political action (Inda 2006, 96–107). On the one hand, contemporary nativisms rely on economic arguments, often under the veneer of pro-labor discourse, to justify political action and lobbying against immigration, especially from Latin America. In these arguments, immigrants are said to use economic and social resources designed for and funded by citizens (De Genova and Ramos-Zayas 2003, 5). These arguments, as Otto Santa Ana (2002) and Lisa Flores (2003) argue, have energized an ethnicized political base that traditionally has sought violence and/or legal remedies to appease their fears (see also D. Gutiérrez 1999). Flores shows how discourses that criminalized Mexican immigration in the late 1920s and 1930s were closely connected to arguments about economics and to the passing of the first immigration law that made undocumented border crossing a felony in 1929 (2003, 376). Nicholas De Genova and Ana Y. Ramos-Zayas (2003), Leo Chavez (1998, 2008), and Mae Ngai (2004) note that the very notion of "illegal" is crafted through immigration laws and deportation practices attentive to corporate need. The term helps create a tractable and vulnerable labor force that can be expelled at will, using nativist rhetoric as justification. The colonization of Puerto Rico in 1898 allowed for racialist discourse to justify the importation of cheap labor from the island to the quickly industrializing urban Northeast. Later, in the 1950s, the island itself was offered as an ideal location for a plethora of environmentally hazardous industries that enjoyed the protection of local governments and Washington, D.C. (De Genova and Ramos-Zayas 2003, 10). Santa Ana (2002) shows nativist reliance on discourses of economics to draft and get support for Proposition 187 in

California in 1993. Similar in outline to the Sensenbrenner Act, Proposition 187 aimed to restrict undocumented and documented immigrants from using social services and deputized law enforcement to act as INS agents. Famously, this proposition would have barred undocumented children from enrolling in public schools, would have denied citizenship to children born in the United States to undocumented parents, and would have restricted most social services, including nonurgent medical care, to undocumented residents (K. Johnson 2008, 1285–1287; Navarro 2009, 118–143). Although Proposition 187 and the Sensenbrenner Act mostly targeted undocumented immigrants, other immigration policies of the time targeted legal immigrants. For instance, in 1996, a Republican-led Congress passed the Personal Responsibility, Work Opportunity, and Medicaid Restructuring Act (PRWORA). This act denied legal immigrants access to welfare, food stamps, and Social Security benefits and made sponsors fiduciarily responsible for immigrants for ten years after their entering the country (Navarro 2009, 132). This commonsense economics is part of the discourses used by a diverse set of nativist organizations including FAIR, the Minuteman Project, and others. Labor also uses a commonsense economics that argues that immigrants lower wages for everybody by supplying unregulated cheap labor to businesses. Contemporary nativist organizations often embrace these labor concerns and actively engage in the recruitment of lower-class white and black Americans to publicly articulate their concerns (Ness 2007, 433). Lastly, corporations and other large businesses have always sought out the cheapest labor and have a huge impact on immigration legislation; corporate interests include constituting an undocumented class that can easily be manipulated and abused and lobbying for guest worker programs when convenient (Ness 2007, 433).

Brokering between nativists, labor, and corporations is the state, which uses techniques of power such as the legal apparatus either to secure borders when convenient or to secure cheap labor when necessary. On the side of corporations, in 1864, the federal government passed the Act to Encourage Immigration, which enabled employers to contract foreign workers prior to their traveling to the United States and allowed this contract to have provisions that would force workers to repay the employer for transportation costs. This act virtually relegalized indentured servitude, hugely affecting Chinese immigration. Nativists succeeded in repealing this law and lobbied for the Chinese Exclusion Act, which passed in 1882. It is no coincidence that in 1882 the rate of unemployment among

European immigrants had increased, which made Chinese immigration relatively unnecessary to the white-controlled economy. Flores (2003) illustrates how during the 1920s, with European and Asian migration at a low level due to the Immigration Act of 1924, which included the National Origins Act and the Asian Exclusion Act, the Southwest briefly turned to Mexican migration to reenergize a flagging economy. Part of this socioeconomic process was carried out with discourses that characterized Mexican immigrants and labor as more desirable than southern/eastern European and Asian immigrants. Constructed as a hardworking, docile people, Mexicans were depicted as ideal for temporary work. "Ignorant, tractable, moderately industrious, and content to endure wretched conditions of life which most white laborers would not tolerate, the Mexican peon has proved a great boon to employers in the Southwest" (S. J. Holmes, qtd. in Flores 2003, 370). As Santa Ana (2002), Flores (2003), and Kent Ono and John Sloop (2002) have shown, the status of Latina/o migration in majoritarian political cultures has always been in close relation to broad national economic markers. In booming times, the state and business communities have sought the legal and undocumented labor pools of Latin America, creating the legal contexts, such as guest-worker programs, to regulate them. In times of crisis, nativisms step in.

As predicted by coloniality and citizenship excess, what has happened in the twenty-first century is then a relative continuation of established ethno-racial liberal governmentality techniques of political and legal power. President George W. Bush's earlier Latino-friendly initiatives, which were open to immigration reform that would have included a path toward citizenship for millions, were couched in the discourses of business and economics, constructing the ideas of justice and legality by reference to labor, profit, corporations, and capitalist drives. Accordingly, Bush repeatedly described undocumented Latino immigrants as "hard workers" wishing to fulfill the American Dream and, in the process, benefiting the U.S. economy (June 26, 2000, and January 7, 2004). Members of the chambers of commerce in Austin, Sacramento, Denver, Tallahassee, Phoenix, and Santa Fe agreed. Post-9/11 Republican initiatives, which eventually became the Bush administration's own, articulated a contrasting position through the discourse of nativism. In the words of Tancredo, who supported his 2008 GOP presidential bid on his xenophobic rhetoric, "illegal aliens" are a "scourge that threatens the very future of the nation" (Tancredo, qtd. in Vanden Heuvel 2006). Although not all nativists use Tancredo's florid language, the general sense among these U.S. citizens is that the nation's future, imagined as a mixture of racial and economic markers of well-being, ought to continue having a white racial and cultural character. In this, they are not alone. According to polling conducted in 2006 and 2007 by *Time* magazine, *USA Today*/Gallup, CNN, and NBC/*Wall Street Journal*, most U.S. citizens have paradoxical views about undocumented migration. *Time* magazine set the trend. According to this poll, 82 percent believed that U.S. borders were not secure enough; 32 percent saw the issue of undocumented immigrants as extremely serious, and an additional 36 percent saw it as very serious; 51 percent believed that the United States would benefit from deporting undocumented workers; 75 percent wished major restrictions in undocumented immigrants' access to public services; 51 percent went as far as suggesting that these immigrants should not be allowed to attend public schools; and 69 percent stated that they should not have access to driver's licenses (Immigration 2006). Contrastingly, 78 percent believed that undocumented immigrants should have a path to citizenship if they learned English, were employed, and paid taxes. So, although at the level of broad support one can read this and other polls as contradictory (most U.S. citizens want more restrictions and penalties on undocumented workers, but most want the resolution sought out by pro-immigrant political positions, which is to have a path to citizenship), even the pro-immigrant position has nativist underpinnings, as suggested by the desire for Latina/o assimilation.[4]

As I noted in chapter 1, Foucault's notion of juridical subjectivity connects the economic and political fields. I apply these ideas to the U.S. case and argue that juridical subjectivity is also in concert with ideas of national membership and race. The political imaginary of populations whose race is already considered central to citizenship as a political and economic franchise permits the formation and reproduction of political and legal cultures that rely on racial and citizenship ascription to mark the boundaries of the social. In this socio-political landscape, Latino immigrants, who are doubly marked by race and immigration, typically become objects, not subjects, of political agency.[5] For Bush, immigrant rights were justified because Latinas/os already contributed economically to the nation-state, not because Latinas/os' political agency had convinced him of their political worth. Alas, a minority of nativist voices ended up weighing much more than those of the millions who marched in 2006. But these voices were given legal and economic weight corresponding of their race, citizenship status, economic/legal location, and media positionality.

Pastoralism is a great metaphor for what I call ethno-racial liberal governmentality because the image of the flock connotes a group joined by biological characteristics. The shepherd should protect the flock, and it is with this logic of beneficence that the ethno-racial liberalism that defines the United States has used legal and economic practices to regulate membership and immigration. When confronted with the history of these legal and economic practices, such as the census and taxation systems, one recognizes that nativism is not an abhorrent expression of the U.S. political system but one of its roots as expressed in our Constitution and legal history. Simply, the technologies of power used by the state are hugely shaped by nativism. This is evident in the history of immigration law, which has organized and disciplined an immigrant population that would be central to the economy and marginal to politics. This is not to say that ethno-racial liberal governmentality is only characterized by nativism. The same legal frameworks that instituted racialized citizenship laws are indebted to, for instance, egalitarian ideas of natural rights and, in more contemporary legal settings, notions of human rights. However, in U.S. history, government has been more responsive to the need to protect the citizenry than to the need to expand egalitarianism. The exceptions have been the result of the sustained efforts and sacrifices of, for instance, abolitionists, suffragettes, labor activists, and the coalition of forces that today we recognize as the civil rights movement. In all these cases, social movements were able to eventually tap into the majoritarian public sphere and thus were able to participate in processes of consensus building. The next two sections analyze the PRM's participation in the public sphere and evaluate its momentary success and eventual defeat in terms of the segments of the public sphere that PRM was able to access and the areas of the public sphere that nativists were able to control.

The Pro-Immigration Rallies

From 2004 to 2012, most state legislative bodies passed anti-immigration policies. At the federal level, things were more complex. The Bush administration continued calling for immigration reforms that in 2005 included a guest-worker program and increased border security. Other national leaders, including Republican senators John McCain and Pete Domenici and Democratic senators Arlen Specter and Ted Kennedy, introduced different bills with different levels of accommodation for undocumented immigrants. Of these, the McCain-Kennedy bill went the furthest in the

process toward becoming law. It was passed by the Judiciary Committee with a vote of 12–6 on March 27, 2005. The bill included a path to
citizenship and a guest-worker program. It was amended by the Hagel-
Martinez Compromise, which also included a path to citizenship but
separated undocumented immigrants into three groups. According to the
Congressional Hispanic Caucus, which opposed the Compromise, the restrictions on two of these groups were too harsh, and too many would
have been disqualified from naturalization. The Hagel-Martinez Compromise went to the Senate floor to be defeated 38 to 62. In December,
the highly restrictive and nativist Sensenbrenner Act (H.R. 4437) passed
in the House, and although it was defeated in the Senate, it fed the impetus of the ultraright nativists, who continued blocking amendments
to the Hagel-Martinez Compromise throughout 2006 and succeeded in
passing several restrictive measures. On May 17, with bipartisan support,
a Republican-led initiative to build a 370-mile-long wall (it also included
500 miles of vehicle barriers) passed 63–34. The following week, the Senate voted on S. 611, an amendment to immigration law that, among other
things, would have made English the country's official language. It passed
on May 25, 62–36, with two abstentions. This amendment to immigration
law (otherwise known as the Comprehensive Immigration Reform Act)
reads, "To amend title 4 United States Code, to declare English as the national language of the United States and to Promote the patriotic integration of prospective US citizens" (Navarro 2009, 300–304; Akers Chacón
and Davis 2006, 203, 227–247; Bacon 2008, 64–70). S. 2611 never became
law because it failed to pass the conference committee. Of all these bills,
H.R. 4437, the Sensenbrenner Act, became the legal symbol that would
energize the pro-immigrant rights movements from January to May 2006.
These social movements succeeded in bringing together the huge March-
through-April rallies.

The 2006 pro-immigration rallies are a great example of how access
to a public sphere can quickly translate into some forms of political citizenship. It is a textbook example of how civil society ought to work. But
it is also a textbook example of the political quandaries faced by ethno-
racially fragmented polities, the ability of civil society to balkanize, and
our political culture's tendency to weaponize techniques of governance to
the benefit of the racial and national status quo.

The rallies were the result of the successful mixture of the organizing
labor of activist organizations and the cultural power of Spanish-language
media (SLM). In this sequence of events, I follow Navarro's narrative,

though I add a parallel analysis of media. According to Navarro (2009), the pro-immigrant movement gained steam after the passing of H.R. 4437 (December 2005), when Elias Bermudez, leader of Inmigrantes Sin Fronteras, succeeded in using the radio airwaves to organize a four-thousand-person march in Phoenix, Arizona, on January 6, 2006. Bermudez, a Mexican immigrant who, at one time, had been the mayor of San Luis, Arizona, launched a ninety-minute radio program in May 2005 titled *Vamos a Platicar*. From 8:30 a.m. to 10 a.m. on KIDR-AM (740), Bermudez engaged in passionate talk extolling the virtues of Latin American immigrants. KIDR-AM is a station that officially embraces a Spanish news and talk format and thus is an ideal platform for Bermudez's political and media goals. But the station was not alone. Other Phoenix stations such as La Nueva (KHOT-FM, 105.9) and Radio Campesina (KNAI-FM, 88.1) also served as vehicles to advertise Bermudez's political views on immigration and helped to organize the march, which speaks to the strength of Spanish-language radio and to the ties this broadcasting system has with Latino immigrant communities (Nuñez 2006; América Rodriguez 1999; Navarro 2009, 318; Panganiban 2007; González 2006; Valdivia 2010, 57). In the weeks following the January 6 march, the National Alliance for Human Rights (NAHR) as well as other pro-immigrant organizations such as the Mexican American Legal Defense and Education Fund (MALDEF), the Central American Resource Center, and Resurrection Catholic Church organized a leadership meeting that was covered by CNN, Univision, Telemundo, and Azteca America on February 11. The result of this meeting was a strategic plan that included national and international goals. Internationally, NAHR would send a delegation to Mexico to meet with President Vicente Fox and Latin American ambassadors as well as with activist organizations. Nationally, NAHR would aggressively engage in lobbying efforts against H.R. 4437, hold a national meeting on March 10, and organize massive mobilization (Navarro 2009, 322).

Navarro (2009) assesses the political moment and historicizes the weeks that followed that meeting all the way to the massive marches. In his view, the relative success of the movement was the result of historical preconditions that pushed undocumented immigrants and hundreds of thousands of their supporters from apathy to action. These preconditions included the rise in violent vigilantism in California, Arizona, New Mexico, and Texas, an increase in human rights violations against undocumented immigrants, increasingly hostile work conditions, and an overall decrease in the future prospects for the success and even survival of undocumented workers. H.R. 4437 "was the straw that broke the camel's back" (315). Navarro, however, credits but does not theorize the importance of media for the success of any of the NAHR goals (329). A social movement of this caliber cannot succeed with political arguments. The media has to broadly disseminate ideas, popularize rhetorical positions, and energize larger numbers of the population (Félix, González, and Ramírez 2008, 622). This role of media is clearly required for mass mobilizations but is also needed for lobbying, which requires the pooling of economic resources not typically found in nongovernmental organizations. Bermudez's own organizing efforts in Phoenix were partly funded by his listeners (González 2006). NAHR and the myriad other organizations, luckily, were able to rely on the growing sector of SLM, first radio and then television, to do the cultural and political task of broadcasting the goals of the organizers.

Spanish-language radio has evolved and grown enormously since its beginnings in the 1920s. In the 1920s and 1930s, América Rodriguez notes, radio stations were not owned by Latinas/os, who, instead, participated in programming on radio stations owned by others (1999, 38). Radio personalities such as Pedro González bought the unprofitable off-hours of the late night and early morning to transmit shows that mixed talk with music. Following this transnational period, the first radio station dedicated to Latino programming was a Los Angeles station that relayed the signal from XEW in Mexico, a station owned and run by Emilio Azcárraga Viduarreta, who eventually founded Televisa, Mexico's largest media empire. Latino control of radio stations increased, and by 1960, 60 percent of all non-English-language radio was in Spanish (ibid., 31–34). By 2008, there were 872 Spanish-language radio stations in the nation. As remarkable, this number was up 64 percent since 1998, a rate of growth which speaks to changes in demography and consumer spending (Albarran and Hutton 2009). This growth is structured by consolidating forces that, since the Telecommunication Act of 1996, have reorganized Spanish-language radio ownership into fewer corporations.

This large Spanish-language radio system and its importance among immigrant populations were the foundations for the successful social advertising effort that was key to energizing and organizing the pro-immigration marches. This radio system behaves like a Latino public sphere, beginning with radio shows such as Bermudez's *Vamos a Platicar* and those of two hugely popular Los Angeles radio DJs, *El Piolín por la Mañana*, hosted by Eddie Sotelo, and *El Cucuy de la Mañana*, hosted by

Renán Almendárez Coello. These were joined by other popular DJs such as El Mandril and El Gordo and shows such as *El Vacilón de la Mañana* (Baum 2006; Félix, González, and Ramírez 2008; Hendricks and Garofoli 2006; Morales 2006, 8; Shore 2006, 8). In addition to the funny names of these radio personalities, their programs shared several key characteristics: they were all aired in Spanish; they were a mixture of morning talk show, entertainment, and local news; they were extremely popular in Los Angeles and other heavily Latino-populated cities; except for *Vamos a Platicar*, they were highly successful syndicated shows with heavy regional or national penetration; they all opposed H.R. 4437; and together they were listened to by millions. The reach of these radio shows gave regional and national platforms to the pro-immigration movement, providing a highly effective and cost-efficient media system to disseminate the goals of the pro-immigration activists.

After thousands marched in Phoenix on January 6, the movement quickly evolved into marches of dozens and then hundreds of thousands, involving more cities and more regions. On March 10, at least one hundred thousand marched in Chicago. On March 24, there were marches in, among other places, Phoenix, Arizona (20,000), Denver, Colorado (20,000–30,000), and Charlotte, North Carolina (5,000) (Navarro 2009, 328). What began with Bermudez advertising on Spanish-language radio continued in the streets of Los Angeles, where, on March 25, 2006, between 500,000 and 1 million came out in support of immigration reform. The marchers blanketed downtown Los Angeles, giving cultural prominence to the political struggle and providing visual evidence to the otherwise abstract census figures of the year 2000, which touted the growth of the Latino population and its new standing as the largest U.S. minority. National media followed local radio as images of the rally occupied front pages in all major U.S. newspapers and were broadcast by most television news programs. For weeks, marches in other cities intensified the political pressure, culminating in a national effort to halt the national economy by stopping Latino/immigrant work on May 1, 2006. On April 10, several marches happened around the nation, and notably, 500,000 marched in Dallas and 100,000 marched in San Diego. In April, marches in Los Angeles, San Jose, San Francisco, Fresno, Sacramento, Albuquerque, Dallas, El Paso, Austin, San Antonio, and Houston mobilized from 10,000 to 100,000 people. On that day, Phoenix saw 250,000 protestors blanket downtown, yelling "Sí, se puede" and "No to H.R. 4437." In Washington, D.C., pro-immigrant groups organized the fourth-largest march in the history of the national capital, bringing 500,000 people to the National Mall. On May 1, 2006, the United States witnessed the culmination of the movement, with the largest labor boycott and one-day mobilization in U.S. history. According to estimates, approximately 2 million people boycotted work or school, and millions marched. Police estimates put the total number of people marching at 1.1 million. According to *La Opinion*, 5 million people participated in one way or another in the protest. Navarro calculates that 3 million people either marched or stopped work or school (Navarro 2009, 341).

Marching in 2006 with thousands of Latinas/os and immigrant allies in Austin, Texas, was the greatest political feeling I have experienced in the United States, Obama's election notwithstanding. But this feeling was also a sour lesson, as we witnessed our political system clamp down and foreclose any hope of immigration reform. These disheartening political retorts surfaced in different ways. First, in the months that followed, ICE increased its efforts to arrest and deport undocumented immigrants with an aggressive effort against businesses. In April 2006, ICE carried out an operation against IFCO Systems, attacking plants in twenty-six states. This resulted in the detention of 1,186 persons suspected of working illegally. These tactics continued during 2006 and 2007, with ICE raiding restaurants (such as House of Blues, Hard Rock Café, ESPN Zone, and China Grill), janitorial services, and food-processing plants. By the end of 2006, ICE had increased its deportation numbers by 20 percent to 221,664. Second, immigration reform at the federal level repeatedly failed, and at the state level legislation became nativist. In Congress, the Hagel-Martinez Compromise failed for the last time in June 2006. In July 2007, conservatives also defeated the Border Security and Immigration Reform Act, which included some provisions beneficial to undocumented immigrants. Later, the Republican-controlled Congress approved the notorious border fence. Nativism became central in several states including Arizona, Oklahoma, Georgia, and Florida; these states passed draconian laws that would negatively affect undocumented immigrants. Third, nativist voices were able to position themselves as being the voice of consensus. The voices of Chris Simcox and Jim Gilchrist, cofounders of the nativist organization Minuteman Project, and the political views of Sensenbrenner and Tancredo dominated the public sphere, and popular media platforms went to the likes of Dobbs, O'Reilly, and Robert Putnam (Navarro 2009, 344–350; Preston 2007). According to Navarro, other factors responsible for the end of the pro-immigrant movement include the absence of a central ideology that could unite the many activist organizations working for immigration reform and the lack of both statewide and national leadership. I want to suggest that these factors marking the decline of the movement are interrelated at the level of civil society and the public sphere. Specifically, I believe that the structure of our civil society roughly corresponds to the structure of a public sphere organized through the governmental logic of ethno-racial liberalism. I also believe, and probably Fraser would agree, that calls for a Latina/o public sphere—as in calls for Latina/o cultural citizenship—must be balanced with calls for the political and civil right to participate in the majoritarian public sphere. Forgoing the latter forecloses the chance for Latinas/os to contribute both to the construction of a national consensus and to the forging of law and policy.

Cultural Citizenship and the Latina/o Public Sphere

Toby Miller (2007) calls for a political economy of cultural citizenship and, others add, of the public sphere. This political economy must define culture in a robust way that can account for culture's material and legal underpinnings. As important, this political economy cannot reduce media to economic interests but must understand that the "political" in a U.S. political economy corresponds to technologies of power that are shaped by ethno-racial governmentality. Let the lessons of 2006 stay with us. Neither the might of Latina/o media, the size of Latina/o audiences, nor the success of the political organizations that brought millions out to march found correlatives in the at-large U.S. political and media cultures, which quickly corrected these anomalies by enfranchising the voices of nativists and amplifying their ability to speak for the majority.

Not once during the months following the pro-immigration rallies, arguably the largest political rallies seen in the nation since the civil rights movement, did the national English-speaking media system allow for the voice of a Latina/o with the same amped, continuous volume regularly given to Dobbs, Limbaugh, O'Reilly, and Beck. This muting of minority speech was made possible, and perhaps even predictable, by a majoritarian public sphere that is predetermined by politics, law, and a political economy of media that follows capitalist and ethno-racial principles. In this section, I want to explore the latter further and to introduce the concept of ethno-racial corporate liberalism to talk about these issues.

The U.S. media system is dominated by capitalist and corporate concerns. Less evident is the way that media are given shape by politics and law. This is amply documented in telecommunication policy research, broadcasting policy research, media law, and media reform scholarship. Together, these approaches teach us that U.S. media industries are the result of government regulation and not the miracle offspring of capitalist entrepreneurship. The work of Thomas Streeter is particularly good for exploring this point. Streeter argues that commercial broadcasting is constituted through political activity, not only because it depends on the use of a public good, bandwidth (regulated by the federal government), but also because from its beginning commercial broadcasters relied on the government to set up rules that would benefit some people over others and, logically, some values over others (1996, xii, 7). Broadcasting is a commercial activity constituted through politics, and not surprisingly, U.S. media makers borrow heavily from the discourse of political liberalism. Liberalism, which emphasizes individualism and independence, often provides the language to justify government action on media regulation. Streeter helps us understand a paradox of the politics of media. Media corporations rely heavily on ideas such as "competition" and "deregulation" and on the notion that the market ought to take care of itself, even while media corporations are seeking government policies that will decrease competition and control the market, making it impossible for newcomers to exist and for new technologies to enter the media environment (ibid., 37).[6] The blurring of media and political environments, Streeter argues, can be called "corporate liberalism," which is a peculiar U.S. blend of capitalism and liberalism that allows for the circulation back and forth of corporate and political language from the political to the economic field and vice versa. "Corporate liberal social organization," Streeter notes, "does not simply mean control by private corporations. It involves a complex, dynamic pattern of interaction among corporations, small businesses, the state, and an electoral polity" (39). Corporate liberalism, as Streeter no doubt would agree, must also be understood as the racializations of the national, political imaginary. I am using here the term *imaginary* in the way that Cornelius Castoriadis (1987) introduced "social imaginary" to political philosophy. According to Castoriadis, one must be able to imagine the social world before one can act on it. By imagining a political world through corporate lingo and a corporate world through political lingo, we construct a social imaginary where actions can be justified and self-regulated according to differing sets of goals as well as a variety of ethical and political imperatives.

As most media scholars suggest, corporate media is partly given shape by government policies. As Streeter argues, the political field is increasingly given form by corporate logics and media concerns. Yet the relationships between the political field and corporate media go beyond their mutual influence. Corporate media and market logic also behave as political tools, etching a media universe atop a political map. For instance, market logic and commercial merit cannot fully explain Latino cultural marginalization, and the case of the 2006 marches gives us yet another pertinent example. The success of the social advertising campaign among Latinas/os was directly related to the impressive commercial strength of Spanish-speaking radio. This fact was invisible to most U.S. citizens, who seemed utterly surprised at the ability of Latino activists and media to organize, so quickly, such huge marches. This surprise was the result of two factors. One is the marginalization of Latina/o politics from the U.S. political imaginary, which tends to favor black versus white understandings of race and which positions immigrants in a political sliding scale where they can go from not yet assimilated to fully assimilated. The second reason was that U.S. media was and is structured as a system in which Latino voices can be heard mostly in the marginal subsystem of SLM, including radio and television. For the non-Latino majority and for the millions of Latinas/os who do not speak Spanish, the Latina/o public sphere is a ghostly presence, and the voices of Latina/o media stars, who have no choice but to represent a significant part of the Latina/o public sphere, are almost nonexistent. *El Cucuy de la Mañana*, the number-one show in Los Angeles that is listened to by millions of others in twenty-six markets across the nation and whose numbers should rightly make host Coello one of the biggest radio personalities in the United States, is practically an unknown for non-Spanish-speaking media audiences, who are more likely to recognize Howard Stern and Rush Limbaugh. In Los Angeles, the second-largest radio market in the United States, *El Cucuy* beats Stern and Limbaugh, day to day. *El Vacilón de la Mañana*, a similarly formatted Spanish-speaking show, hosted by Luis Jiménez and Raymond Broussard, also beats Stern and Limbaugh in New York, the largest U.S. radio market. These DJs' success notwithstanding, to most U.S. citizens, they are still unknown, and their irrelevance outside Latino communities must be understood in terms of a corporate culture that relies on the politics of ethno-racialization as much as it relies on corporate merit. To recognize the political and cultural power of Stern and Limbaugh while failing to even recognize the name of *El Cucuy de la Mañana* is to live in a social imaginary where the corporate world is political and heavily racialized.

Paraphrasing Etienne Balibar, the majority of U.S. citizens share a "fictive" ethnicity that has definite racial and linguistic markers (1991, 96). This suggests that the term *corporate liberalism* cannot fully capture a political world that is always already ethno-racialized. Which brings me back to a serious limitation in Foucault's theory of liberal governmentality. His liberal governmentality seems incapable of anticipating multinational, multiracial, and multilinguistic states, and this becomes even more evident in his notion of the juridical.

In Foucault, the juridical system organizes the economy and political field with the goals of creating a climate of security and prosperity. These goals are the precondition for political stability. Extrapolating these ideas to media, we can see that telecommunication research, media law, media reform research, and Streeter provide basic steps for explaining the relationship between citizenship, Latinas/os, and the public sphere because they explain media as a structure partly constituted through law (and policy) and partly organized to benefit those individuals and communities for whom the law works better. Hence, the political stability of the state is achieved through ethno-racialized notions of security and prosperity that legal frameworks help concretize. I refer to law here as more than the written words that can be found in government decrees and judges' rulings. Law links citizens to the goals of the state; yet law is also an embodied social structure that is subject to political and social control by specific groups and that in our nation-state has consistently been dominated by economic, racial, and sexual elites (Brown 1993; C. Harris 1997; Cheah and Grosz 1996, 8–16; P. Williams 1991); lastly, in liberalism, law constitutes a specific type of juridical subjectivity central to liberal governmentality, and thus law becomes a modality of being associated with citizenship (Balibar 1991, 94; Gordon 1991; Foucault 1991, 2007; Hong 2006, 6).

These three variants on the juridical open up the spaces that we typically associate with state liberalism, energizing the relative fluidity of power in liberal arrangements. The barriers to participate in lawmaking are not the result of straightforward legal prescriptions, which, if such laws existed, would contradict our most liberal impulses. Instead, this elusiveness is constructed through many smaller laws and policies that, quite effectually, constitute subjectivities that embrace, or at least consent to, the unequal distribution of educational, social, cultural, and economic resources among peoples, reconstituting, generation after generation, the legal realm's particular racial, gender, and class memberships. Given this reality, insofar as citizens are subject to the law, they are made subject by the law and the particular values of those who write it and those who interpret it. This structural reality impacts the public sphere in a very real, tangible way, helping regulate the material structure that media is (as to who buys what media company) and the discourses that it generates.

Undocumented immigrants are impacted by this state of affairs not only because the Latino public sphere is marginal to national political processes of consensus but also because the juridical is not designed to secure the prosperity and safety of noncitizens in general and undocumented immigrants in particular. In February 2009, the National Hispanic Media Coalition (NHMC) and the Institute for Public Representation at Georgetown University Law Center filed a petition to the Federal Communications Commission (FCC) to investigate the pervasiveness of hate speech against undocumented immigrants and its impact on hate crimes against the Latino community. The hate speech that these organizations were referring to include comments by radio personalities such as Michael Savage (Talk Radio Network), who argues that undocumented immigrants are "raping" the nation, or John Stokes, who has used KGEZ 600 to argue that "Americans" should cut off the limbs of anyone who does not speak English: "Romans 15:19 says that if they break into your country, chop off their leg. We have to forcibly get rid of them" (qtd. in O'Grady 2009).

In the NHMC and Georgetown Law Center petition, hate speech has a possible effect on Latino life, and this is evidenced in the rise of hate crimes against Latinas/os who are believed to be undocumented (e.g., the killings of Jose Sucuzhanay, Eduardo Ramírez Zavala, and Marcelo Lucero) and in the multiplication of radical nativist groups which, according to the Southern Poverty Law Center, have appeared by the hundreds in the past few years. The petition is as revealing in what it asks from the FCC as in what it does not ask. It asks for an official study that could shed light on these complex connections. It does not ask for the FCC to regulate speech, which would make the petition poisonous to an FCC deeply invested in ethno-racial corporate liberalism. Evidencing a disinterest in giving legal basis to claims by racial minorities, women, and homosexuals, the FCC follows the leadership of the U.S. Supreme Court, which has been reluctant to regulate hate speech and has struck down local ordinances that do so, as in the case of *Brandenburg v. Ohio*, *Skokie v. National Socialist Party of America*, and *R.A.V. v. City of St. Paul* (Kagan 1993, 873). In each of these instances, the Court emphasizes the protection of free speech and the fear that in regulating hate speech, local, state, and federal authorities may overreach into the regulation of legally protected speech. In each of these cases, the Court reconstituted the legality of free and injurious speech of white populations (however radical) over the relative mainstream concerns about personal safety of racial and ethnic minorities. It is important to note that in each of these cases, the Supreme Court (or in the case of *Skokie*, the Seventh Circuit Court of Appeals—the Supreme Court declined to take on the Seventh Circuit's decision, hence confirming it) reversed local rulings, which speaks to the legal process in its complexity and the tensions between localism and federalism. Like the Supreme Court, the FCC has also played a role in the structural production of hate speech. For decades now, the FCC has been set on stultifying competition through the legalization of broadcasting consolidation (e.g., the 1996 Telecommunication Act), which has generated less local competition by lifting the cap on the number of radio stations that large media corporations can own in any given market and has made it structurally easier for a syndicated show such as Savage's to have national syndication. The irony here is that consolidation has also given national markets to *El Cucuy* and *El Piolín*, but their participation in the public sphere is limited by audiences organized around linguistic and ethno-racial lines as well as by a similarly organized radio-star system in which *El Cucuy* and *El Piolín* play marginal roles regardless of their numeric success with listeners.

Being attentive to the public sphere means also being attentive to the ways in which self-regulated media industries, such as printed news, regulate racialized discourse. From 2005 to the present, the discourse of nativism has dominated our news landscape and has strongly influenced institutional policies, foreclosing the possibility of using majoritarian news outlets to launch a pro-immigrant rights offensive. This is evidenced in the way the basic terminology of "illegal immigrant" has become incorporated into the normal journalistic practices of printed news outlets. In 2008, the *AP Stylebook*, one of the key sources for journalistic language use, approved this problematic term and assured that the term "illegal immigrant" should be preferred over "illegal alien" or "undocumented worker." Although the National Association of Hispanic Journalists, the Asian American Journalists Association, the Native American Journalist Association, and the National Association of Black Journalists have strong guidelines on the matter (always to avoid "illegal immigrant," "illegal," and "illegal alien"), these organizations have clearly lost the battle. Today, these terms can be heard on Fox, yes, but also on ABC and CNN; they can be read in the *Washington Post* and even in the paper nativists love to hate, the *New York Times*. The result is a public sphere that normalizes derogatory language against the advice of all minority journalistic organizations. These uses have real effects in the public sphere, shaping the way discourses about immigration are created and re-created. I teach a class called Latina/o Media Studies, and my students cannot immediately see the logic of why I am asking them to use "undocumented" instead of "illegal" in their papers. "They did cross the border illegally, didn't they?" is often their argument. Moreover, in the past couple of years, I have witnessed my students reproduce the notion that there are only two types of people, citizens and "illegals," often forgetting that most Latina/o immigrants who are not citizens are here with legal documents such as green cards. So, when they hear the term "noncitizen," they also hear "illegal," a racialized mental schema that proves that the normalization of nativist terminology and the tone of hegemonic discourse around immigration have profound repercussions on juridical subjects.

Conclusion

I define citizenship in chapter 1 as a series of processes (legal, cultural, economic, and political) that allow a class of people to shape the state's social and political reproduction. I use this definition because it forces us to immediately ask the question of excess. What happens if the state is narrowly defined and those who control the political and legal processes that secure it decide that the state ought to have an ascriptionist base? The simple answer to this question is that they can and they have. Nativism has been part of U.S. governmentality from the beginning, helping the state define itself in ethno-racial and linguistic terms. Nativism is to ethno-racialization what patriarchy is to juridical and political sexism. Nativism is inscribed in our laws and has helped regulate the social, political, and economic resources of the nation. From the census to media, nativism is a deep organizing framework in the juridical and economic fields.

As Rogers Smith (1997) has argued, the role of ascriptivism (and nativism) is often ignored by theorists of the state, who prefer to concentrate on the Western roots of liberalism and republicanism. Foucault, I note, is no exception. His elegant theories of governmentality theorize liberalism and help us to understand the important role of the juridical, the interiorization of the law, and the relationship of the juridical to prosperity and security. Law is important here because it is central to the subjectivity of individuals shaped by liberal democracies such as our own. Indeed, what Foucault calls the juridical-legal subject is, as other have noted, the citizen of liberalism (Burchell 1991).[7] Hence, the citizen's legal formation is also a type of legal subjectivity that, as I show in the following chapters, is constituted and maintained through media and discourse. The mental metaphors Foucault uses to make his points, such as the pastoral, reduce the state to an ethnonationalism that, arguably, is the basis for nativism. But Foucault does not follow this train of thought and instead concentrates his theoretical energies on understanding liberalism. For this reason, we can see Foucault's work as limited by methodological nationalism, that is, the sense that analyzing society means analyzing the nation-state. This is a failure that Foucault passes on to those who apply his ideas. By extension, this failure is part of some of the best and most recent work in media and citizenship, including the work of Liesbet van Zoonen (2005) and Ouellette and Hay (2008). This translates into an inability to deal with issues of politics and media in relationship to noncitizens and immigrant populations. To borrow from another work by Foucault (*The Archaeology of Knowledge*), the discourse of the nation-state is based on a set of propositions that formally marginalizes the noncitizen. This discourse of the nation-state includes the following propositions: society equals state; liberal states are organized by law; liberalism relies on citizens willing to abide by law; coercion should not be central to liberal governmentality; politics is the field where distributive systems are negotiated; the citizen is the political agent, the social actor, the grantor of legitimacy to the nation through the social contract, the sovereign, and the benefactor of distributive justice. Checkmate. Fifteen million undocumented immigrant Latinas/os just fell off the chessboard and have no right to get back on it.

Was there ever a consensus for or against immigration reform? No. But the nativist voices succeeded at every step. Not only did they block immigration reform that would have built a path to citizenship for undocumented immigrants, but they also managed to change immigration law to the benefit of nativists. Instead of exemplifying the hope of liberalism, the PRM's success was quickly overshadowed by its dramatic defeat. The political behavior of these Latinas/os, it would seem, was antithetical to the rules of liberal governmentality, which underscore the importance of consensus, prosperity, security, and civil society, all discourses that reference a close-knit community with self-legitimated political agency. In a sense, Foucault was right. Stock, following the pastoral metaphor, was central to giving nativists extraordinary powers and to helping nativist discourse take center stage in our political and media world, as in the quick dismissal of the pro-immigration movement, the normalization of hate speech, and the legitimization by AP of the term "illegal immigrant." This was citizenship excess at its most subtle and in its nastiest manifestations.

3

Hutto: Staging Transnational Justice Claims in the Time of Coloniality

The genesis of a system of works or practices generated by the same *habitus* . . . cannot be described either as the autonomous development of a unique and always self-identical essence, or as a continuous creation of novelty, because it arises from the necessary yet unpredictable confrontation between the *habitus* and an event that can exercise a pertinent incitement on the *habitus* only if the latter snatches it from the contingency of the accidental and constitutes it as a problem by applying to it the very principles of its solution; and also because the *habitus*, like every "art of inventing," is what makes it possible to produce an infinite number of practices that are relatively unpredictable . . . but also limited in their diversity.
—Pierre Bourdieu, *The Logic of Practice* (1990, 55)

In the aftermath of the pro-immigration reform rallies of 2006, we witnessed an array of measures taken by city, state, and federal officials aimed at curtailing the immigration problem. The Sensenbrenner Act, which further criminalized behavior associated with undocumented labor, remained in the Republican agenda, and versions of it were voted on until late in 2006, when it was finally defeated. The *habitus*, which Bourdieu defines as "systems of durable, transposable dispositions" that "function as structuring structures," was "inventing" new political ways of reconstituting difference (1990, 53). Other successful legal provisions invented by the *habitus* allowed for workplace raids, the building of fences along the U.S.-Mexico border, and the indefinite detention of undocumented immigrants in centers that have been locations for legal exceptions and that exist beyond the reach of citizen or human rights. So, if up to this point I have been critical of law and the nation-state as the sole arbiter of justice, that does not mean that I wish to be in the absence of law, because to be in this absence is to be at risk of losing our very humanity, which is a type of juridical subjectivity much more tenuous than citizenship. *Homo nationalis*, the playful term used by Etienne Balibar (1991), trumps *homo sapiens*.

This chapter reflects on one of those exceptions to justice. I use the term *exception* inspired by the work of Giorgio Agamben. To him, some features of contemporary governmental responses to crisis are quite troublesome because they border on the tyrannical. In particular, Agamben is interested in how a state of emergency allows for the displacement of legal precedent and the centering of exceptionalist law aimed at addressing the emergency with little or no regard for a nation-state's juridical tradition. "In every case, the state of exception marks a threshold at which logic and praxis blur with each other and a pure violence without logos claims to realize an enunciation without any real reference" (2005, 40). Agamben exaggerates to make a point. The *habitus* in the field of politics is engaged in the "art of inventing," as Bourdieu writes it, and of reacting to "pertinent incitement[s]" with the furnishing of creative practices that accommodate and contain the exception within the limited diversity of political traditions. Referring to discursive behaviors carried out by President George W. Bush to justify the indefinite detention of "enemy combatants," Agamben notes that the administration practically created a new legal entity, an unclassifiable being not protected by national or international laws but, I would note, respectful of the rules of racialization and in the tradition of coloniality (Hong 2006, 41; Lowe 1996). According to Anibal Quijano (2000), this tradition constitutes modern liberal governmentality and the knowledge practices that give it rational consistency. In the aftermath of 9/11, enemy combatants were not the only people treated in novel and tyrannical ways by the U.S. government. Examples of legal vacuums obedient of old racializations and coloniality were among us, and in the United States, the majority of these examples were created by the complex interrelations of immigration law, international law, and hegemonic media systems.

Starting in 2006, children, including toddlers, have been incarcerated in the T. Don Hutto Correctional Center in Taylor, Texas. Not since the detention of Japanese Americans during World War II has the U.S. government jailed children en masse, without criminal charges against them.[1] Reminiscent of World War II, these shameful policies and quasimilitary actions against a civilian population came at a time of perceived state emergency, a post-9/11 of paranoid securitization during which it has been culturally acceptable to use mainstream media to express the most xenophobic views about immigrants, in particular migrants from Latin America. To the credit of American society and as a testament to the potential ethical benefits of state liberalism, much of the legal community has opposed the federal government's use of immigration law and the clear overriding of human rights law in the case of Hutto and the many other detention centers that have sprouted up around the nation to detain undocumented immigrants. Regarding Hutto, the ACLU and the University of Texas School of Law sued the government in 2007 and won a settlement on August 27 of the same year that included the ability to monitor the facilities. Just as important, the results of the lawsuit mandated the release of twenty-six of the children. But others remained. The practice itself was not ruled illegal. The legal and political communities that controlled the state and federal congresses remained complicit. On August 11, 2009, the new executive branch under President Barack Obama forced the Department of Homeland Security (DHS), the government agency now in charge of safeguarding immigration law, to change detention practices. The DHS has since promised to close Hutto, but this has not yet happened at the time of this writing. Even in the wake of these positive developments, it is worth asking questions of justice, law, and media. Let us not forget that as President Obama ends the practice of jailing children, hundreds of thousands of undocumented immigrants will remain in detention centers without recourse to some of the most basic legal rights. Outside the purview of citizen law, outside the reach of human rights jurisdiction, they are desubjectified, living in spaces of exception.

This chapter analyzes the case of Hutto in terms of the historical, legal, and media traditions that constituted it. It argues that the root of this state of exception is the heavily ideological link between justice and citizenship, a link unlikely to be challenged by the hegemonic public sphere and the media field. A second argument is that successful analyses of media and citizenship and of media and Latinas/os cannot be performed without a framework that, like coloniality, understands the nation form as furthering the traditions of colonialism that gave it legal and economic power. The nation and its media are political organizations and in times of crises will revert to staunch polis-centrism. A state of exception is partly the result of mediated discourse, and its existence is dependent on the ability of the nation to narrowly define security, prosperity, and danger. Media systems join political and legal cultures to reproduce the *habitus* of the field of politics by participation in the production of some level of consensus and legitimization for states of exception, opening certain venues for public discussion and closing others. As German Nazis demonstrated in the 1930s and 1940s, Spanish Nationalists proved from the 1930s to the 1970s, and liberal Americans showed in the 1940s, the nation and its media will not only partner to fight beastly war enemies; the nation and its media will use sheepish fear to criminalize innocent populations, be they Jews, Gypsies, Basques, or Japanese Americans.

The following sections function as a criticism of the nation form, the universalism of rights, and lastly, the media field. First, I examine the Hutto case in its historical and political contexts. I also include an over-view of the news coverage of Hutto in relationship to the practice of jour-nalism. Noticing the endemic weakness with which journalism engages on behalf of the rights of transnational populations, I follow by investigat-ing the universalism of rights talk. I argue that the idea of universal rights rhetorically centers citizenship in the discourses of justice. Justice can be differently conceived, and Michael Walzer's (1983) approaches to justice are suited for a critical understanding of the link between citizenship and justice. For Walzer, justice depends on what he calls "complex equality"; however, this complex equality cannot be reached if a dominant good (e.g., citizenship, wealth) towers over different social fields. That is what happens with citizenship dominating the media field, a disciplinary effect that I illustrate with alternative media practices around Hutto. Each sec-tion locates administrative and legal practices within traditions initiated at times when colonial logic was central to imagining the social.

Hutto

The legal and political moves that allow for anti-human-rights policies to become legal and somehow normal must be understood as part of the process of securitization that followed the 9/11 attacks. Continuing the metaphor of the pastoral that Foucault so evocatively uses to illustrate lib-eralism, the sheep were in danger, and the beasts had to be pushed back (see chapter 2). President Bush's executive branch, Congress, and loud media voices succeeded in linking the immigration problem to terrorism, justifying the disbanding of the Immigration and Naturalization Services (INS) and placing the U.S. Citizenship and Immigration Services (USCIS) under the jurisdiction and extraordinary powers of the DHS. So it was in the spirit of security and a benevolent government (benevolence toward the citizen, not benevolence per se) that the detention centers were cre-ated. In following our legal and traditional political processes (though not without heavy dissention), President Bush succeeded in gaining enough legitimization for the new laws and institutions (USCIS; Hutto). He connected with the juridical subjectivities of Americans who accepted the new state of securitization that immigrants were placed in and who implicitly consented to the state's unusual exercise of anti-human-rights powers. *Unsurprisingly, benevolence to some became tyranny to others.* This pastoral paradox is the heart of liberalism that Foucault so astutely identifies and the reason governmentality must remain one of the theoretical instruments used to dissect the nation.

Administering the detention of undocumented immigrant families has traditionally been a difficult task for the U.S. government. The current system, in which Hutto has played a strategic role, is a type of procedural escalation that began in the aftermath of 9/11. Prior to 2001, the INS would release, pending hearing, the great majority of families detained without documentation. Beginning in 2001, already under the aegis of securitization, the INS began using the Berks Facility in Leesport, Pennsylvania, to detain undocumented immigrant families. A former nursing home, the Berks Facility provided a relatively adequate setting for the custody of families who tended to stay only short periods of time, often less than sixty days. In 2002, the Homeland Security Act broke the INS into three discrete agencies, and the care and custody of unaccompanied alien children (UAC) was entrusted to the director of the Department of Health and Human Services' Office of Refugee Resettlement (ORR), the organization also in charge of assisting refugees, asylees, and victims of human trafficking. The Homeland Security Act also created the DHS, which became the administrative and policy agency overseeing immigration. In 2003, the DHS created Immigration and Customs Enforcement (ICE), an organization substituting the already problematic INS, and intensified the central goal of securitization to the mission of administering immigration. Also in 2003, the DHS released ICE's first strategic long-term plan for illegal immigration. Stupidly called *Endgame*, this national "Final Solution" to illegal migration amped up the role of expedited removal and downplayed the complex administration of undocumented immigrants and refugees vis-à-vis U.S. immigration legal traditions and international law (Bureau of Immigration and Customs Enforcement 2003). Mindful of the state of exception authorized by the *Endgame*, in 2004, ICE began the practice of separating arrested families, "holding the parents in adult facilities and their children at ORR facilities pending removal" (Nugent 2006, 230). Responding to Congress's investigation in 2005, the DHS claimed that the separation of children from parents was necessary because the agency had found undocumented migrants who, aware that the DHS tended to release families, would rent children in order to cross the border with them. In a bizarre turn of logic, the DHS decided that all detained families were somehow guilty of this practice and treated the children as if they were unaccompanied minors, making them proper subjects of ORR administration (Women's Commission 2007, 5–6).[2] This practice, which trampled over U.S. law pertaining to the welfare of children and over international human rights law (see Article 5 of the United Nations' *Convention on the Rights of the Child*), came under Congress's scrutiny in 2005, when new policies on the matter were levied:

> The Committee is concerned about reports that children apprehended by DHS, even as young as nursing infants, are being separated from their parents and placed in shelters operated by the Office of Refugee Resettlement (ORR) while their parents are in separate adult facilities. Children who are apprehended by DHS while in the company of their parents are not in fact "unaccompanied"; and if their welfare is not at issue, they should not be placed in ORR custody. The Committee expects DHS to release families or use alternatives to detention such as the Intensive Supervised Appearance Program whenever possible. When detention of family units is necessary, the Committee directs DHS to use appropriate detention space to house them together.[3]

It is within this context of detaining whole "family units" that the DHS and ICE responded to the need for creating new detention facilities, besides Berks, that could accommodate families with children.

In January 2006, ICE reached an agreement with Corrections Corporations of America (CCA) to house up to six hundred undocumented immigrants, including children, in the underused T. Don Hutto Corrections Facility. Hutto became only the second such facility in the nation, after Berks. This contract was just another step in the ongoing process of privatizing the institutional arrangements required to deal with undocumented immigrants. CCA has detention centers in nineteen other states including California, New Mexico, and Colorado (Corrections Corporation of America 2007). The agreement with ICE paralleled an agreement with Williamson County, which was to receive one dollar per day per inmate. This could mean up to $200,000 of yearly revenue for the county if Hutto was at full capacity (Humphrey 2006). This money would become part of the general revenues, which also benefited when CCA hired locals to administer and maintain the prison.

Prior to January 2006, Hutto was a medium-security prison, and its infrastructure showed it. After the agreement with ICE, CCA made minimal changes to the facility, including adding extra padding to beds and installing playpens and cribs where necessary. CCA also committed to providing space appropriate for instruction and personnel capable of teaching the "inmates," the term that these procedural realities forced on children (Humphrey 2006). Cheaply done, the changes to the infrastructure did not change the physical sense that this was a prison, something that would later be harshly criticized by activists and human rights advocates. Regardless of the commonality of the term "illegal" (see chapter 2), being in the United States without documents is not a criminal offense. It is an administrative offense that merits different standards of detention, according to U.S. legal traditions and to international law. But lowering these standards was expedient at the time, particularly as CCA was overseen by a government agency, ICE, set on reducing undocumented immigration to a security issue. The economic benefits to CCA have been substantial and immediate, with its net income jumping from $20.8 million in the third quarter of 2005 to $26.1 million in 2006, an increase of more than 25 percent over the course of a year, due greatly to CCA's ability to secure contracts with ICE (Corrections Corporation of America 2007; Talbot 2008). According to Simona Colón, ICE's officer in Hutto, from January 2006 to February 2007, roughly two thousand people were detained in the 512-bed facility, more than half of them children (Castillo 2007b). To make matters worse, roughly 40 percent of those detained in Hutto were asylum seekers who had already passed the first screening test that would qualify them as deserving of asylum status.

Discourse, Media, and Hutto

To justify Hutto, the DHS and ICE have used a discursive stage whereby their legal and procedural behaviors seem reasonable performances of civitas. In this stage, social actors such as Michael Chertoff, then secretary of the DHS; John Torres, ICE's director at the time; and David Aguilar, chief of the Border Patrol, speak of how their actions are in strict obedience of President Bush (disciplinarity) and in response to the nation's need for heightened security (pastoralism). In addition to using disciplinary and pastoral language, their speeches are invested in a sort of coloniality of political discourse, evidenced in the systematic use of de-humanizing language, including the widely mediated animalistic meta-phor of "catch-and-release." In an extensively distributed report on DHS practices, Chertoff used this metaphor to refer to the practice of detain-ing undocumented immigrants and immediately releasing them on bond. In this report, Chertoff explains that Hutto was part of the plan by the DHS to stop "catch-and-release" and part of the implementation of the new policy of "catch-and-remove." He continues by explaining that non-Mexicans could not be "removed" immediately, nor could they be held in custody (Remarks by Secretary of Homeland Security Michael Cher-toff 2006). To "remove" these non-Mexicans, the DHS was increasing the number of detention facilities that could allow ICE to detain noncitizens until legal proceedings were carried out and logistic processes were put in place for their deportation. Hutto was one of these facilities. In using animalistic metaphors, Chertoff and others associated with the DHS and ICE continued on the tradition noticed by Otto Santa Ana (2002), who observed that the metaphoric system used in California in the 1990s to pass the highly xenophobic referenda for Proposition 187 included animal metaphors. Santa Ana argues that these metaphors invite listeners to use a knowledge system based on animals that reduces immigrant activities to thoughtless, violent disturbances to the social order, enacted outside a shared ethical system (86). In addition to inviting a hierarchical and racist relation to immigrants, something Santa Ana observes, these metaphors reduce the rational scope used to evaluate proposals about immigrants, inviting solutions to the problem that immigrants represent that are le-gally questionable and weak.

News coverage of Hutto was relatively scant, and the majority came from print news. (In the following sections, I expand on radio and televi-sion coverage.) From 2006 to the end of the Bush administration in Janu-ary 2009, Hutto was written about only 110 times. Sixty-nine of these news items came from Texas; forty-two were published in the *Austin American-Statesman*; twenty-eight were written by Juan Castillo; twenty-seven re-ports and wires were by AP, mostly written by two reporters, Anabelle Garay (Dallas bureau) and Suzanne Gamboa (Washington bureau). These AP reports and wires were reprinted in a variety of news outlets, includ-ing *ABC News*, *USA Today*, and smaller print and online sources such as the Dallas Peace Center website. A mere fourteen times did newspapers outside of Texas dedicate their shrinking resources and use one of their reporters to write on Hutto. These fourteen reports were a warning sign about hegemonic institutional commitments of the time, painting a predictable picture of a liberal-left news media, represented by the four pieces written for the *New York Times*, which was still reeling from the political challenges brought about by two Bush administrations (Valdivia 2010, 40). The only newspaper located in a state that voted Republican in the 2004 presidential elections that sent a reporter to write on Hutto was the *Mobile Register* in Alabama. All the other papers were in states that voted Democratic. This gives us a glimpse into a set of media institutional practices all too concerned with political ideology in the newsroom and in the readership. What was written is also informative, for it gives us a glimpse into the repertory of arguments, narratives, and knowledges available to journalists and editors with regard to undocumented immigration.

On December 15, 2006, Castillo wrote his first news piece on Hutto when he reported about a protest march that would go from Austin to Taylor, Texas. He used the expert voice of activists and legal professionals interested in ending the practice of incarcerating undocumented children and commented that the incarcerated children were losing weight, getting ill, and experiencing psychological trauma. In addition, he wrote, the only instruction the children were receiving was one hour of English. A relative rarity, Castillo left in the text several quotes referring to ICE's practices as violations of human rights, and he wrote with a relatively high level of specificity about things that had to be interpreted as legal infractions ("psychological trauma," lack of education, improper health services). In the following two years, Castillo continued his reporting on Hutto, publishing more than two dozen stories that often referred to specific legal issues and detention practices that violated human rights or U.S. law. Central in these reports was the American legal precedent of *Flores v. Reno* (also known as the *Flores* settlement), which had given the INS the legal rules by which to detain minors. In the great majority of the news reports that followed, roughly three-quarters of the writers avoided specific legal claims in favor of listing vague complaints about inhuman or immoral treatment. This is evidenced in Suzanne Gamboa's piece for AP (February 22, 2007), which serves to illustrate her point of view and her power as a journalist to select, from among the possible quotes available to her, those that fit her views:

> Immigrant families, many with small children, are being kept in jail-like conditions in Texas and Pennsylvania, according to advocacy groups that say the Texas facility *is inhumane* and should be shut down.

In a report being released Thursday, the groups seek the immediate closure of the T. Don Hutto Residential Center north of Austin, the Texas capital. The center, which opened in May, used to be a jail.

The groups, Women's Commission for Refugee Women and Children and Lutheran Immigration and Refugee Services, based their findings on their members' visits and interviews with detainees. At the Hutto site, a child secretly passed a visitor a note that read: "Help us and ask us questions," the report said. *The groups reported that many of the detainees cried during interviews.*

"What hits you the hardest in there is that it's a prison. In Hutto, it's a prison," said Michelle Brane, detention and asylum project director for Women's Commission for Refugee Women and Children. . . .

The groups suggested that immigration officials release families who are not found to be a security risk, and said the federal government should consider less punitive alternatives to the detention centers, such as parole, electronic bracelets and shelters run by nonprofit groups.

"Unless there's some crime or some danger, families don't belong in detention," said Ralston H. Deffenbaugh, president of the Lutheran Immigration and Refugee Service. "This whole idea of trying to throw kids and their parents in a penal-like situation is destructive of all the normal family relationships we take for granted."

The Homeland Security Department defended the centers as a workable solution to *the problem of illegal immigrants being released, only to disappear while awaiting hearings.* Also, *they deter smugglers who endanger children,* said Mark Raimondi, spokesman for Immigration and Customs Enforcement, the DHS division that oversees detention facilities.

"ICE's detention facilities maintain safe, secure and humane conditions and invest heavily in the welfare of the detained alien population," Raimondi said.

White House press secretary Tony Snow said last week that finding facilities for families is difficult, and "you have to do the best with what you've got." (emphasis added)

Gamboa's piece is a typical way of presenting the issues by the majority of the news reports. The two sides that she is presenting to us are represented, first, by the findings of the Women's Commission for Refugee Women, which seems to argue, if we only rely on Gamboa, that the Texas facility is inhumane. To give weight to these findings, Gamboa mentions that many of the interviewees cried. On the other side, Gamboa uses quotes from ICE's officers and from White House press secretary Snow, which seem to present in better detail the positions of the administration. Snow sums it up: "you have to do the best with what you got." The Women's Commission report that Gamboa is referring to is a compelling legal document and a scathing criticism of the government; it lists specifically what national and international laws are being broken, and though it briefly uses the word "inhumane," it mostly argues against practices that are illegal. Gamboa erases the report's legal specificity in favor of a dramatization that pits the well-being of the families against the reasonably worded position of the government represented by ICE's officers and Snow. In so doing, she reproduces news practices that normalize a political world where governmental power is traditionally accepted.

In stating this, I am not trying to replicate functionalist arguments such as those by Edward Herman and Noam Chomsky (1988), who argue that the role of the press in the United States is eminently propagandistic and functions to "mobilize support for the special interests that dominate the state and private activity" (xi). Rather, I am siding here with Michael Schudson (2002), who points out that the political role of journalism is partly defined by journalism's systemic reliance on government sources as one of the main wellsprings of information (255). This means that, over time, journalists' language and ethical commitment are shaped by interactions with government officials. Schudson correctly notes that the "reliance on government officials does not guarantee pro-government news" (257), but on this point, his argument is weak. He supports his argument by citing research that shows that government officials also serve as sources for journalism that is critical of the government. Here, Schudson insinuates that independent journalism is evidenced in negative government reporting. But negative coverage of the government does not equal a journalism that freely argues against government wrongdoing in the same way that journalists freely argue against other kinds of wrongdoing. Consider the quotation from Gamboa, a phrasing that was highly typical of the coverage that Hutto got. In what other social and/or legal context would the mistreatment of children not be followed by a call for immediate legal action and the jailing of those responsible? Why is Gamboa avoiding the specific legal language used by the Women's Commission report?

The journalistic practices of Gamboa and Castillo are the result of a *habitus* that Rodney Benson (2006) calls the "journalistic field." The field is a methodological and theoretical shortcut that characterizes broad

institutional settings as social systems with structural properties. In Bourdieu's work, which Benson reflects on, the journalistic field occupies a
subordinating position to the field of power (the system of power relations
or the "ruling classes") (1993, 15). The intellectual class that constitutes this
field lacks economic and political power, and for that reason Bourdieu
refers to it as a dominated segment of the dominant class. Benson notes,
echoing Schudson, that the journalistic field also is closely linked to the
political field, an observation fully supported by the coverage of Hutto,
which consistently printed the points of view of ICE's and the DHS's officers (2006, 106). Holding the field together, Bourdieu continues, is the
field's *habitus*, which structures dispositions and practices within the field.
In the case of Hutto's coverage, journalistic practices and institutional arrangements predetermined the type of reporting that Hutto would get,
including the type of sourcing that would be common (for instance,
government officials and recognized activist organizations such as the
ACLU) and the type of frame that would help constitute it as a specific
news narrative. For instance, the call for mild remedies, such as the closing of Hutto instead of the jailing of Chertoff, belong to a frame where the
activities and life pursuits of immigrants are reduced to the immigrants'
relation to American legal structures. These journalistic traditions include
a general agreement that U.S. government officials are not prosecuted for
human rights, an awareness that human rights law is not a framework
typically associated with the legal procedures that Americans uphold, a
recognition that government wrongdoing toward marginalized populations is not punished severely, and central to my claims, an assumption
that undocumented people do not have the rights that we typically associate with citizenship.

Like any evidence of a social practice, Gamboa's writing sits at the intersection of institutional and discursive histories that she does not control and that she cannot simply disregard. Her professionalism was at
stake, and she behaved professionally. In so doing, she, like almost every
other journalist covering Hutto, replicated an American style of nationalism that is conservative, parochial, unwilling to engage fully with international law, committed to emphasizing the legal difference between
citizens and noncitizens, and incapable of entertaining the possibility that
the justice claims of undocumented people rest firmly on a legal basis.

The idea of the *habitus* allows Bourdieu to circumvent the dichotomy
of subject versus agent, for it assumes that some actions within the *habitus* are experienced not as subjection or obedience but as agency. Agents

exist in positions from which they are constantly enacting and modifying the *habitus*; they are always structuring and restructuring it from sites of regulated freedom. Agency does not fully explain why certain choices are more viable to some agents than to others. One possible way to explain how choices follow from "dispositions," a term Bourdieu uses, is to consider that all individuals are formed by a multiplicity of identities and, potentially, can engage with their *habitus* in multiple ways depending on the aspects of identity activated in the agent (Isin 2002, 25). For instance, Gamboa's style of writing was not the only expression of professionalism. Castillo represents another one, but one that was not very popular. In my interview with Castillo (2010), it became clear that his style of professionalism had been crafted alongside identity markers that were not primary for Gamboa. As a senior Latino journalist born on the border of Texas and Mexico, Castillo's identity was formed by a multiplicity of ethnic and national allegiances. Castillo's Latinidad was central to his style of professionalism. But this is not the only factor to explain his disposition. After all, Gamboa is also a Latina journalist who wrote with enough empathy to make that fact clear. But Gamboa's empathy was discursively produced through journalistic writing that followed a larger set of journalistic traditions, including embracing language more submissive to the political field. Castillo's language, though hardly revolutionary, required the use of more professional capital, and this was partly the result of seniority and education. Two decades of working as a journalist, mostly in Texas, had given him some accumulated professional capital that he used to further separate himself from his peers. In 2001, Castillo got a grant to study for one year at Stanford University, on border issues and immigration. Working under the guidance of Professor Luis Fraga, he came back with a new knowledge set that included the history of immigration law and its repercussions on border life. Upon his return to Austin, Castillo negotiated with the *Austin American-Statesman* the creation of the immigration beat, one of the first of its kind in the nation. From that beat, and with the historical and theoretical background he received at Stanford, Castillo was able to delineate a way of being professional that included a more direct engagement with legal issues about immigration.

In outlining the creation of Hutto and its news coverage, I am taking a step toward the delinking of citizenship from justice, making sure that I can glimpse the political act of jailing children en masse in its bare significance. To do this delinking, I have to contrast two styles of news writing that are only slightly different. Both are empathetic to the children of

Hutto, but their empathy is manifested differently. Gamboa emphasizes moral issues; Castillo places law more at the center of his writings. To different degrees, they both follow journalistic traditions about human rights, undocumented immigrants, and citizenship (Hong 2006, 50). A nation-centric social practice, Gamboa's writing sits at the intersection of institutional and discursive histories that she does not control and that she cannot simply disregard. In upholding professionalism, she normalizes hegemonic discourses and practices that place the justice claims of the undocumented immigrants outside national law. Is it really so absurd to think that the children of Hutto should have had inalienable rights? And even if they do not, could they not still suffer injustices?

Rights

With few exceptions, the coverage of Hutto failed to mention rights, and when rights were mentioned, there was a lack of specificity as to what specific rights Hutto had infringed on. For sure, the legal transgressions that Hutto represented stood in contrast to the commonly held tradition of speaking about rights in terms of universalism. If children's rights are universal, what were these children doing in prison? This question highlights how important it is to understand the pastoral character of liberal governmentality as political performance. When political and legal hegemonic voices speak of universal rights, they are performing the care required by pastoralism. These performances are rhetorical and, often, simply strategic. We tend to rhetorically argue that universal rights are species rights (humans have them), but we only selectively believe that. More precisely, universalism is a rhetorical tool that legitimizes the nation-state episteme's constrictive definitions of justice by linking the figure of the citizen to universalizing ideas of rights and political agency. Under coloniality, universalism is both the ground for citizenship excess and the reason for the peaceful reproduction of the state.

Rhetorically powerful, universalism convinces most people that the laws, rights, and justice provided by the nation-state are beyond reproach. Yet even the universalisms that are at the root of our modern nation-states, such as founding documents, are contradictory and ambivalent. Let me cite three quick and clear instances found in arguably the three most cited nation-founding documents. The most grandiose and universalizing American text is the Declaration of Independence (1776), which famously reads, "We hold these truths to be self-evident, that all men are

created equal, that they are endowed by their Creator with certain un-
alienable Rights, that among these are Life, Liberty and the pursuit of
Happiness. That to secure these rights, Governments are instituted among
Men, deriving their just power from the consent of the governed." Here,
the expansiveness of "all men are created equal" is given limits by the size,
power, and jurisdiction of government to secure these rights. Unlike the
Declaration, the U.S. Bill of Rights (1786) is much more modest, techno-
cratic, and administrative in tone and nature. But even this document
goes back and forth between expansive universalisms and particularisms.
The Fourth Amendment starts with "The right of the people"; the Fifth
Amendment begins with "No person"; and so on. The second article of
the Declaration of the Rights of Man (1789), the document that signaled
France's arrival to the new club of nation-states, reads, "The principle of
all sovereignty resides essentially in the nation. No body nor individual
may exercise any authority which does not proceed directly from the nation." The French use very expansive language to define the rights and
privileges of citizens and the state, but even in this declaration, rights
are not universal. If anything, there is an inherent ambivalence between
its claim to define "mankind" and its provincial jurisdiction. In each of
these cases, the documents establish that what they refer to as "man" and
"people" is actually the more modest and much more troubling figure of
the citizen, the actual bearer of rights who mutually constitutes the legitimacy of government and law. The semiotic slippage between people
and citizens, which confuses even the smartest readers, is evidence of a
colonial legal ontology that defines personhood based on subjection to
the monarch and the colonial epicenter. This slippage is also an important
element of liberalism as a political technology, for it helps to normalize
the discursive and social practices that allow for citizenship excess as political capital accumulation and disavowal of noncitizens. If the nation is
the grantor of justice, should not then the good of the nation take prece-
dence over everything else? This is the logic used by President George W.
Bush in support of extraordinary rendition and torture, and it is the same
logic used by the Minuteman Project in its vigilante practices at the U.S.-
Mexico border.

If we consider that these three political documents are seminal to our
understanding of rights, we must then also assume that our legal and political understanding of *citizen* is the product of the same ambivalence,
caught between expansiveness and exclusivity. Typically, universalism
rests on one form or another of naturalized inequality, adjudicating race,

sex, gender, or other as the sufficient legal standing to grant citizenship to the bearer (Calabrese and Burgelman 1999, 2). Always sitting atop an abstraction, as Wendy Brown comments, universalism "is ideologically achieved by turning away from and thus depoliticizing, yet at the same time *presupposing* our collective particulars, not by embracing them, let alone emancipating us from them" (1993, 392; emphasis in original). Our individual particulars, our difference, be it race, age, gender, or place of birth, are only recognized as political if they have been presupposed and codified in our political and legal imaginaries.

According to Brown, the inability of liberalism to account for uncodified or uncodifiable particulars dissipates with the increasing influence of capitalism and disciplinarity in contemporary forms of governance. In today's liberal governance, universalism recedes in the background, like the ghost in the shell, and other bureaucratized and commercialized processes step up to give it legitimacy.[4] This does not mean that universalism is gone. Its phantom survives in at least two variants. Universalism is present in the language of rights, which continues giving energy to the justice claims of much identity politics, including a notable section of Latina/o politics. Brown (1993, 2004) has theorized extensively on this style of justice claim, noting that rights produce the paradox of opening avenues for equality as they force their claimants to normalize their difference. She writes, "rights secure our standing as individuals even as they obscure the treacherous ways that standing is achieved and regulated" (2004, 430). With "treacherous ways," Brown implies the second way in which universalism is present in today's liberalism. *Universalism is resemanticized under bureaucratic and legal language that uses administrative logic to produce the same or similar results as traditional, essentialist universalisms.* Our standing as individuals is made law when the legal apparatus is able to fashion the governmental specificities that constitute personhood, such as universalizing birth certificates, passports, driver's licenses, and Social Security numbers. This way of seeing rights, universalism, and the bureaucratization of the juridical imaginary means that coloniality will have some of its most surreptitious and, perhaps, dangerous manifestations in administration and policy frameworks, not only in cases that, for instance, have the legal weight to reach the Supreme Court.

The bureaucratization of rights impinges on cases such as Hutto by greatly reducing the scope of legal problems and remedies that Hutto may represent to the legal system. This is evident in the legal framework used by the ACLU and the University of Texas School of Law during the lawsuit against Chertoff et al. In the specific legal complaint filed by the ACLU on behalf of the nine-year-old Saule Bunikyte (one of several dozen plaintiffs) versus Chertoff et al., the ACLU's Vanita Gupta argued for the reinstatement of Saule's legal rights, drawing on everything from the expectation of her release under conditions of supervision to her violated right of privacy (Civil Action No. 1:07-cv-164-SS, Western District of Texas, March 19, 2007). Ms. Gupta's strong and precise lawsuit was filed in the court of Judge Sam Sparks, who originally expressed sympathy for the plaintiffs and declared, "This is detention. This isn't the penitentiary. . . . [Detainees] have less rights than the people I send to the penitentiary" (Castillo 2007a). Judge Sparks proceeded to immediately remove restrictions on attorney visits and set an expedited trial. His decision came on April 10, and in the two weeks that had passed, his tone had already changed. By then, the rights of the children had been weighted against the rights of ICE to pursue its work of securing the borders. In a decision that did not order the release of the children but did order the improvement of detention conditions, Judge Sparks stated that "the court cannot say that [the Department of Homeland Security] has abused its mandate by exploring family detention," thereby foreclosing the possibility of punitive charges against the defendants. Based on this ruling, ICE's spokesperson Marc Raimondi could rightfully state that Judge Sparks had recognized that "detention of families is an important part of ICE's work to remove illegal aliens from the U.S." Sparks's decision performed several roles on behalf of the U.S. government. First, it reduced the legal scope of the argument on behalf of the detained children by citing only one precedent (*Flores v. Reno*) that could be used to argue for the plaintiffs. The *Flores* settlement established detention parameters for minors detained by the INS, and though it eventually meant an improvement in the conditions in which Saule and other children lived in detention, the *Flores* settlement also served to frame the legal issues away from international human rights law, specifically provisions within the Universal Declaration of Human Rights, the International Covenant on Civil and Political Rights, and the Convention on the Rights of the Child.[5] Second, Judge Sparks's decision bureaucratized the already reduced rights of the detained children, calling for administrative solutions (for instance, more education) without recognizing that CCA and ICE administrators were breaking laws every time that the children were denied their rights. Not a single bureaucrat, official, or CCA employee was further prosecuted, fired, or even officially reprehended. The impunity with which the state and its corporations can break laws contrasts starkly with the harsh detention of the children due to the minor administrative infractions committed by their parents. Third and last, by not ordering the immediate release of the children and by siding with ICE's overall political goals, Judge Sparks produced a broad legal framework for the state of exception, and instead of ending it, he gave legal precedent to its reproduction.[6]

Although the rights of citizenship have been expanded (e.g., now citizens have civil rights and some economic rights) and are now given to more people (most liberal nations have some version or another of the Fourteenth Amendment to the U.S. Constitution, which grants citizenship based on birth, disqualifying the excluding power of race), the equation of citizenship and political franchise, central to liberal governmentality and coloniality, has remained constant. Today, as during the time of ancient Greece, the French Revolution, and Marx, an individual's ability to participate in the politics of the state is typically understood as dependent on citizenship, which becomes the primary repository of abstractions that the state recognizes as the political in the individual. Such abstractions have included being propertied (central to political agency in the beginning of our union), white (ibid.), male (1920; should I say more?), mature (children cannot enter into contracts, nor can they behave as political agents), law-abiding (most prisoners lose political rights), and in possession of the "proper" mental faculties to exercise politics. These abstractions can activate political agency only in cases where the mother of all abstractions is present, citizenship. The likeliness that the equation of citizenship and political agency will remain central to our political discourses is directly related to the ability of states to use the language of liberalism and justice to self-adjudicate legitimacy.[7] Hence, the government's rationale to jail children need not be questioned once the state and hegemonic mediated discourses have proven that undocumented immigrants represent a threat to the well-being of the populace. The important question that the citizens opposing the government (including the ACLU and the lawyers involved in the suit, the many legal scholars using their academic status to advocate on behalf of immigrants, and the many activists who day in and day out protested in front of the front gate at Hutto) could ask was "how?"

Although the contemporary application of liberalism is increasingly the bureaucratization of the juridical imaginary, liberalism's appeal remains its universal calls to freedom and emancipation (Dussel 2006, 498; Marx 1975, 212–241). On this, liberalism is in consort with the language of modernity, which defines progress as a teleology toward Western definitions of the good life and the good society (Quijano 2000). At this level, the citizen is the actor of modernity, for only through the juridical-legal position of the citizen can the universalist claim of emancipation come alive. This is a central reason why it is so hard to dislodge our hopes for political betterment from the figure of the citizen and to imagine a justice outside state laws. Reflecting on similar problems of ethnicity, nationality, and the state, Marx proposed the following: "Only the critique of political emancipation itself would constitute a definitive critique of the Jewish question itself and its true resolution into the 'general question of the age'" (1975, 215). Most people fail to query emancipation, and the result is that insofar as the state is conceived as the forum for distributive justice, as in the case in Foucault's work on governmentality, one is forced to trust in the ethics of the state or, at the very least, in the state's ethical potential (Walzer 1992, 281). And trust we do. So from Marx's time to today, the best theoretical tools to distribute justice and national political betterment have been citizenship reform and the expansion of rights. But if the politics of betterment depends on trusting the state, as the Hutto case illustrates, then undocumented immigrants and their supporters live in the age of tragedy.

Lodged in the figure of the citizen, our hopes for political betterment have given way to a set of extremely dangerous and, I suggest, tragic dispositions, including those that structure our willingness to believe that the citizen is, and should remain, the only arbiter of rights. These dispositions, popularized in the field of politics and reconstituted in popular culture, constrain the imagining of political progress to one social organization: the nation-state. The citizen, objectified political history, mutually reconstitutes the legitimacy of the large institution that is the nation-state. Like Marx, Foucault, and many media scholars, those who trust the politics of the state, state revolution, democracy, liberalism, emancipation, or political reform are also implicitly trusting of citizenship, citizenship's political power, citizenship's potential, and/or citizenship's ability to improve and transform the community of nationals. This closes the system to radical critique, for it creates conditions of immanence. The nation, the citizen, law, and justice legitimize each other from within the system of nation, the national episteme, and only claims launched from within are recognized as proper political parley. This functionalist haven is, of course, a discursive construction. And predictably, as Nicholas De Genova (2005) notes, the discourse of citizenship is produced and disseminated from the subject position of the citizen. From this position, which is almost exclusively occupied by natives (Tocqueville notwithstanding, naturalized citizens rarely occupy this position; noncitizens are basically excluded), the citizen authorizes her- or himself to talk about citizenship, "illegal" migration, and the law and is authorized to frame all of these issues in terms of "what is good for 'the nation'" (7). The citizen as the juridical subject narrowly defines the political actor, helping constitute a politics of recognition that makes political agency a "good" unevenly distributed among citizenship populations and often absent from noncitizen populations.

Media and the Dominant Good

There are universalisms that inspire ("life, liberty, and the pursuit of happiness") and others meant to be whispered. In 1792, James Madison published in the *National Gazette* a now famous essay titled "Property," which reinterprets the role of government as the management of property and expands and redefines the very notion of property. He wrote,

> In its larger and juster meaning, [property] embraces every thing to which a man may attach a value and have a right; and *which leaves to every one else the like advantage.*
>
> In the former sense, a man's hand, or merchandise, or money is called his property.
>
> In the latter sense, a man has property in his opinions and the free communication of them.
>
> He has a property of peculiar value in his religious opinions, and in the profession and practice dictated to them.
>
> He has property very dear to him in the safety and liberty of his person.
>
> He has equal property in the free use of his faculties and free choice of the objects on which to employ them.
>
> In a word, as a man is said to have a right to his property, he may be equally said to have a property in his rights. (Madison 1997, 83)

So, if in chapter 1, I reference the idea that citizenship is a tradable good, I am simply following the logical thread of one of the central features of American legal and political thought (see also my use of Cheryl Harris's work on whiteness as property and my argument on political capital accumulation in the following chapters). Moreover, if by universalism we mean to say that some essence should be or is shared by everybody, then the alchemic transformation of life essence into property easily qualifies as the most universalizing feature of the nation-state (Hong 2006, 4, 41; Marx 1975, 229). We are property, and our political valence is ultimately measured, paraphrasing Madison, by the very quantity of things and rights that constitute our citizenship.[8]

That citizenship is a good does not mean that citizenship has to be a dominant good. According to Walzer (1983), citizenship becomes a dominant good when it is capable of structuring other social fields. Echoing Bourdieu's ideas on interconvertibility explored in chapter 2, Walzer's concern is that while all goods exist in specific exchange structures governed by discrete distributive processes, dominant goods transcend their particular structures, creating a chain reaction of power that can end up producing tyranny. This significantly reduces the egalitarian possibilities of any political system. In theory, egalitarianism is better served by having checks and balances, hence by having strongly independent exchange structures. If not for coloniality and liberalism, politics (the purview of the citizen) should be different from justice, and both should be different from media. But if the citizen is at the center of these three systems, equality is hardly possible. Walzer observes that most societies are empirically organized around a sort of gold standard: "One good or set of goods is dominant and determinative of value in all spheres of distribution. And that good or set of goods is commonly monopolized, its value upheld by the strength and cohesion of its owners" (1983, 10). Our society is organized around the gold standards of wealth and citizenship, the goods central to the economic and political fields. Having citizenship gives you the right to trade in other social markets and thus an a priori condition of capital, cultural, and political accumulation. The absence of that good, as the Hutto captives exemplify, displaces you from the relative comfort of being legally read as a juridical subject and transforms you into a legal cipher impenetrable to discourse, someone who is, to reference Madison, nonproperty and nonpropertied.

Walzer proposes a theory of justice that can accommodate the complex distribution issues of contemporary societies.[9] He argues that in complex societies, "simple equality" is not possible. Even if ideal societies existed where all had access to every good, human difference would soon form distributive systems based on merit (different merits, different spheres) that would quickly challenge any simple distributive system (1983, 13–16). Instead, the challenge is to create a theory of justice befitting our complex societies. First, this theory should recognize the multiplicity of distributive systems. For instance, there is such a thing as a distributive system for education (e.g., education field), where access to the good of education is granted on the basis of different principles, including educational merit and parents' financial success. One who recognizes the multiplicity of the distributive system would have to craft a notion of justice proper to each system. Walzer calls this notion "complex equality," which can only be achieved if the systems follow two principles: First, "personal qualities and social goods have their own spheres of operation, where they work their effects freely, spontaneously, and legitimately." Second, "disregard of these principles is tyranny. To convert one good into another, when there is no intrinsic connection between the two, is to invade the sphere where another company of men and women properly rules. Monopoly is not inappropriate within the spheres" (19). Returning to the educational field, the dominant goods of sex, race, citizenship, and money have been consistently used to distribute the good of education, and Walzer, like most observers, argues that this is a type of tyranny. How then do we think of citizenship as a dominant good? In light of the normalized theoretical inability to consider justice beyond the nation, should we not reevaluate citizenship as the most nefarious of all tyrannies? For centuries we have criticized the tyranny of wealth, the second most powerful dominant good in liberal democracies, but citizenship, for the most part, is simply immune to radical criticism, our hopes for justice too invested in a legal world dominated by politics and the nationals.

When citizenship dominates politics, law, and media, tyranny is not only possible; it is also predictable. Citizenship excess is its result. Immigrants are always in peril, because at any time they can become unworthy subjects in these important spheres. As Foucault has noted in his studies on prisons and mental hospitals, some people are simply subject to power, outside the purview of political agency, and incapable of engaging in the trade of political goods. In my way of seeing techniques of governance and distributive justice, the undocumented immigrant occupies a position similar to the mad person or the criminal sentenced to death; the constitution of their particularism (Brown 1993) makes these subjects legally, discursively, and politically unworthy of recognized social agency and power. Undocumented immigrants may have some power in the private sphere and within marginal national social and labor markets, but clearly they are not competing for goods in the markets that matter most. Hence, the children of Hutto cannot exist in legal discourse without the intervention of American citizens (think the ACLU, the Texas School of

Law, journalists, and the myriad protesters and video archivers who have made it possible to learn about this detention center), and their best hope for justice is to become proper objects of compassion.

The case of Hutto shows the dominance of citizenship outside the political field, in particular, the harmony between the political and legal fields and the media world. Consider this: in Hutto, reporters had a case involving the mistreatment of children and human rights violations that the government tried to keep secret for months (Castillo 2010). All the ingredients for a drama were there, but the story never became what in today's media world we call "viral." This was not for lack of opportunity. The *New York Times* reported on it four times; twice was Hutto in the *Washington Post*; the *New Yorker* published a compelling article on the matter. Although subtle ways of marginalizing the story were common even in Texas, where Castillo's work, for instance, was mostly published in the Metro/State section and not with the rest of the national or international news, the story was there for the networks to grab. Yet, from 2006 to end of the Bush administration in January 2009, Hutto was mentioned only forty-two times in television and radio news.[10] Of the forty-two mentions, thirty-two were in Texas or on Spanish-language television (Univision and Telemundo). Hutto was mentioned ten times on broadcast or cable news channels. NPR engaged with the issue three times. Dan Rather, at his post-CBS televisual outfit HDNet, produced a show on immigrants in which he briefly mentioned detention practices and Hutto. Most of these reports were brief, though some are poignant (listen to NPR's *All Things Considered* of February 9, 2007, or watch Univision's *Despierta America* of February 23, 2007). Given the huge amount of television and radio news in America, the result of these searches is evidence of a systemic absence of this issue in national media news organizations. Ironically, the only two private, English-language, national television media that addressed Hutto extensively were Fox and CNN, where Bill O'Reilly and Lou Dobbs, two of the nation's most xenophobic voices, talked about the detention center in their own powerful, ethnocentric, and racist voices. Dobbs dedicated three programs to Hutto on February 23, March 6, and March 8, 2007, and he alone produced more televisual text on Hutto than the rest of English-language television combined. The children, he noted in his February 23 program, are better off in this prison than at home, where abject poverty is the norm. The humanitarian and civic organizations speaking on behalf of the children, he continued, are colluding with pro-immigration forces to get amnesty for those whom he calls "illegals."

Unsympathetic and, arguably, vicious, Dobbs presented all issues of legality from the point of view of the ultraright. Supportive of Chertoff and ICE and self-congratulatory of the fact that these facilities were so much nicer than the places where these children would have to otherwise live, Dobbs was rabidly critical of all organizations and people involved in defending the children.

The overall effect of this media coverage was that for most Americans who were not on the right, Hutto never made it onto their radar. Mainstream media shape the majority's sense of ethics and justice. In this case, it did so through the repetition of nationalist and ethnocentric agendas and also, and perhaps more poignantly, through its silences: those aspects of life and reality that never made it onto the evening news. If we consider side by side the relative silence around Hutto at the national level and the timid way with which print journalists typically engaged with the story, it is possible to understand the state of exception as the product of a political culture of exceptionality fostered and produced by mainstream media.

Alterity and Alternative Media

In political theory and in politics, hegemony and tyranny are hardly the same thing, but the presence of one does not preclude the existence of the other. Here, they coexist. The hegemonic, agonistic aspect of American politics and American media found spaces to voice some discontent. A small number of people and organizations showed that they cared about Hutto and used small media and guerrilla tactics to challenge ICE and the government. Many of these activists were at the entrance of the prison daily protesting Hutto's detention practices. Others came on weekends, brought their cameras and banners, recorded footage, and posted it on sites such as YouTube. Most are local to central Texas. YouTube was one of the few relatively public, relatively general forums that allowed for events such as Hutto to be videoed and distributed. In the site's almost nihilistic way of structuring things, YouTube provided space for an array of different video genres, contrasting viewing traditions, and counterpublics. The range of videos on Hutto that are available on YouTube includes some in which the camera is used as the most simple recording device, in its rawest power, without editing or artifice, à la Lumière. Typically shot by people not heavily involved with media production, these videos were filmed outside the prison and record the protests themselves as well as the surrounding landscape. The makers, clearly, did not have access to

Hutto's interior or to officials involved with the detention center. A few other videos on YouTube were formal, traditional minidocumentaries that used documentary conventions to produce powerful narratives in an attempt to engage viewers' emotions and reason. In "Children Confined—Immigrant Detention Center at Hutto," the most viewed of the Hutto videos, the filmmakers interview a child and her mother to harness the emotional force that will make the listing of UN provisions rhetorically powerful (acluvideos, March 23, 2007, http://www.youtube.com/watch?v=HBCAgSCGMo4). In two minutes, this video, sponsored by the ACLU, shows the perspective of immigrants and of the UN, and it casts the government's actions as violations of the basic principles of American justice.

As powerful as "Children Confined" is, I find "T. Don Hutto—Footage from ICE" to be the most eerie video of all. This is a strange documentary presented by Docubloggers, a video initiative sponsored by KLRU, Austin's public-television broadcasting station. According to text accompanying the video, Docubloggers requested footage from ICE, which Docubloggers presents without editing and without sound (May 17, 2007, http://www.youtube.com/watch?v=bFo24cB6kHU). Although I am sure the footage was provided by ICE to address criticism and to show the world the quality facilities and positive living conditions of Hutto, the effect is quite the opposite. For four minutes, we are allowed to see inside Hutto; in silent images, children wearing prison garb play, eat, and color. The only faces shown are blurred or filmed at a distance, providing just enough visual information to communicate that these are brown bodies, brown families, and brown children.

Docubloggers decided to show ICE the footage as is, partly because they believed in the power of the visual image to communicate much more than ICE intended. They were right. There is something about the video that is excessive and that the images cannot seem to contain, information that is unruly and that subverts the makers' intentions. Let me give you two instances. There is a point (1:26) when the video shows a series of people walking in front of the camera on an extremely clean floor, dressed in extremely clean green prison garb, and wearing brand-new shoes. We only see them from the knees down, an adult followed by several small sets of feet. I found these seconds of footage quite unsettling and could not quite point to the reason. But then I realized that these images of disembodied feet were disturbing because they remind me of some prison movies set during World War II, in which prisoners are meant to be rehabilitated through the rigors of fascist über-discipline, which is shown through rhythmic images, repetition, and obsessive cleanliness, just as in ICE's video. In a similarly excessive fashion, we later see the aseptic reality of a cell (2:21) that includes four items: a toilet, a sink, bunk beds, and a crib. This image, empty of life, is meant convey "humane" living conditions to viewers; instead, it reminds us of a morgue. Its emptiness becomes scary, its cleanliness absurd. The overall effect of the video is partly reached by an invitation to intertextually connect the footage of Hutto to fascist images and videos of criminals, which often blur the faces of criminal subjects or cover them with hoods. Intertextuality, however, has its weaknesses, for it necessitates a degree of viewer competency and ideological willingness. Some viewers, thus, may have interpreted the footage as simply indexing a high degree of cleanliness and, hence, as evidence of ICE's care for the children. But for those who read "T. Don Hutto—Footage from ICE" through the codes of fascism, the video is a reminder that a rhetoric of development, progress, and care through hygiene cannot legitimate the inhumanity inherent in jailing children.

Relying on these videos to make an impact on the public sphere is not advisable. As powerful as some of the videos are, they have been viewed only a few thousand times. The ICE video had been viewed twenty-three times at the time of this writing. These activists and their videos were and are marginal; they have little to no chance to impact our nation's mainstream culture. This is an example of how the agonistics of hegemonic processes in the national realm engender tragedy. These activists are on the fringes of our video culture, barely existing. They are marginal to the nation's political pursuits, their goals irrelevant, their voices dim. To the great majority of Americans, the children of Hutto remain safely absent.

Conclusion: Reimagining Hutto

If rights are property, as Madison suggests and Grace Hong (2006) theorizes, and the law and government are invested in the protection of rights, undocumented immigrants are always in danger of signifying the lawless but not as defined by the now popular, and still offensive, term "illegal." The lawless here exist in legal vacuums where tyranny is not only possible but the rule (Hong 2006, 41). What is justice in this transnational problematic? Justice, at least justice to the immigrants, is not part of the ethical repertoire implied in the social transactions between immigration law enforcement and undocumented immigrants. Justice, always implicitly concerned with the relationship of law and the citizen, stands as the dark spot concealing the automatic dismissal of the other from the political. In securing, protecting, and franchising the citizen, justice depoliticizes the immigrant, producing a rightless, propertyless, and lawless individual, more closely resembling the archetypical legal object of the slave than of the human. Is it then surprising that the legal remediation of Hutto was so mild? The children have remained rightless, and though the ACLU tried to argue for their humanity (and used the Human Rights Chart as legal backing), the courts did not agree. The undocumented immigrants, like slaves, were inscribed in law and interpreted by legal discourses as things, not humans; they were seen as capable of entering the physical space of the nation but unable to enter the imagined space of the national community. Because it is possible to see connections between the undocumented immigrant and the slave, it is worth reconsidering the children of Hutto from the perspective of coloniality, legalscapes, and exceptional neoliberalism, all of which provide explanatory logics to the children's ethical quandaries.

The work of coloniality is partly to make transhistorical some specific solutions to the contingent problems of governing colonial subjects. Connecting past to present, the colonial residues found in bureaucracy, law, and epistemology carry on the dirty work of fragmenting, disenfranchising, and exploiting populations given legal character by the nation-state and, often, democratic processes dependent on consensus. As Quijano notes, racial discourses are the product of colonialism. Under coloniality, racial difference is subsumed under the national umbrella, and as I argue, it becomes part of modern governmental liberal techniques that produce supple and stealthy forms of racial exploitation while participating in the discourses of consensus and democracy. Undocumented immigrants, unlike other marginal populations, suffer the most severe forms of coloniality, for they are rightless and not needed for the legitimacy of national democratic processes. Their labor can thus be appropriated by the nation with impunity, and Lou Dobbs can exist as a legally protected voice of reason. To make matters worse, Latin American undocumented immigrants carry the double stigma of having also been colonial subjects of the United States; they are ingrained in U.S. history as the defeated subjects of the Mexican-American wars and the dozen coups d'état "sponsored" by the United States in Central and South America. Latin American undocumented subjects are subjects produced through the colonial administrative logics that governed the Southwest for a century and the economic and cultural colonialisms that the United States imposes on Latin America still today.

Expanding Quijano's criticism of contemporary nation-states to citizenship produces troubling possibilities, for it means reevaluating law in relationship to coloniality. In Western and Westernized nation-states, the discursive and cultural construction of the citizen goes hand-in-hand with the social production of citizenship as a juridical subjectivity. Law, therefore, occupies a central role in constituting subjects, and unsurprisingly, law, as a national construct, becomes central to discussions of justice. As Thomas Streeter (1996) and Bernard Edelman (1979) have noted, law is the most effective technology for producing subjects. Even Althusser, when he attempted to illustrate the effectiveness of ideology, used the image of the police officer "hailing" a person. We are certainly hailed by ideology, but the hail of the law is powerful, effective, and constant. To disobey ideology may be dangerous to the hegemonic system; to disobey the law is physically dangerous to us. Law, which is manifested in myriad ways, brokers our relationship to others (by setting protocols of polite interaction), to the economy (by defining the rules of labor), to politics (by establishing political rights and defining political subjects), and to culture (by legally establishing the basis for media industries, cultural policies, and cultural franchise). Law, which subjects us from before we are born (through health policy, sexual policy, and educational policies that establish the field of medicine), is, however, not everybody's purview. In coloniality, law is a social and political field created by and for the citizen. Moreover, law expands and, I would argue, hides the logic of colonial administration behind the Taylorization of rights that Brown observes, producing the suppleness that Foucault notes is central to liberal governmentality. Coloniality facilitates the epistemological and social rationales at the base of the reproduction of law and legal structures, furnishing the social scripts that make unsustainable the justice claims of the children of Hutto.

4

English- and Spanish-Language Media

The modern world-system was born in the long sixteenth century. The Americas as a geosocial construct were born in the long sixteenth century. The creation of this geosocial entity, the Americas, was the constitutive act of the modern world-system. The Americas were not incorporated into an already existing capitalist world-economy. There could not have been capitalist world-economy without the Americas.
—Quijano and Wallerstein (1992), qtd. in Mignolo (2000, 219)

Latinas/os have never owned much media in the United States. Today, although Latinas/os are 15 percent of the population and their buying power stands at roughly $1 trillion, lack of ownership persists. As Catherine Sandoval (2005–2006), Kent Wilkinson (2009), and Leonard Baynes (2009) have noted, Latinas/os own roughly 1 percent of radio stations and only 1.25 percent of television stations (for a general picture, see Valdivia 2010, 54–63). Majorities, dominated by ethno-racially white interests, own all major broadcasting networks in radio and television, and the future of the ownership landscape seems equally dystopic for Latinas/os, who face the challenge of economically competing for ownership and an unfriendly regulatory apparatus. Spanish-language media (SLM) have changed hands repeatedly, and the Federal Communications Commission (FCC) has never made a priority to frame the sales in terms of minority ownership. That is, the FCC does not treat SLM as minority media; instead, in radio, the FCC treats Spanish-language radio as a format, a definition that links

SLM more to taste cultures (e.g., jazz and country are other formats) than to an ethnic and political identity. This has meant, according to Sandoval, that FCC restrictions on the number of stations that can be owned by a single corporation do not apply to Spanish-language radio. This has translated into the conglomeration of Spanish radio in the hands of large radio corporations such as Clear Channel and Hispanic Broadcasting Corporation, now owned by Univision. Similarly, the FCC has treated television as any other for-profit media, a simple commodity, allowing Spanish-language media corporations to change hands without respect for the basic notion that to have a successful public sphere, minorities ought to own and control their own media. Currently, Univision, the largest Spanish-language media corporation in the United States, is owned by a financial group headed by a number of equity firms. Telemundo, the second-largest Spanish-language media network, is owned by NBC.

In this chapter, I investigate this state of affairs and begin with the observation that the utter commodification of SLM is intimately linked to SLM's political devaluation. I also note that in contrast, English is politically overvalued and treated as the U.S. national language. The political devaluation of SLM happens at the intersection of economics and politics, an ambivalent space where SLM is measured against two contrasting definitions of public interest. The first definition of public interest is rooted in neoliberalism, a way of thinking that trusts in the ability of the market to deliver individual and public goods. In neoliberalism, the public interest is served when media is regulated with attention to market competition, and the wishes of audiences are represented in ratings and advertising revenue (Aufderheide 1990; Rowland 1997; Simone and Fernback 2006, 290). The proper role of the Federal Communications Commission under neoliberal understandings of the public interest is to ensure vibrant market competition, to reduce the likeliness of monopolies, and to assure that corporations invest in infrastructure and technological innovation. Under this definition of public interest, all media, including SLM, are depoliticized. The second definition of public interest is fully political, rooted in ethnonationalism and the proposition that the security of the nation-state depends partly on establishing sovereignty over media (see chapter 2). In this definition of the public interest, media is the place where cultural citizenship happens, and it becomes a symbolic territory that the FCC will protect with ownership rules. In the neoliberal definition of the public interest, SLM is simply a commodity; in the ethnonational definition of the public interest, SLM is all politics because it is the media of foreigners and of immigrants. Both definitions of the public interest politically devalue SLM. I argue that both definitions of the public interest are rooted in the linguistic frameworks of coloniality that have established Spanish as a particular object of state regulation. These are the same linguistic frameworks that have made English the U.S. national language and the basis for ethnonational forms of neoliberalism.

In this chapter, I show that the political devaluation of SLM and the linguistic frameworks of coloniality that regulate language are clear examples of citizenship excess. The result of this excess is that Spanish in general and SLM in particular are weak platforms for citizenship rights and that as Spanish is weakened, English and its media accumulate greater political capital. The political capital accumulation involved in making English and ELM hegemonic in history, law, and politics is citizenship excess that depends on erasing the history and juridical location of Spanish and SLM in the United States. The relationship of English to Spanish and of ELM to SLM marks spaces where political practices and struggles demarcate national belonging.[1] Like all politics, these spaces are multidimensional and expressed in law, culture, economics, and social relations. Here I am interested in the juridical and the way language becomes an object of regulation. In the United States, language policy structures the political field, as when we officially sanction the printing of bilingual voting ballots, and the educational field, as when we declare that bilingualism is a state or federal goal. Less often do we think of media policy as language policy. Yet media are fundamental to the live expression, reproduction, and vitality of languages. For these reasons, in this chapter, I link media policy to language policy and explore the connections between the political marginalization of Spanish and SLM policy.

In the first section of this chapter, I apply coloniality to the media field and argue that an ethnonational linguistic political technology is at work in broadcasting policy, an issue that has long-lasting implications to Latina/o life. Then I historicize the practice of treating Spanish as a foreign language and place it within a politics of the state constructed around ethnonational goals. These ethnonational goals are tied to coloniality and to processes of governmentality that use language as a political mechanism to separate peoples and to define resource allocation. I introduce multicultural liberalism, a political framework that has the potential to expand the linguistic claims of Latinas/os by repoliticizing Spanish at the national level. Lastly, I examine the types of political effects that could be expected if SLM and Spanish were treated as linguistic, political, and cultural rights.

Depoliticizing SLM

Neoliberal and ethnonational definitions of the public interest have depoliticized SLM and are the immediate reasons for the shape and limitations of the Latino public sphere. Under neoliberalism, SLM becomes a deregulated commodity and the FCC a state agency in charge of facilitating trade and market competition. The result of neoliberal definitions of the public interest have affected all media, but they have affected SLM in very particular ways that speak of a neoliberalism that is also invested in ethnonational agendas. In this section, I note that this mixing of neoliberalism (capitalism on steroids) and ethnonationalism is a common feature of coloniality, a claim that I continue exploring in following sections. I used Quijano and Wallerstein in the epigraph to this chapter in order to illustrate this very point and to note that nation-states are as much political organizations as they are economic territories meant to regulate, police, and administer a national economy. Nikolas Rose argues this point when he states that since Adam Smith and David Ricardo, it is common to

> presuppose that an economy is more or less coincident with the territorial boundaries of a nation state. . . . It was thus only in the nineteenth century that we can see the birth of a language of national economy as a domain with its own characteristics which could be spoken about and about which knowledge could be gained. Once such an economy had been delineated, it could become the object and target of political programmes that would seek to evaluate and increase the power of nations by governing and managing "the economy." (1999, 33)

Rose helps us see that, in the West, the development of capitalism happens alongside liberal governmentality and that questions of how to govern have often been paralleled by questions of how to organize society to the benefit of industrial, corporate, and financial interests. In his chapter on "advanced liberalism," Rose also argues that what we term *neoliberalism* is an evolving form of liberalism that seeks to further enmesh state functions with the goals of private economic development (138–140). Rose and Quijano and Wallerstein also propose that the rise of capitalism and the nation-state are ethnic and racial projects in which politics, economics, and law were instruments key to the disciplining, categorizing, and administering of racial others. Based on these scholars, it is fair to assume that neoliberalism itself is partly a racial project meant to reconstitute vertical hierarchies and an ethnonational project meant to push away immigrant populations with xenophobic laws. With this assumption in mind, this chapter proposes that economic terms such as *commodity*, *market*, and *trade* are anchored in ethnonational discourses. The evidence, as I show, comes from the slippery way in which SLM has been treated in majoritarian political and legal circles and the contradictory definitions of public interest that are used to evaluate its worth.

The neoliberal notion of public interest that regulatory bodies use with SLM reduce it to its commodity status without regard for the effects SLM has on its users. I am not suggesting that regulatory bodies should treat SLM as a noncommodity. All things that are subject to trade are commodities, and this includes privately owned media such as SLM. However, some commodities are defined in complex social and political ways and thus are subject to different government regulations. Medicine, food, alcohol, and tobacco are all commodities subject to different complex sets of regulations. Often, as in the case of medicine, food, alcohol, or tobacco, regulation is meant to protect users from, among other things, the dangers of substandard products. So when I note in dismay that SLM is primarily being defined as a commodity, I mean that SLM is not defined in terms of what it does or what it does not do for its "users." Regulatory bodies have approved sales of SLM without recognizing that SLM is central to Latinas/os' cultural and political life (F. Gutiérrez 1985). Most media scholars believe that, as with food or medicine, the state ought to be involved in the process of selling and buying of media companies and that, as with food or medicine, the main principles behind media trade regulation should be a broad understanding of the negative effects that a substandard product will have on society's well-being. This is the primer for critical definitions of public interest, which argue that media are central to democracy because they create the space where public debate happens and broad political consensus is formed (McChesney 1993, 2004; McMurria 2009; Miller 2007; Napoli 2001; Noriega 2000; Perlman 2007; Schudson 2002; Simone and Fernback 2006; Valdivia 2010). Over the decades, the principles around which the Federal Radio Commission (FRC) and, later, the Federal Communications Commission (FCC) regulated media have changed; the definition of "public interest" is after all subject to political control as well as social and historical transformation.[2] Yet since the civil rights movement, these principles have included the recognition and protection of diversity of programming and the sense that to foster diversity in programming one needs to foster diversity in media employment and diversity in media ownership (Baker 1998; Corbett 1996; Eule 1990; Perlman 2007; Simone and Fernback 2006; Weinberg 1993). So my position here is that a notion of public interest that includes the idea that minorities ought to own their own media is part of the FCC tradition, and what is surprising is how this tradition is rejected by the FCC when it comes to SLM.

Simply put, SLM has been subject to weak public interest standards. As such, SLM is regulated following whatever capitalist lexicon is popular at the time. Today, this lexicon, inflected by neoliberalism, includes terms such as *convergence, deregulation,* and *transnationalism,* all terms that define SLM as a particular type of commodity of little cultural or political importance for the unimportant transient immigrant communities that it serves. In the spirit of deregulation and convergence, in 2003 the FCC allowed Univision to purchase the Hispanic Broadcast Corporation (HBC), the largest Spanish-language radio network in the United States, creating a mammoth media conglomerate that Latino critics saw as diluting media options for Latinas/os and narrowing down programming diversity (Dougherty 2003, 72; Valdivia 2010, 56–59). Although the FCC has policies (e.g., H.R. 3207 and S. 1563) to safeguard ethnic, non-English media, these were not enough to frame the issue in political terms, and the sale was approved. The FCC's policies require a hearing anytime a transfer of ownership affecting minority languages is imminent, which forces the FCC to produce a report to Congress. Yet these safeguards are clearly not enough. Although Latino civic organizations and legal suits challenged the sale, the government sided with Univision and its market-driven logic. The result is a Spanish-language mediascape dominated by Univision, a situation that activists and corporations fear will permanently endanger Latino political culture and consumer rights. This result is an outcome predicted by critics of deregulation, such as Philip Napoli, who argues that technological convergence provides new ways of decreasing competition and limiting access, further hurting nonhegemonic communities (2001, 90–93). Napoli also reminds us that the "diversity principle," which has the goal of maximizing sources of information and points of view available to citizens, has become a rhetorical tool to justify policy outcomes (2005, 350). Despite evidence that the new Univision conglomerate would dominate 75 percent of revenue from SLM, the FCC declared that the merger "would not adversely affect competition or diversity in any media market" (Dougherty 2003, 72). Kristin Moran (2007, 18), who has researched Spanish-language news after the merger, argues that the oligopoly status of Univision is partly at fault in making the Univision news more like English-language news, making it responsive to some needs of the Latino community but overall embracing the corporate values of other language news organizations.

Echoing similar disregard for the importance of SLM to Latino communities, in April 2002, the FCC approved the sale of Telemundo to NBC for $2.7 billion, formalizing what was already clear, that the FCC's commitment to minority ownership was lip service only (Valdivia 2010, 58). The last betrayal by the FCC of its stated goal of providing the ground for minority ownership policies happened in March 2007 with the approval of the $12 billion sale of Univision to Thomas H. Lee Partners, the Texas Pacific Group, Madison Dearborn Partners, Providence Equity Partners, and the billionaire Haim Saban. Like the Black Entertainment Network before it, Univision shares the fate of other ethnic media under post-Reagan neoliberalism, which defines media as corporate institutions, not as cultural spaces. Today, a weak definition of competition becomes the central good that the FCC dispenses to the public. Who controls media and to what ends become secondary issues. Clearly, if the FCC understood SLM as central to the exercise of Latino cultural citizenship and language rights, who controlled SLM would be a more relevant matter.

The commodification of SLM did not begin with neoliberalism, nor has it been a straightforward process of defining SLM only within the discourse of the market. Different media have a different history of commodification. Spanish-language newspapers and radio were often simultaneously commodified and politicized. América Rodriguez (1999) notes that early Spanish-language newspapers in the nineteenth century, for instance, were supported by the economic interests of marginal but active Latino communities. Although chiefly advertising driven, some of these newspapers were subsidized, especially in California, where local and state policies treated them as necessary instruments for internal colonization in the wake of annexation (F. Gutiérrez 1977, 39). Most of these privately owned newspapers defined themselves in terms of ethnicity and nationality and often became political advocates of Latino interests. This was true of papers such as *El Clamor Público* (1850s, Los Angeles), *El Heraldo de México* (1916–1920, Los Angeles), and *La Prensa* (1913–1957, San Antonio). Similarly, early Spanish-language radio was chiefly a commercial enterprise that behaved as political media and that engaged with issues relevant to the local Latino community they served (see chapter 3). From its beginnings in the 1920s, Spanish-language radio stations behaved partly as what Dolores Inés Casillas calls "acoustic allies" of Spanish-dominant listeners, who benefited from radio programming encompassing advocacy-oriented issues and entertainment (2006, 19).

Unlike newspapers and radio, Spanish-language television has a history of depoliticization, and this is evident from its beginnings in 1961.[3] Highly commercialized and dominated by Mexican media interests, the Spanish International Network (SIN) was a vehicle for Televisa's programming and advertising. Conceived as an extension of Televisa, Latin America's most influential Spanish-language television company, for the first two decades, SIN did not produce local programming except for a few low-budget talk shows. Evidencing a lack of interest in servicing the national or local cultural and political needs of Latinas/os, SIN's hypercommodified practices even included the importation of news programming from Mexico. SIN, in short, behaved as if the Spanish-speaking Latinas/os it served did not have national or local interests.

Ironically, the depoliticizing of Spanish-language television was happening at the same time that other mass media were becoming politicized. The 1960s and 1970s were characterized by civil-rights-influenced media activism seeking to influence the FCC and other regulatory agencies in charge of structuring the media landscape. In 1964, the United Church of Christ (UCC) partnered with the NAACP to try to withhold the broadcasting license of WLBT-TV in Jackson, Mississippi, for failing to serve the cultural and political needs of the substantial African American community (Horwitz 1997). Though the FCC ruled against UCC and NAACP, the victory in the appeal process gave communities the right to stand before the FCC. Having gained the right to stand in front of the FCC—that is, to have a say on processes of license renewal—communities and activist organizations exercised that right through broadcasting media advocacy. Processes of license renewal became the bread and butter of media activism during the following years. As important, the notion that television ought to serve the public interest became a more central part of the legal imaginary. In the 1970s, this notion also included the logical proposition that to best serve the public interest of minority communities, some media needed to be owned by members of the minority community. During this period, the FCC created rules to energize minority ownership, including the provision that when television stations were put on sale, the FCC would favor bids by minorities. Specifically, bids by minorities would be considered equal even if they included smaller upfront payments and more payments in installments (Forty megahertz 1995, 1150).

Public interest FCC policies and the type of broadcasting advocacy common during the 1960s became quite relevant to Latinas/os in general, as Chon Noriega (2000) narrates in his book on Latino media. However, only once since 1961, the year SIN was founded, have Latinas/os had an opportunity to buy a large SLM corporation. The FCC chose the non-Latino bid. SIN was put on sale in the mid-1980s, and Latino groups believed that the FCC would use minority-ownership policies to make the buy possible. Frank del Olmo, from the *Los Angeles Times*, organized a bid and framed it in the following terms:

> There are many thoughtful Latinos in this country who think the network could do a far better job than it does. Most of the entertainment programming that the network gets from Mexico is no better, and often much worse than the sophomoric pap television from ABC, NBC, and CBS. As for community involvement, Christmas telethons to help poor families in the barrio are wonderful. But it would be nice too, if local news outlets like KMEX had bigger budgets. Then they would report all year long on the causes of the poverty, like school dropouts, and the consequences, like gang violence. (del Olmo, qtd. in América Rodriguez 1999, 62–63)

Despite significant pressure from Latino activists and business groups, civic rights organizations, and the Congressional Hispanic Caucus, and as a testament to the rise of neoliberalism and Reaganism in media policy, the FCC chose the nonminority bid by Hallmark, the giant greeting-card company. Under Hallmark, SIN became Univision.

The neoliberal commodification of SLM is partly constructed through discourses that depoliticize it within the nation while framing it as an international political threat or issue. So, in a sense, SLM is not regulated as a medicine; it is regulated as a fighter jet, a commodity that cannot be sold to enemy nations but could be traded with allies. This implies a notion of public interest that is national, defined in a world-system, and meant to protect the nation from foreign threats. This type of regulatory approach and this understanding of the public interest goes back almost a century, and it has involved radio and television. When reviewing this history, it is also clear that this notion of public interest is not simply national but is also defined ethnically and must be considered ethnonational.

From early radio broadcasting to the present, SLM has been partly constructed in relationship to a "'Latin' culture outside U.S. borders"

(Casillas 2006, 25; see also F. Gutiérrez 1985). In particular during the 1930s, when President Franklin Roosevelt's Good Neighbor Policy shaped U.S. relations to Latin America, Spanish-language radio was part of the tactical arsenal used by the United States to construct solidarities with Latin American nations. As Catherine Benamou (2007) notes, these solidarities, in turn, would facilitate U.S. economic, political, scientific, and military influence in the region. These radio ventures, which included major broadcasters such as NBC and the built-to-purpose two Pan-American Union radio stations, helped constitute Spanish as a political international language, foreign yet allied. In a different political spectrum, Latinas/os in the Southwest had been producing Spanish-language radio programming since the early 1920s. As Casillas writes, "Physically present within the 'real' public sphere, yet imagined as largely foreign within the landscape of radio," Latinas/os of Mexican origin constructed shows that mixed entertainment with community service (2006, 39). These early radio efforts were commodified political performances that gave cultural solidity to longtime Spanish-speaking citizens of the region and newly arrived immigrant populations (América Rodriguez 1999). Their origins roughly coincided with the rise of anti-Latino nativism in the 1920s. This nativism was exacerbated by the economic imperative of the Depression era, a period of systematic deportations. These deportations were nothing less than labor purges that majoritarian political and nativist communities rationalized with fantastic claims about the negative effects of immigrant labor in the Southwest. In 1930, President Herbert Hoover went as far as declaring that Mexicans were one of the main causes of the economic depression (Casillas 2006, 43). Opposing this hateful environment, commercially organized Spanish-language radio became one of the few public spaces in which Latin American immigrants and Latino citizens could experience belonging and a sense of limited but meaningful political power and franchise.

Early Spanish-language radio was greatly affected by the FRC's and the FCC's ethnonational agendas. During the late 1920s and the 1930s, these regulatory bodies imposed stricter controls on what they referred to as "foreign"-language programming, including Spanish-language radio. Foreign broadcasters were deemed subversive, a potential threat to the nation. Often within the context of war and threats to sovereignty, early ownership restrictions were formalized first in the Radio Act of 1912 by forbidding foreign nationals from owning broadcasting stations and, later, by prohibiting foreigners from owning more than 25 percent of a licensee's company stock (I. Rose 1995, 1194). In an effort to dodge these restrictions, during the 1930s, a large portion of Spanish-language radio moved to the Mexican side of the border, exacerbating its foreign character. These same broadcasting restrictions affected Spanish-language television. But the effect of ownership restrictions did not end then. As América Rodriguez (1999) recounts, SIN was put on sale in 1985 because FCC administrative judge John H. Conlin ruled it was controlled by foreign interests, specifically, Televisa. As George Ramos writes in the *Los Angeles Times*, Emilio Azcárraga, owner of Televisa, "and his family had created an 'abnormal relationship' that made the Spanish-language stations in the United States dependent on their influence and direction. The relationship, according to Conlin, stemmed from the long association between the Azcárraga family, which controls the giant Televisa TV network in Mexico, and Anselmo, a U.S. citizen who was an export division manager for Azcárraga's company in the early 1960s" (1986; see also I. Rose 1995, 1197). Up until 1985, the FCC had turned a blind eye to Azcárraga's influence and, at least partial, ownership of SIN. Politicizing the sale of SIN in nationalistic terms, casting it in terms of the threat of foreigners, did not preclude the FCC from approving the sale purely in market terms. Hallmark was the winner and, as a testament to the context of the sale, immediately got rid of the name Spanish International Network. Univision was created, and its neoliberal commodity status has been held constant to the present.

The worst consequence of defining SLM in nationalistic terms is that SLM's role as a cultural and political platform for Latinas/os is diminished. I also believe that overplaying the SLM's foreign status reconstitutes a notion of public interest that marginalizes Latinas/os, who are treated as immigrant, transient populations not central to the nation and not deserving of the right to have and control their own public sphere. When SLM is treated in relation to its connections to foreign media, Latinas/os lose. What is startling is that most people in the United States treat SLM this way, including academics. I mention academics because academia tends to monitor, affect, and often define good discursive practices. Academia is partly in charge of crafting the discourses that widely define media as an economic and/or political issue. And yet academics here are at fault in defining SLM in these dangerous ways.

A quick illustration of this national/foreign frame in academia is found in work by Robert Kent and Maura Huntz and by Kenton Wilkinson. When Kent and Huntz introduce their study of Spanish-language newspapers, they begin with the following:

Throughout the history of the United States most immigrants have arrived speaking only their native language. When population concentra-
tions who spoke the same language arose, foreign-language newspapers
often appeared to serve them. Typically, these newspapers terminated
publication once the group gained command of the English language
and when the influx of additional group members in the area subsided.
The Spanish-language press, however, is different from other foreign-
language publications. Spanish-language newspapers were published in
New Orleans as early as 1808, and their presence in the Southwest pre-
dated the United States' territorial acquisition in the wake of the 1848
Mexican-American War. (1996, 446; internal citations omitted)

Well intentioned, Kent and Huntz grant Spanish antiquity but never question its status as foreign. Similarly, Wilkinson concludes his chapter on
bilingual media as follows: "Since its origin early in the nineteenth century, Spanish language media in the United States has helped its audiences
stay connected with *their cultures of origin*. . . . Publicly supported media
in Spanish are few and far between, likely because of the general expectation that immigrants to the United States learn English" (2009, 14; emphasis added). Like Kent and Huntz, Wilkinson rearticulates the notion that
SLM is foreign immigrant media and should be treated as such. Other
examples abound. During a recent visit to a giant media library of a pres-
tigious research university, I was informed by the head of acquisitions that
the library's massive collection contained not a single Spanish-language
U.S. television program. She kindly stated that "foreign-language programming" is typically acquired by faculty request. In 2010, I presented a
paper on Spanish-language television at the Society of Cinema and Media
Studies, a top conference in my field. Instead of being placed on a panel
with other ethnic or racial media, the leaders in my field placed me on a
panel with foreign television, which included papers on Norwegian and
Palestinian television. Ironically, the conference was held in Los Angeles.

Perhaps because SLM is frequently imagined as foreign, it is often absent from academic discussions of national television. When most academics talk about U.S. television, they are referring to English-language
television. This is clear when we consider the discursive practices of trade
press and academia. Let me illustrate this with the following example. On
November 9, 2007, I entered the following search terms in LexisNexis:
"television *and* network *and* CBS *and* ABC *and* NBC *and* WB *and not*
Univision." The results were a staggering 1,766 entries that in one way or

another discuss U.S. network television without mentioning Univision (or any other Spanish-language television network such as Telemundo, Azteca America, or Galavision). I then used the Boolean operators to add Univision to the search ("television *and* network *and* CBS *and* ABC *and* NBC *and* WB *and* Univision"), and the search engine returned 229 entries. Of the almost 2,000 total articles and trade news items, less than 12 percent included Univision in their discussion of U.S. broadcast television. Even more startling, the vast majority of the 229 news pieces about Univision were ratings reports. These data refer to the televisual map predating the creation of the CW in 2006 (the WB and UPN merged to form the CW on January 24, 2006). Next, I conducted a similar search with more contemporary names or terms, typing "CW" instead of "WB," and the results were somewhat different. A total of 983 reports excluded Univision, and 470 included it; or roughly 31 percent of news and trade press included the Spanish-language network. The press perhaps was atypically interested in Univision at this time, as the company was being bought and sold and was involved in legal battles with Nielsen, the giant ratings corporation.

Another example of Univision's conspicuous absence comes from academic tools and institutions. The differences here are much more startling. I searched the Communication and Mass Media Complete database, restricting the search to peer-reviewed articles. I typed "Univision *and* television": 59 entries. I then typed "UPN *and* television" (remember that UPN is now defunct and never enjoyed substantial ratings): 142 entries. I typed "Fox *and* television": 2,463 entries. The results with CBS, ABC, and NBC were all above 3,000. I was very surprised to learn that the number of articles about Univision was 1.5 percent of the number of articles about CBS. I searched syllabi on television studies within media studies departments across the United States and discovered that the vast majority did not include research on Spanish-language television, and only a few departments even offered courses addressing Latino media. The only journal dedicated to the subject, the *Journal of Spanish Language Media*, is not indexed by any of the major databases such as EBSCO or JSTOR.

I do not believe academics are willfully trying to define the public interest in ethnonational terms, and some of the aforementioned scholars are the life and blood of SLM research. However, when discussions of SLM treat it as foreign, they sideline the fact that SLM is *the* Latino media, and when discussions of national television ignore SLM, they definitely constitute the U.S. viewer in ethnonational terms. Ultimately, the chances that Latinas/os will have a more energetic public sphere are weakened by the two oddly contradictory and complementary definitions of public interest that go into media regulation: neoliberalism and ethnonationalism, which are hardly the same but work in tandem.

In chapter 3, I explored detention centers for undocumented immigrants and refugees and the systems of justice that consider them legal. I noted that it was common for people to think that the legal protection of foreigners was not equal to the legal protection of nationals. Similarly, here I argue that when Spanish enters the political framework of the foreign-versus-national, its political potential is skewed. Fueled by decades-old nativist hysterias, the position that a foreign SLM ought to be treated in the framework of the liberalism of rights or within the purview of First Amendment protections is not likely to succeed. Contrarily, placing SLM in a foreign-versus-national framework reenergizes the sense that Spanish in general is a threat to the national character, which is defined in English-centric terms. So, the foreign-versus-national frame is a net loss for Latinas/os and a net political gain for ethnonationalists. In an attempt to rearticulate a position from which Spanish and SLM function as net political gains for Latinas/os, in the next sections, I problematize the treatment of Spanish as a foreign language and link it to systems of coloniality and ethnonationalism all too common in U.S. history. The goal of these sections is to reintroduce Spanish within the liberalism of rights and then to evaluate its national political potential. I will also consider the effect that Spanish's reintroduction would have on the discourses defining SLM.

English and the Notion of Foreign Languages

Modernity is, for many (for Jürgen Habermas or Charles Taylor) an essentially or exclusively European phenomenon. In these lectures, I will argue that modernity is, in fact, a European phenomenon but one constituted in a dialectical relation with a non-European alterity that is its ultimate content. Modernity appears when Europe affirms itself as the "center" of a World History that it inaugurates: the "periphery" that surrounds this center is consequently part of its self-definition. The occlusion of this periphery (and of the role of Spain and Portugal in the formation of the modern world system from the late fifteenth to the mid-seventeenth centuries) leads the major contemporary thinkers of the "center" into a Eurocentric fallacy in their understanding of modernity. *If their understanding of the genealogy of modernity is thus partial and provincial, their attempts at a critique or defense of it are likewise unilateral and, in part, false.* (Dussel 1995, 65)

A central thread in philosopher Enrique Dussel's work is that the eminent content of European modernity is alterity. Hence, the epistemology produced by this modernity partly revolves around the dialectical understanding of the European against non-Europeans. This provocative idea that functions to recenter colonialism and racialization in modernity serves to recontextualize myths of European origin central to nationalism and capitalism. Among these myths is citizenship itself, which has often been theorized, in the U.S. context, in terms of its links to liberalism and republicanism, that is, in terms of the relation of the community to itself. Rogers Smith (1997), Bonnie Honig (2001), and Engin Isin (2002) have criticized this type of theorization and have argued that more complex processes of alterity were and have been at play (see chapter 1). Smith has shown that ascription, which concretizes theories of alterity into the juridical and social processes of colonialism and slavery, has been also at the center of our legal and cultural ideas about citizenship. Honig shows that the images of the foreigner and of the immigrant have been central to the very imagining of the possibility of U.S. liberal democracy. Isin, in examining the historical and philosophical roots of citizenship, also uses the notion of alterity. He argues, echoing Dussel, that we must not only consider citizenship as constituted by processes of exclusion and inclusion but also consider citizenship in relationship to its alterity. In these works, citizenship's fluidity is expressed as a dialogical process of constitution between the citizen and its others. If Smith, Honig, and Isin are correct, language, a central feature of identity and national membership, is equally constituted through processes of alterity. Thus, the national and the foreign are more than systems of inclusion and exclusion. They exist in dialogue and are co-dependent in systems of co-creation. If Dussel is correct, U.S. modernity is expressed in discourses about language that *occlude* the role of languages other than English in their history, modernity, and knowledge systems. In this section, I engage with the idea of English as a national language. Contrary to nation-centric approaches, my approach assumes alterity and, in particular, a dialogical relation between English and Spanish.

How does alterity relate to language? Alterity is manifested in the recognition that our relationship to *our* language is dependent on the way we see, understand, and define the other's relationship to our language. Regarding English and Spanish, alterity works both ways. Our linguistic sense of self can only exist because of and with the other. Let me offer a quick illustration. Starting on September 15 and extending to October 2009, CNN dedicated a lot of time and institutional energy to exploring Latino reality. Since 1988, the thirty days following September 15 have been recognized as Hispanic Heritage Month. CNN has participated in this celebration of the contributions and cultures of Latinas/os with special reporting and a documentary (aired on October 23, 2009), which was featured ion CNN's website (http://cnn.com) under the header "Latinos in America." On October 16, Ruben Navarrete, one of CNN's Latino commentators, wrote a piece in which he argued that forty-seven million Latinas/os are quickly integrating into U.S. life, becoming successful economic and political actors. Although Navarrete is a writer whom I consider to be conservative for his ongoing reliance on the discourses of assimilation, he apparently crossed a threshold with this celebratory piece.[4] In the comments and opinions section at the bottom of the page, the huge majority of the comments (on the CNN website, this feature allows for only fifty comments) were anti-Latino and anti-Navarrete. One could quickly see that most of the complaints were about language. "Learn English," wrote Mike, an immigrant of Indian descent. Similarly, Debra R. corrected Navarrete by stating that "Latinos will assimilate [*sic*] if they learn to speak, read, and write english [*sic*]." Candi agrees—"learn the language"—and so does Frank B: "You came here. We didn't go there. So learn the language and press one for English." J.R. pleads, "Yeah, we can't ignore you, it's too bad, because I am sick of hearing people chatting loudly in spanish [*sic*], asking me questions in Spanish, and having to hit the 'English' button all the time on the internet, at ATM's and on the phone. I am sick of hispanics [*sic*], they're everywhere." Of the fifty comments, two were positive. Together, the negative, angry comments evidence a sense of English as a national language—a felt right not to have to select an English option, a desire for English to be the only option (or an assumption that this is the proper order of things, the contract these men and women signed) (Petersen 2011). The comments also show that to these men and women, Spanish takes them away from feeling at home in the cities and spaces they inhabit. It is as if Spanish clashed with a sense of self that is fragile, contingent, and in danger of being overtaken by the other. Spanish seems to force a redefinition of self that these men and women have not chosen, thus undermining the sense of personal sovereignty that is the basis of their ontological security. To these men and women, their home is changing, and unless they embrace a personal change, they will feel estranged, like foreigners in their own home. This is alterity at its clearest, a structure where self and other are mutually constituted not simply in terms of inclusion and exclusion but in a more fundamental sense. Alterity explains that the sense of self these men and women have constructed is based on affective ("I am sick of Hispanics"), spatial ("you came here"), biographical ("We didn't go there. So, learn the language"), and practical ("you . . . press one for English") determinants. As an immigrant, I am familiar with these feelings and with how challenging it is to remain oneself in a different political/linguistic environment. The difference between these English-centric respondents and me is that I do not assume that a threat to my sense of self should be corrected by changing the world around me (Ana Rodríguez 2002, 114). Contrarily, the arguments against Spanish that these men and women put forth assume that a threat to one's sense of self ought to be addressed at the level of political membership. This infantile assumption clearly shows that to these men and women, the ethno-linguistic characteristics of their selves are equal to and should remain equal to the nation as a political organization.

The responses to Navarrete are indicative of some important features of current anti-Latino discourse and the way alterity, the other, threatens, constructs, and becomes the very environment in which the self defines itself. To these respondents, the sense of personal threat activated by Spanish and Spanish speakers translates into a political rhetoric centered on three ideas that try to give a rational veneer to their reactions: being in this society means, among other things, speaking English; Spanish is injurious to the aesthetic of the nation-state; and Spanish is a foreign language. These three propositions together constitute the backbone of much nativist rhetoric, which uses the other to overvalorize the centrality of English to the nation-state. Ideas about how Spanish speakers renege on the privilege of linguistic assimilation ("learn the language") confirm to nativists that the ineffable value of English is not for everyone but is for the exceptional. English brings nativists together. Organizations such as the American Immigration Control Foundation (AICF), the National Organization for European American Rights (NOFEAR), ProjectUSA, and V-Dare may lobby, research, and publicize on a variety of issues, but they tend to coalesce around the linguistic issue, arguing for English-only policies at the federal and state levels.

The core of the three propositions—that is, the one proposition that serves as anchor for all—is the last proposition, the notion that Spanish is a foreign language, a proposition that is widely held by Americans of all political inclinations and sympathies. As mentioned earlier, that SLM is understood as foreign by head librarians and lead academics in media studies exemplifies the provincialism that Dussel refers to in the epigraph. In this provincialism, I find the convergence of Anglocentrism, ethnonationalism, the disavowal of U.S. history vis-à-vis English and Spanish, the mapping of state language over the television world, and the faulty liberal accommodation of justice claims to fund, maintain, and educate in Spanish.

The U.S. mainstream idea that Spanish is a foreign language is not a historical claim; it is a claim about the preferred histories we enjoy using to justify our present. It is a myth. It is connected to the traditional socio-political location of Spanish speakers in the social grid, just as it is connected to the socio-political location of English speakers (Achugar 2008). Simply, the socio-political location of English speakers has for a long time given them control over most official (schooling and law) and private (media such as newspapers, magazines, and the telegraph) institutions in charge of producing the official histories and myths of origin that most populations accept as truthful history. The National Park Service, for instance, advertises Jamestown in this fashion. The first paragraph on the historic site's website states, "Come, walk in the steps of Captain John Smith and Pocahontas as we explore America's beginnings. Here is where the successful English colonization of North America began." That Pocahontas lived in the area before the arrival of the English is quickly dismissed, in typical Eurocentric fashion, which does not consider Native Americans to be part of the founding culture or myth of origin. Instead, the National Park Service publicizes the most common Eurocentric myth of origin, but even this myth is highly ideological and not based on historical fact. Questioning this common myth of origin, Anna Brickhouse (2008, 714) shows that the area of Jamestown was a successful Spanish settlement in 1570, thirty-seven years before the English arrived to the area and seventeen years before the failed British colonization of Roanoke in interior Virginia. Similarly notable is the fact that Juan de Oñate began the settlement of San Juan, located in today's New Mexico, in 1598; Santa Fe was founded in 1610. In spite of this history, most U.S. citizens recognize only the British myths of origin and regard Anglo roots and English language as natural expressions of the nation's beginning and its continuation.

This ethno-racial myth of origin depends on the disavowal of racial others (African American slaves, Native Americans, and Latinas/os) and also on the disavowal of ethnic others, such as the Dutch, Irish, Germans, Jews, and others participating in the colonization of the Americas. Simply, people forget that European migration to the British colonies did not mean only British migration. For instance, as James Crawford (1992) narrates, German immigrants were a huge concern among the elite. In 1753, Benjamin Franklin wrote a letter to British Parliamentarian Peter Collison complaining, "Those [Germans] who come hither are generally the most ignorant Stupid Sort of their own Nation, . . . and as few of the English understand the german Language, and so cannot address them either from the Press or Pulpit, 'tis almost impossible to remove any prejudices they once entertained" (B. Franklin [1753] 1992, 19). Germans, who maintained a lively German press and fought against the British for independence in German-language battalions, eventually gained Franklin's respect, and he helped promote and establish the first German-language institution of higher education in the United States: Franklin and Marshall College. In 1787, the college's founding year, German was a language of instruction and continued to be one throughout the nineteenth century. Today, German is again a foreign language. But what made it foreign was clearly not its lack of rootedness in the United States but the socio-political location of Germans, who were subject to majoritarian cultural and political pressures (World War I purges and ethnic profiling) that forced this important population to disidentify with its past. I taught in Texas, a state with one of the largest German heritages in the nation. None of my students took German for heritage reasons. That, very literally, made no sense to them. But it would be a mistake to think of this outcome as cultural, because it was furnished partly by Texas linguistic policies that, for instance, made English the official language of instruction in 1856 and that made German instruction a criminal offense in 1918 (Soltero 2006).

What is foreign is not equal to what comes from the outside, and the history of German, Dutch, Zulu, Spanish, and Mohican is evidence of that. Everybody's sense of the domestic, of the native, is discursively constructed in alterity. Informed by preferred histories (e.g., our nation was a British colony) and fictional narratives (e.g., captive narratives of the nineteenth century), the discourses in charge of producing a strong sense of the domestic and the foreign tend to spin around the axis of ethnonational identity, a relational style of being that relies on the ongoing monitoring of self and others to mark boundaries of belonging and kinship.

Let me be clear: I am neither arguing for ending ethnonationalism (that is a project for utopianism) nor interested in calling it unjust or burdened with ethical problems. With Jacob Levy (2000), I understand the feelings, discourses, and identifications of ethnonationalism to be part of social and political organizing and the source of both good and evil.[5] Although I do not believe that ethnonationalism is, in principle, problematic, in the United States, white ethnonationalism *is* a problem because of the ability of this ethnic group to control the corporate, legal, cultural, and political fields and, more broadly, because of its ability to claim itself equal to the state. Hence, white ethnonationalism produces citizenship excess. The notions of foreignness are rooted in this centralizing power, a modern fallacy that equals one ethnonationalism, one nation, to the state. Here, I use the terms *nation* and *state* in their formal definitions. *Nation* refers to a group of people who believe they are connected to each other and have been so for a long time. Thus, by this definition, *nation* is closer to the term *kin*, which connotes stock and ethnicity. However, Balibar (1991) reminds us that these connotations of kinship and ethnicity are socially and culturally constructed, and so he uses the term "fictive ethnicity" to refer to nation. This fictive ethnicity, which uses language and race as its most recognizable characteristics, is a precondition for becoming a people (see chapter 1). Fictive ethnicities help organize our political values, affective structures (Whom do we love? Whom do we hate?), and juridical subjectivity (see chapter 2). When a nation becomes equal to the state, fictive ethnicities also draw the boundaries of state. Balibar writes, "The 'external frontiers' of the state have to become 'internal frontiers' or—which amounts to the same thing—external frontiers have to be imagined constantly as a projection and protection of an internal collective personality, which each of us carries within ourselves and enables us to inhabit the space of the state as a place where we have always been—and always will be—'at home'" (1991, 95). The resulting cultural and affective processes generate and rely on the discourse of foreignness, which becomes part of a process of recognition whereby nationals project their own sense of collective kinship onto others and evaluate their worth on the basis of whether the other reflects back the projection. Ethnonationalism can be seen as a hermeneutics that helps establish intersubjectivity and gives form to social life. And language, as one of the preeminent markers of ethnonationalism and the primary means for intersubjectivity, becomes central to kinship and foreignness.

While nations are fictive, states are relatively arbitrary political, geo-graphical, and social institutions (Connor 1994, xi). Most modern states are multinational, multilingual, porous, and changing, and the United States is one of the most multinational and multilingual states, sharing this arbitrary characteristic with other states born through empire, such as the United Kingdom, Russia, and Mexico. However, the territorial and impe-rial expansionism that defined the United States in the nineteenth century brought the territories of Louisiana (1803) and the Southwest (1846) and the island colonies of Puerto Rico, the Philippines, and Guam (1898) into the state. With these new territories, the state became composed of hun-dreds of thousands of nonwhite ethnics. In the Southwest, the Mexican-American War resulted in the 1848 Treaty of Guadalupe Hidalgo, which gave international legitimacy to the annexation of the territories of Cal-ifornia and New Mexico, including today's states of Colorado, Arizona, and Wyoming. The treaty also formalized the annexation of Texas, which Mexico had not yet recognized. As in other colonial enterprises, the an-nexation of these territories and the treaty that formalized it changed U.S. membership. The treaty granted citizenship to roughly 116,000 Mexican citizens residing in the area.[6] This number was between 25 and 30 percent of the total population of the area that also included Native Americans, free and slave African Americans, and a growing ethno-racially white population.[7] As Rodolfo Acuña (1988) has shown, Article IX of the treaty guaranteed Mexicans all the rights of citizens. Lynn Perrigo adds, "In other words, besides the rights and duties of U.S. citizenship, they [the Mexicans] would have some special privileges derived from their previ-ous customs in language, law, and religion" (qtd. in ibid., 19).

Extending citizenship in 1848 to previously Mexican citizens meant two things that challenged the white fictive ethnicity. It reclassified Mexi-cans as white (to legally codify them within a system of law insistent on not recognizing nonwhites as citizens), and it legally recognized the citizenship of Spanish speakers (Almaguer 1994, 54). This type of clas-sification accounts for a contradiction that still persists at the center of the Latino experience, a contradiction enabled by coloniality. Latinas/os have been U.S. citizens, with Spanish, for roughly 160 years, and Spanish-speaking Latinas/os are still treated as a foreign population that speaks a foreign language. One of the roots of these cultural and political practices is found in the weaponization of administrative logic, exemplified here by linguistic policies in general and media policies in particular. In the next section, I show the processes that led to English becoming the national language and the role ethnonationalism and race played in discursively constructing Spanish as a foreign language.

Coloniality and Spanish

Coloniality locates a stealthy colonialism in today's systems of administration, policy, and law. Governmentality argues that governmental techniques rely on citizens' interiorization of policy and law. Hence, the psychic mapping of contemporary citizens, Foucault obverses, can be described with the term *juridical subjectivity*. If coloniality and governmentality are sound arguments about politics and civic life, then the juridical subjectivities of U.S. citizens are interiorized colonialism toward ethnic and racial others. In the previous section, I showed that conceiving of Spanish as a foreign language, and grafting that conception into law, are examples of ethnonationalism and of complex legal practices. This section expands on this idea and links ethnonationalism to coloniality. Although a legal treaty should have compelled government and the judicial system to protect the citizenship rights of Mexican Americans and Puerto Ricans, other quasi-juridical racialist thinking served as the base to forgo legal principle and to engineer contradictory law. English became the official language of instruction to Spanish-speaking citizens, and linguistic discrimination became legalized. Ironically, coloniality in the United States exists alongside democratic liberalism; so one must reflect on this linkage and consider the potential that liberalism has for erasing or at least diminishing the effects of coloniality in language.

In principle, the liberalism of rights, legally engineered on top of Lockean natural rights and statist legal rights, is imperfect ground for the juridical subjectivity of coloniality. One horizontal, the other hierarchical, the contradictions between liberalism and coloniality have forced periodic reevaluations of the legal grounds of national membership. Instead of straightforward broadening of the category of national membership, the results of these reevaluations are deeply invested in a pragmatism that has regularly foreclosed avenues for radical critique in favor of reformist, accommodationist, or plainly conservative approaches to rights, justice, and politics. From Jefferson's and Madison's accommodations of slavery to the U.S. Constitution (which institutes the independence of Americans from British rule while denying the right to property and citizenship to Native Americans) to the recognition that to sign the Treaty of Guadalupe Hidalgo would mean legally codifying Mexicans as white (so that they could be made citizens), the United States' elites have publicly relied on pragmatism toward their colonial others and have allowed themselves to forgo democratic/liberal principles for self-interest. The debate in Congress about whether to expand citizenship to Mexicans in the newly conquered territories of the Southwest is one clear example. Although the letter of the treaty did not differentiate between races (or between sexes, though it was widely accepted at this time that only males could be citizens), the spirit of the treaty and ensuing legislation was quickly racialized. Senator John C. Calhoun (South Carolina) passionately declared soon after the treaty's ratification,

> We have never dreamt of incorporating into our Union any but the Caucasian race—free white race. To incorporate Mexico would be the first instance of the kind of incorporating an Indian race; for more than half the Mexicans are Indians, and the other is composed chiefly of mixed tribes. I protest against such a union as that! Ours, sirs, is the Government of a white race. The greatest misfortunes of Spanish America are to be traced to the fatal error of placing these colored races on an equality with the white race. That error destroyed the social arrangement which formed the basis of society. (Qtd. in Nieto-Phillips 1999, 53)

As extreme as Calhoun's words may sound, they accurately foretold the direction of racial and linguistic politics in the United States and territories and the type of citizenship rights that would be given to nonwhites. On this, David Montejano (1987) carefully documents how during the nineteenth and twentieth centuries, naturalization and citizenship notwithstanding, Mexicans in Texas, Tejanos, were systematically disenfranchised by white immigrants (yet full U.S. citizens) and residents with the acquiescence and/or cooperation of the U.S. legal and judicial systems. This disenfranchisement took the form of white citizens appropriating the land, the labor (indentured servitude), and the cultural, political (many, but not all, Mexicans were declared racially equal to blacks, and in accordance with U.S. conventions, their political rights were severely reduced), and social rights of Mexican Americans. Language was a factor: George Martinez notes that although the treaty guaranteed the property rights of Mexicans, the courts forced Mexicans to prove their rights in a language that was not theirs, and this provided the grounds for many land claim losses (2000, 42). Although an opening existed to welcome Mexicans into a liberal state via the pragmatic application of citizenship rights, it was quickly shut by reference to colonial understandings of citizenship, which relied on cultures of law when needed and on cultures of legal impunity when required. Both the institution of law and impunity were central to what Angela Harris calls race law, "law pertaining to the formation, recognition, and maintenance of racial groups, as well as the law regulating the relationships among these groups" (2000, 88).

Although German was allowed to thrive, at least for some of the nineteenth century, Spanish was not. A language of the colonized, not of the immigrant, Spanish was treated as a foreign language in the Southwest as soon as the treaty's ink had dried, and its foreignness became the basis of systematic injustice (Grasfoguel and Georas 2000). Soon after a few common schools were organized in 1855, the California State Bureau of Public Instruction declared English the exclusive language of instruction. In 1856, Texas legalized English as the language of instruction, though in rural areas, away from government oversight, schooling continued in Spanish and in German (MacDonald 2004, 54). The exception to this legal enfranchisement of English was in the territory of New Mexico, which did not create specific linguistic provisions, legally permitting education in Spanish throughout the century. The erosion of this legal possibility, however, was accomplished through other administrative and political provisions that legalized English as the language of administration, government, and law. By the beginning of the twentieth century, English had become the exclusive and official language in schools, administration, and law in mainland America. The exception was Puerto Rico, which continued to recognize Spanish and English as official languages.

New-century nativisms produced even more draconian linguistic laws. In 1903, fourteen states had laws making English the official language of instruction. By 1923, the number had multiplied to thirty-four states that had legalized English as the educational medium. Anti-German sentiment during and following World War I led to discrimination against German Americans (and other linguistic minorities) and to the passage of laws forbidding the teaching of German, even the conviction of teachers instructing in German. The Supreme Court reversed some of these convictions, as in *Meyer v. Nebraska* (1923) and *Bartels v. Iowa* (1923), arguing that the First Amendment included the protection to teach non-English languages (Soltero 2006, 185). Following anti-German and anti-Latino sentiment, Texas's English-only law of 1918 made it a criminal offense for teachers, principals, and other school personnel to teach in languages other than English. Supreme Court decisions notwithstanding, draconian rules continued. In the decades that followed post–World War I English-only laws, children who dared to speak Spanish in schools were routinely punished, and despite the concerted efforts of Puerto Rican parents in New York and of Chicanos in the Southwest, the practice of forbidding Spanish grew. The outcome of this history was an educational *habitus*, constituted through ethnocentric measures of academic success such as intelligence testing, that cemented the official view that Latino Spanish-speaking children were simply backward (MacDonald 2004).

In contemporary America, coloniality, expressed in race law, continues forging a population stratified by race and ethnicity. Language provides coloniality the perfect opportunity to do so. Ethno-racially white animosity has played out in linguistic policies that pit the legal status of English against that of Spanish. The 1960s brought some positive changes, including national antidiscrimination provisions in the Civil Rights Act of 1964 and the Voting Rights Act of 1965, which also translated into linguistic protections. In education, the Bilingual Education Act of 1968 legitimized instruction in Spanish and set the basis for the bilingual education system that survives until today. It should be noted that the goal of the educators who are the backbone of bilingual instruction is to ease Spanish speakers into English educational, professional, and academic environments. Hence, bilingual education works within an assimilationist paradigm that deflects, if not outright negates, the value of Spanish as such. Recently at a conference on the anthropology of education, I confirmed that the most courageous educators, who have no problem risking careers and advancement to advocate on behalf of Latino Spanish-speaking children, consider that the educational and economic future of these children depends on their command of English. Spanish is not in and of itself a language of instruction, in spite of the fact that the United States is part of the Latin American languagescape, the term used by Terhi Rantanen (2005). Within this languagescape, only Mexico, Colombia, and Argentina have more Spanish-speaking people than the United States. However, there is an ongoing denial of this fact. According to the 2010 U.S. Census, there are thirty-eight million U.S. Spanish speakers of different proficiencies who do not have access to schools, K–12 or college, organized around the goal of learning, mastering, and creating art and knowledge in Spanish. An additional six million people are learning it (Instituto Cervantes 2011, 4). Much as the institution of slavery used linguistic imposition to cut the links between slaves and their history, linguistic colonialism has been at play against Latinas/os, who, in losing their language, lose the possibility of intimately experiencing their past and the bonds they might have with today's Latin American cultures.

Linguistic colonialism is present in other social arenas, including Puerto Rico (Pérez 2004, 108). Though dozens of states have embraced bilingualism in education and law (although not without ongoing conflict), by 2002, twenty-seven states had selected English as their official language. These states include California, Colorado, and Florida, all of which have gigantic Latina/o populations. In 2007, Arizona, for a third time, voted to join this special club. Lawsuits have challenged the right of these states to issue English-only policies and provisions in administration and the workforce, including *Lau v. Nicholas* (1974) in California, *Arizonans for Official English v. Arizona* (1997), and *Alexander v. Sandoval* (2001) in Alabama. However, the Supreme Court has refused to rule directly on the constitutionality of states declaring English their official language, resolving all of these cases in narrower terms (Soltero 2006, 185–193). This has meant the de facto legality of these discriminatory policies that are clearly at odds with Title VI of the Civil Rights Act of 1964, which prohibits discrimination based on nationality, and that disproportionally affect Latinas/os and Asian Americans.

As a testament to the strength of white ethnonationalism, no state has officially adopted Spanish as its official language. (Spanish and English are the official languages of Puerto Rico, but, alas, Puerto Rico is not a state.) In 2006, the U.S. Senate passed an amendment to immigration law that came within an inch of declaring English the federation's official language. The stated purpose of an amendment to S. 2611 of the Senate reads, "To amend title 4 United States Code, to declare English as the national language of the United States and to promote the patriotic integration of prospective US citizens."[8] This measure passed sixty-two to thirty-six, with ten Democrats joining every Republican in the Senate. It never became law because it was not reviewed by the conference committee, but its passage marked a threshold confirming that nativism and the English-only movement had gained mainstream political status.

Ethnonationalisms have some fluidity and accept new members, change character, and at times, embrace otherness. Yet this fluidity is often, if not always, structurally and discursively related to assimilation. And why should this not be so? Hoping that new members assimilate is consistent with attributing value to one's culture. However, when an ethnic group takes over the state, assimilation becomes an undue burden on people of other ethnicities. As most immigrants will testify, they have moved here to live in the United States, not to become ethnically white. Because of the way the state is organized, and because of its embodied character, many Americans conflate the ethno-racially white nation with the state and seem convinced that assimilation, including linguistic assimilation, is a just burden placed on people of other ethnicities. This position is also shared by a portion of African Americans, Latinas/os, and others, who are willing to place the burden of assimilation to white ethnic markers on the newcomers, disregarding the assimilation asymmetry that they have been part of historically. Latinas/os or blacks who assimilate to ethno-racially white markers cannot remedy their racial difference and must enter into unequal social contracts with whites, who continue having a disproportionate control of systems of power and language policy tools (e.g., educational, legal, and media institutions).

As should be clear by now, one of the major systems of political control is language itself. In political theory debates, language is often discussed in relationship to rights—"Is language a right?" When a language is legally defined as a right, that language will receive protections not granted to other languages, such as the creation of affirmative actions for its preservation, reproduction, and diffusion. In post-Franco Spain, for instance, Catalan became an element of the portfolio of rights, and the state has provided subsidies for writers interested in writing in Catalan and for publishers interested in publishing those writings (Van Jacob and Vose 2010). Now, the issue of whether any language should be defined as a right is a different matter subject to ample debate. As Helder De Schutter notes, some people believe that language is a nonissue, and others go as far as supporting linguistic assimilation so that ethnic minorities may enjoy equal social and economic benefits (2007, 4). Often based on traditional views of liberalism, the latter position (which today is dominant) argues that the state should not prioritize between communities and institute policies that privilege only certain groups. This is not the same as the liberal argument that ethnic communities have no specific rights but rather is an argument that community rights should derive from the state's broad and effective protection of individual rights. Thus, according to De Schutter, in matters of language policy, the state should foster the equal ability of individuals to have and use a language but cannot interfere on behalf of communities needing and wanting state support for the protection or promotion of a specific language. Here, state neutrality and noninterference is the standard of justice.

Opposing these views are theorists such as Will Kymlicka (1995, 45–46), who uses communitarianism to produce what is often referred to as "multicultural liberalism." His influential position is that the liberal ideals of autonomy and individuality require the protection of the individual's cultural context of choice (e.g., ethnic or subcultural contexts). With Alan Patten, Kymlicka argues that the state must provide the structure of justice by protecting the ability of groups to exist in meaningful ways in horizontal arrangements. Thus, cultural minorities have the right to state support and protection of their cultural context of choice, including language (Patten and Kymlicka 2003, 26–31). Although Patten and Kymlicka are rightfully concerned with the need to foster horizontal ethnic arrangements, their examples and arguments are meant to address more clearly defined political spaces, such as debates against English becoming the official language of the United States or bilingual education. Media, however, is not their concern. Yet Patten and Kymlicka's ideas can be expanded from the notion of the context of choice to what is formally known as "cultural citizenship." Drawing on a communitarian and multicultural perspective, William Flores and Rina Benmayor define cultural citizenship as activities that help Latinas/os "claim space in society and eventually claim rights. Although it involves difference, it is not as if Latinas/os seek out such difference. Rather, the motivation is simply to create space where the people feel 'safe' and 'at home,' where they feel a sense of belonging and membership" (1997, 15). The examples that Flores and Benmayor use are not corporate media. Yet, in thinking about the social stakes of cultural citizenship, Nick Stevenson argues that cultural citizenship must include media structures and the expectation that these structures are relatively free "from the excesses of the free market" (2001, 3). Returning to Patten and Kymlicka's expectation for horizontal ethnic arrangements, it is possible to briefly sketch a multicultural liberal perspective on media and language. First, in today's society, cultural citizenship is partly articulated through corporate media. Second, following Stevenson and Flores and Benmayor, one may note that Latinas/os can only experience the freedom to be who they are when mediatic contexts are properly provided and structured around political, not corporate and market, logic.

Within the framework of liberalism, a multicultural liberal perspective may be the best political project to ameliorate the negative effects of coloniality in language. But as I suggested in previous chapters, all liberalisms rely on legal frameworks that are national and thus cannot fully resolve the injustices that immigrant communities endure, particularly when these communities have significant numbers of undocumented immigrants. Aware of this limitation, in the following section, I explore what it means to bring SLM within the framework of multicultural liberalism; in particular, I examine the political roles that Univision plays in favor of Latinas/os.

Repoliticizing SLM

Up to this point, I have argued that the commodification of SLM is related to its depoliticization within the discourse of liberalism and its strident politicization within the discourse of ethnonationalism. A multicultural liberal perspective provides a path out of this impasse and points to a political future without the heavy baggage of coloniality. The path is not without obstacles. Reimagining SLM as a corporate media structure that participates in the politics of liberalism to the benefit of Latinas/os, not nativists, has to account for factors that push SLM away from the political. Most of these factors relate to the corporate practices that SLM carries on and that give it a capitalist (as opposed to political), transnational (as supposed to national), and Latin American (as opposed to Latina/o) identity.[9] But as I have argued for most of this chapter, several of these dichotomies require closer inspection. These dichotomies do the work of discursively depoliticizing SLM, which is the linguistic and cultural context of choice of millions of Latinas/os and others.

Earlier I showed the linguistic provincialism patent in the way trade press writers and academics imagine their objects of analysis and their disciplines. Here I argue that this provincialism is partly related to ethnonationalism and the colonialist result of imagining Latinas/os and Spanish as foreign and as transnational. Ironically, a closer look at the most successful SLM, Univision, supports the notion that Latinas/os and Spanish are foreign. Much of Univision's programming is either Mexican or Venezuelan or is otherwise imported from some other media system. Even the national programming is marked by transnationalism. The long-running Univision show *Don Francisco Presenta* stars Mario Kreutzberger Blumenfeld, a Chilean star. Likewise, Mexican and Venezuelan stars populate many of the sitcoms. If anything, Univision is a great example of a multinational media system built on the strength of transnational markets, converging media systems, and Latin American diasporas. But as I show with the argument on coloniality, imagining Spanish as foreign is a way of reconstituting political hierarchies between languages and people, an ethnonationalist optic that renders invisible the other's political worth and meaning. Even a media corporation such as Univision, which indeed is transnational and corporate-centric, deserves a focused gaze. This gaze quickly reveals that Univision's programming is partly transnational, but it is also significantly political at the level of the nation. The case of the pro-immigration reform rallies discussed in chapter 1 implicitly argues this. But there are more reasons.

Univision is not only the most successful of the Spanish-language networks and the fourth or fifth most important network in America; it also functions as a primary element of Spanish-speaking Latinas/os' political culture. The Project for Excellence in Journalism, sponsored by the *Columbia Journalism Review* (*CJR*), rates Univision's news division at the same level as the news divisions of English-language networks in terms of quality and professionalism. However, there are two significant differences that speak to the role of Spanish-language television broadcasting in Latino political culture. First, Spanish-language news is more likely to present foreign news from the point of view of other nations (chiefly Latin America) and to deal with issues such as immigration in a sustained fashion and from a Latino and international perspective. Second, in places where Spanish-language networks can afford local crews (and they have them in all large markets), they present the point of view of local Latinas/os in ways that no other network does (Alexandre and Rehbinder 2008, 99–101). Federico Subervi-Vélez's and América Rodriguez's research on Spanish-language print and broadcasting news support the *CJR* findings. According to Subervi-Vélez, Spanish-language news addresses the particular needs of Latinas/os in issues such as health and politics on a more consistent basis and with more cultural sensibility than do other media (Subervi-Vélez et al. 1988; Subervi-Vélez 2008). As important, Rodriguez observes that Noticiero Univision, with bureaus in Mexico City, Lima, Bogota, and El Salvador, dedicates almost half its airtime to news from Latin America (1999, 100–102). Because of this, and because Latino journalists are better at reporting on Latino local issues, Rodriguez argues that Spanish-language journalistic practices have been essential for Latino cultural maintenance and the creation of a Latino symbolic space in U.S. culture (73–106). In all of these cases, SLM, even with its deep-rooted flaws, its commercialism, and its tendency to address a weakly defined Latino audience, is significantly better than ELM at addressing the particular needs of Latinas/os. And these news broadcasts do not go unnoticed. According to Louis DeSipio, 84 percent of bilingual Lati-

nas/os use Spanish-language news, a percentage that speaks to the importance viewers place on language and ethnic perspectives (2003, 11). Jorge
Ramos, the top anchor of Univision's evening news and host of the weekly
El Punto, is acquiring the gravitas of a respected television journalist and
is becoming a spokesperson for Latinas/os across the televisual landscape.
For example, he co-hosted the Democratic presidential debate sponsored
by Univision on September 9, 2007, and, with CNN, co-hosted a second
debate on February 21, 2008, at the University of Texas–Austin. In 2007,
Univision joined forces with the National Council of La Raza in a voter-
registration drive that aspired to increase the number of voting Latinas/os
in the 2008 presidential election. They succeeded, with the Latino vote
increasing 28.4 percent from the 2004 to the 2008 elections. In each of
these instances, Univision is performing as a politically responsible ethnic
media firm, aware that its mission is not only to seek profit but also to
enfranchise its viewers.

In spite of Univision's inability to be a full alternative to mainstream
English-speaking news, it and other SLM do cultural and political work
that no English-speaking broadcaster is willing to do. Hence, SLM can be
and must be understood as a cultural and political asset for Latinas/os,
one required for the construction of a national public and central to Latino political participation. As previously mentioned, Univision aired the
first bilingual presidential debate for the Democratic Party in 2007. The
Democratic field included Hillary Clinton, Barack Obama, John Edwards,
Mike Gravel, Bill Richardson, Christopher Dodd, and Dennis Kucinich.
Of these, Richardson, a Latino from New Mexico, and Dodd spoke Spanish fluently, but they were not allowed to demonstrate that fluency during the debate. At one point, Richardson asked permission to use Spanish, and Jorge Ramos, the moderator, responded in his Mexican Spanish
that it was not possible and that those were the rules agreed on by everybody. But why should the talking field be equal? When perfectly ac-
cented English is imposed on everybody wanting to have a "national"
platform, why cannot Spanish be imposed on candidates wanting our
(Latino) votes? Univision made history hosting the first bilingual presidential debate, but all the candidates were presented as speaking English.
Only the hosts (Maria Elena Salinas co-hosted with Ramos) and listeners
used Spanish. Regrettably, this is still an imperialist script and one that
assumes English to be the state language. This script is partly constituted
through media convergence and deregulation, the two policy principles
that shape Univision's current configuration, wealth, and unique position

in the Spanish-language mediascape. It is also a script that requires or as-sumes linguistic assimilation for political participation. With the support of Univision, this replicates the idea that one ethnonationalism should "naturally" rule over the other.

Conclusion

As Angharad Valdivia (2008) has noted, there is a tension brewing be-tween the transnational and the national in media and Latina/o studies. As rates of media exchange continue to grow, as populations become more mobile and likely to migrate, as cultures seem to shift from national to transnational, global, and regional, it is common and perhaps necessary to imagine the future in terms of transnationalism and globalization. This is happening at the same time that the nation and the political world that it has created come under attack. In chapters 2 and 3, I used some of the arguments attacking the nation to point out the radically faulty ways in which political and legal cultures engage with Latinas/os. In particular, I showed that the pastoral character of democratic liberalism is the ground for a nativism that by now has been sedimented in law and political tradi-tions. In this chapter, I continued this line of argumentation and showed the pastoral character of democratic liberalism through the prism of eth-nonationalism and linguistic policies and practices. I also showed that the marginalization and commodification of Spanish and SLM are partly the result of being defined as the foreign linguistic practices of transnational, immigrant populations. So, in the cases of Spanish and SLM, the prob-lems of citizenship excess are related to transnationalism and to ethno-nationalism; in a sense, linguistic citizenship excess is the worst manifes-tation of the tension between the national and the transnational.

The transnational delegitimizes the political character of Spanish and SLM, while the ethnonational reconstitutes a staunchly provincial and ideological fictive ethnicity that marginalizes and weakens a huge seg-ment of the Latino public sphere. Among others, I use the case of the sale of Univision in 2007 to Saban and associates to illustrate my point. The way the FCC treated Univision is consistent with the way one treats an apolitical commodity. Though the buyers were Saban and associates, the first suitor was Rupert Murdoch, the owner of Fox and the corporate agent most responsible for furnishing media nativism against Latinas/os. Saban, a billionaire with a history of donating to the Democratic Party, sup-ported a voting drive sponsored by Univision which registered millions of Latinas/os and gave an extra edge to the candidacy of now president Barack Obama. Because Saban was able to buy Univision, the Democratic Party was able to count on more Latino votes. Latinas/os traditionally vote Democratic, and increasing the Latina/o vote is a way of increasing the standing of the Democratic Party.[10] I do not think Saban and associates bought Univision to secure Democrats in the White House. That was a fortuitous byproduct that Saban likely enjoyed. However, I do believe that if Murdoch had succeeded in buying Univision, the political future of Latinas/os and of the Democratic Party would have changed, perhaps permanently. Treating SLM as a commodity has profound political implications that affect the present and future of Latina/o political cultures and the ability of Latinas/os to participate in mainstream politics.

Although linguistic citizenship excess is one of the worst manifestations of the tension between the national and the transnational, I propose that a linguistic multicultural liberal perspective is likely to ameliorate the significant injustices in our current linguist and ethnic media landscapes. A linguistic multicultural liberal approach is a way of imagining national reform, but this is different from arguing for the nation. The nation, as I showed in previous chapters, is at the base of many of the injustices Latinas/os have endured, including some at the level of epistemology, politics, and ethics. In chapter 1, I framed this issue in relationship to the problem of reification, that is, confusing the abstraction that the nation is with reality. It is partly because of reification that some people can argue that English is the national language while Spanish is a foreign one. The histories and laws that define the communities living in this territory prove otherwise.

A multicultural liberal perspective would produce affirmative actions to protect the right of Latinas/os to express their cultural and political lives in the language(s) of their choice. For millions, without question, the language of choice would be Spanish. For dozens of millions, the linguistic context of choice would be plural, a bilingualism equally attentive to English and to Spanish. But before having this Spanish, bilingual, or plurilingual legal and political world, a multicultural liberal perspective must be able to politicize Spanish, to make it subject to political debate and contestation, to reevaluate its status as a citizenship right, and in the process, to denaturalize the English-centric way of defining political rights.

What I propose is different from arguing that only true inclusion in the nation-state will remedy the linguistic problems facing Latinas/os. I believe that only the concretion of transnational systems of governance can one day address issues of justice in our globalized world. But at present, transnational social and media realities, for the most part, lack systems of transnational citizenship and transnational rights. The nation-state, as Gayatri Spivak notes, remains the arbiter of rights and citizenship dispensations and is thus the main broker for issues of justice—globalization notwithstanding. Given this, it is necessary to continue using the nation as the base for justice claims and as the basic architectural metaphor for imagining egalitarianism.

For the here and now, constituting a national Latino public becomes a necessity for accessing equal rights, and media is a primary means by which to achieve a national Latino public. However profit driven networks such as Univision, Telemundo, and Azteca America may be, they are nevertheless in a unique position to address a Latino nation-state-wide viewership and are Latinas/os' best hope for engendering an informed public. This is not to replicate the fallacy that all Latinas/os speak Spanish but to assert that the political needs of Latinas/os, regardless of their language(s), are *not* served by English-language broadcasters.

Perhaps the most important issue supporting my argument that Spanish and Spanish-language media should be properly politicized is that we need to recast Spanish-language media as cultural and political platforms so that we can produce the studies, research, and arguments that will convince the FCC to consider it as such. On this, my position is closer to what Ruth Rubio-Marín (2003) calls "instrumental language rights." She recognizes that at issue for the state are not only ethical and political principles but types of decisions and policies that can best accommodate the needs of a reasonable majority. Our union includes hundreds of languages, but the state and the economy need, for their better functioning, to operate on a number that is reasonable, albeit while providing minimum accommodations for all people to participate in government and markets. Due to the number of Spanish speakers and the historical contexts in which Spanish was absorbed by the state, it is reasonable to think of Spanish-language media as a right and to believe that its status as such can be reasonably accommodated by policies that are not cumbersome or costly to other ethnonationalisms. I agree with Rubio-Marín when she states that "language should not be a liability in the enjoyment of one's general status of civil, social, and political rights and opportunities in society" (2003, 63). The benefits of treating Spanish-language media as a right are significant. Let us briefly consider the potential benefits of this position.

If Spanish-language media is a civic and cultural right because it is the linguistic context of choice for millions of U.S. citizens, then that right can function to alter the basis by which language policy happens today. Instead of producing policy that tries to accommodate Spanish speakers and minimize their linguistic marginalization, we would be forced to find ways in which Spanish speakers can exercise their right to equal access to the same cultural and political structures that English speakers currently enjoy. Because Spanish speakers do not have a territorial concentration (or claim) like the Quebecois or the Kurds, the only reasonable way by which to enable ethnonational political positions is national media. I believe that this could be the basis for forcing the FCC to redefine Spanish-language media as a political and cultural right. So, for the here and now, I propose a new model of regulation that more forcefully takes into consideration the relationship of media to nationhood while abstaining from equating the nation-state to ethno-racially white markers. We need to reimagine the reality of our changing populations and to shift our media from espousing corporatism to functioning as a plurinational public sphere. However, a plurinational public sphere will always be in danger of disappearing without adequate legal protections. Spanish, I believe, should be so protected by the FCC, not as a language for commerce but as a language for community and politics.

Sadly, the FCC is not the only institution at issue here. Media studies departments across the United States consistently disregard Spanish-language media in their curricula and research agendas. When SLM receives any treatment at all, it is handled as a foreign-language issue. This disciplinary positioning is a naturalized violation of the right of Spanish speakers across the nation-state to have their language understood as constitutive of the federation and constitutive of our educational system. This chapter is a plea for reform and is offered with the hope that we reevaluate the way academic social practices in the here and now reconstitute Latino disenfranchisement.

PART II

Conditions of Inclusion

5

Labor and the Legal Structuring of Media Industries in the
Case of *Ugly Betty* (ABC, 2006)

Ethnonationalisms are flexible and can welcome others under certain
conditions. Processes of inclusion are political but also cultural, and
media participates by giving a few members of society the ability to construct the narratives that matter to the entire polis. This chapter reflects
on processes of cultural inclusion by investigating the show *Ugly Betty*
(ABC, 2006–2010) and by asking the questions, what can *Ugly Betty* tell
us about the conditions Latinas/os have to fulfill in order to be part of
mainstream English-language media? and, as important, what can these
conditions tells about the relation of Latinas/os, mainstream media, and
citizenship excess?

Before trying to answer these questions, let me frame the show in
terms friendly to citizenship excess. Early in the first season of *Ugly Betty*,
we learn that Betty's father, Ignacio Suarez (played by Cuban American
actor Tony Plana), is having some problems with his Health Maintenance
Organization (HMO). He is ill; his medicine has run out, but he does not

want to urge the HMO for a new prescription. In the episode "Fey's Sleigh Ride," Betty (America Ferrera) must go in person to the pharmacy, where she discovers that her father has been using a fake Social Security number. Up to this point in the narrative, Ignacio has been depicted as an unusual man and father. He is the primary caregiver to his two daughters: he cooks for them, stays at home, and shows kindness and emotional wisdom not typically associated with an older working-class Latino male. He has been made sympathetic through softening (or perhaps feminizing) his masculinity. But the plot throws a monkey wrench in the narrative when we discover that he is an undocumented immigrant, one who has committed what the legal and immigration system of the time tried to define as a felony.[1] Perhaps because of this sympathetic representation of an undocumented immigrant, perhaps because the show cast Latinas/os in key production, writing, and acting positions, *Ugly Betty* was seen in the media world as an example of good media corporate ethics. However, *Ugly Betty* was the only one-hour show centered on and at least partly produced by Latinas/os on prime-time English-speaking television. This makes *Ugly Betty* different from other ensemble cast shows such as *Desperate Housewives* (ABC, 2004–present) and *Modern Family* (ABC, 2009–present). These shows include Latinas/os, but they are not centered on, produced by, or written by Latinas/os. Ironically, *Ugly Betty*, by its very existence, has helped ABC maintain a respectable reputation regarding diversity programming. In the show's exception and in the discursive positioning of it as good corporate ethics, *Ugly Betty* illustrates some of the key conditions Latinas/os have to fulfill to be incorporated in mainstream English-language media, conditions that include fitting into neoliberal definitions of diversity that further devalue the political and cultural capital associated with Latino narratives and Latino labor. It is in this convergence of narrative and labor that citizenship excess is manifested. Its result is the political and cultural capital accumulation of anti-Latino media practices and labor policies.

Ugly Betty is a text in which different ideas about labor and Latinas/os intersect. It narrativizes the life of a Latino undocumented worker; it is a work-place dramedy with a Latina at its center; it is the product of the labor of immigrant Latinas/os; and it is hailed as an example of labor diversity, in an industry often criticized for labor conservatism. Although each of these aspects of labor are important, in this chapter, I consider the text to be the product of specific cultures of production and political imaginaries. With the example of *Ugly Betty*, I argue that current ideas of

diversity and labor in media reproduce processes of political capital accumulation to the benefit of a citizen defined in ethno-racial ways. These
ideas on diversity and labor craft pathways of inclusion that naturalize
unjust labor systems and that, like alchemy, turn the racist political and
labor practices of mainstream media into political gold. Giorgio Agamben (2005) theorizes how inclusions can be used for exclusions and how
"inclusive exclusions" constitute nation-states. Diversity fits Agamben's
parameters for inclusive exclusions. Instead of being publicly shamed for
embracing labor practices that systematically marginalize racial and ethnic minorities, mainstream media such as ABC use the disciplined public
performances of Latinas/os, who are often thankful for the privilege of
inclusion, to accumulate political capital. In short, *Ugly Betty's* circulation
as an exemplar of mainstream media ethics relies on the systemic marginalization of Latino labor in the industry and on a definition of diversity tuned more to corporate interests than to social justice (Brown 2004,
423). In the fusing of political and capitalist goals, the public circulation
of this dramedy exemplifies processes of racialized political capital accumulation under the guise of what Thomas Streeter (1996) calls "corporate
liberalism." This term refers to the deep influence of capitalist logic on the
egalitarian philosophy of liberalism and to the framing of political values
in the language of capital. In the case of *Ugly Betty*, racialized political
capital accumulation and corporate liberalism impact the legal production of citizenship by defining the show through media legal frameworks
that normalize ideas of diversity and corporate civics that are unlikely to
improve the overall social standing of Latinas/os and other minorities.

The following section links political capital accumulation to media,
thus providing the general framework of analysis for the case. The next
four sections speak to *Ugly Betty* as an exception to two rules about labor
and politics: Rule 1: Controlling the meaning of labor and of labor laws is
political capital. Rule 2: The power to control and narrativize labor is an
intrinsic part of media cultures that use this power to marginalize Lati-
nas/os. The four sections are organized dialectically in terms of the two
rules, alternately explaining a rule and then discussing how *Ugly Betty*
managed to circumvent or negotiate that rule. The first of these sections
discusses the first rule and explains how political capital is extracted from
the control of the meaning of labor and from labor law. This section starts
with discussions of labor and race at the birth of the nation and ends with
contemporary nativist media discussions on undocumented labor to
ultimately show that being able to shape the discourse on labor is great

political capital. The following section investigates how *Ugly Betty* was able to participate in narrativizing citizenship, law, and labor. In particular, this section notes the textual concessions that *Ugly Betty* had to embrace to be part of prime time. The second rule is investigated in the next section, which argues that traditionally Latinas/os have been disenfranchised, and it shows two historical shifts in the way this happens. Starting in the late 1960s, new civil right legal frameworks allowed for more ethnic minorities to participate in mainstream media. This positive legal development did not last and, during the past three decades, mainstream corporate and media interests have worked hard at weakening civil rights labor provisions. The result is a new language of diversity that is ethnocentric and neoliberal. In the last of these four sections, I show how *Ugly Betty* fits within this new definition of diversity and unintentionally undermines civil rights gains. In short, this chapter presents two rules and two exceptions that speak to the way citizenship excess is activated in media labor and contemporary practices of diversity.

Political Capital Accumulation and Media

The notion of political capital accumulation assumes that political capital is distributed unequally and implies that this inequality is patterned. In particular, I am interested in investigating the manners in which media labor connects with political capital accumulation. Citizenship excess proposes that law and policy, including labor policy, regulate access to political capital. Citizenship excess is also a theory of media that argues that, because of media's impact on culture and because of its role in constituting what Max Weber calls "prestige," those who produce media are central to the distribution of prestige and social, cultural, and political capital. The media worker, in short, is a key player in processes of political capital accumulation, an argument that is consistent with Marxian theories of culture and political power. Beyond that, my contribution in this chapter is to acknowledge the political capital of fictional mainstream media, the way the cultural field is given shape by the political field through labor law, and the intricate relationships between media, discourse, and law.

Fictional mainstream media closely relates to labor laws and political capital accumulation. This is so because fictional mainstream media, understood as speech, is patterned after the speaking political positions of media makers, who occupy locations in the media field that are structured by labor laws. Labor laws are the means by which the political and juridical fields distribute resources, a factor that makes labor a type of politics and thus subject to citizenship excess. Fictional media is speech that has a political, economic, and legal basis. Examples of citizenship excess include the normalization and continuation of sexist, classist, racist, and ethnocentric textual traditions (Aparicio and Chávez-Silverman 1997; Fregoso 2003; Santa Ana 2002; Ramirez Berg 2002; Molina-Guzmán 2010; Beltrán and Fojas 2008; Valdivia 2000). But citizenship excess also exists in the way labor laws organize speakers, easing the path of some while blocking the advance of others. In media, labor laws help define hiring, firing, and advancement processes, which are attentive to political capital. Equally important is that labor laws and labor equity are normalized (and at times, challenged) through media; that is, we learn to relate to labor laws through media. Ultimately, the effects of labor laws and the effects of discourse on labor are multigenerational, structural, and material. Reconstituting each other, labor laws can become social inertia and the materiality of discourse.

So, what can *Ugly Betty* tell us about Latino participation in mainstream media? First, it is clear that *Ugly Betty* is unusual, and thus the issue becomes what labor and narrative factors made *Ugly Betty* a good candidate for occupying a spot in prime-time English-language television. Before addressing *Ugly Betty*'s uniqueness, I need to explain Rule 1, which argues that controlling labor and the discourses of labor is political capital. In the next section, I present labor, labor law, and labor discourse as interlinked technologies of power used by the state to the benefit of some and the detriment of others. I also show that these technologies of power have traditionally been organized around racial and sexual axes that enable them to effectively construct a hierarchical economic world that uses labor as a political tool.

Rule 1: Controlling Labor and Its Meaning

The way we think and produce wealth today is the result of capitalism and its juridical counterpart, the nation-state. Nowhere is this more evident than in the way ideas about wealth, and the social concerns of the wealthy, became inscribed on modern notions of citizenship, and on this, the American case is particularly instructive. As many observers have noted, including Rogers Smith (1997), Grace Hong (2006), Judith Shklar (1991), and Evelyn Nagano Glenn (2002), the birth of the United States is bound to the social and discursive repositioning of the wealthy landowning class as the naturalized ruling class. No longer believing that any subject of the British monarchy was in a natural position of authority, the wealthy land-owning class of the United States redefined itself as a group of indepen-dent individuals who were united and empowered by consensus. In the process, these American elites engaged in repeated and spirited debates on the meanings of wealth as it pertained to civics, politics, and leader-ship. The results of these debates were codified in law that gave political franchise, or citizenship, to various types of wealthy subjects, then dis-cursively constructed as northern European males with either property or monetary assets. As Hong notes, "The concept of property defines the subject and also constructs the subject's relationship to the state—the state is narrativized as guaranteeing the citizen's right to property" (2006, 11). In the process of debating and legislating these ideas, American elites gave legal shape and social value to whiteness as a relatively newly minted racial category that was judicially discussed as property and thus as wealth, and to maleness as the natural possessor of the political and economic franchise of men *and* women (Nelson 1998; Shklar 1991, 39–42; Glenn 2002, 22).

Dana Nelson (1998) has convincingly argued that the racial category of white manhood was central to establishing a fraternity of citizens that was large enough to counteract the potential power of Native Americans and slaves.[2] Throughout the eighteenth and nineteenth centuries, discourse on white manhood increasingly supplants that on national and ethnic ori-gins, and Dutch, British, and Scottish men become pooled together under the umbrella of the white race. Discourse became law, and during the nineteenth and twentieth centuries, citizenship legislation drew on (and co-generated) the relatively nascent racial category of whiteness to craft the socio-biological boundaries of national membership. This movement toward enfranchising northern Europeans cut along national and ethnic lines but also along class lines. At one point in American history, citizen-ship and political franchise (suffrage) were given only to propertied males or, quoting Thomas Jefferson, to the "responsible and virtuous electorate" (qtd. in Shklar 1991, 3).

Consequently, of the eight states admitted into the Union between 1796 and 1821, only six had universal suffrage for white adult males, but by the mid-nineteenth century, all states had adopted the principle of universal suffrage for white adult males (Glenn 2002, 27). This broadening of the category of full citizenship was only possible, following Glenn (2002), through the discursive repositioning of whiteness at the center of white laborers' concerns for their identity, franchise, and independence. At issue was how to justify the political franchise to a population of people who, by the very legislative debates about franchise happening in the 1770s, lacked the necessary economic independence to make reasonable political choices. The laborer's economic dependence precluded him from the independence of will needed to carry out the political duties and responsibilities of full citizenship, namely, suffrage. According to Jefferson's standards for political agency, only owners had the will and freedom to exercise responsible electorate decisions. However, this way of interpreting political agency placed the new Union at risk by narrowing citizenship credentials to a population too small to defend it. So, in the spirit of securing a larger number of citizens and potential defenders of the Union, states allowed for the universal suffrage of white adult males, regardless of their laborer status. White male universal suffrage was only possible when white laborers could substitute their discursive deficit (economic dependence) for a surplus, here argued as a racial identity discursively spoken as follows: white manhood allowed northern European men to sell their labor *freely* and to eventually acquire property, which differentiated them from slaves and other nonwhite indentured servants.

Two things ought to be remarked on in regard to this racial discursive surplus that is so key to understanding American racialized political capital accumulation. The repositioning of whiteness as central to laborers' identity relied on the mythology of racial independence as necessary and sufficient to economic and political freedom. Regardless of indentured servitude, impressment, apprenticeship, convict labor, farm tenancy, or wage labor, all white males came to be discussed as having the potential to become propertied, a racial mythology that influenced what later became known as the American Dream myth (Hong 2006, 4; Roediger 2007, 25). Second, the binding of white manhood to freedom and to property becomes legally codified and, as Cheryl Harris argues, manifested in the American legal tradition of interpreting whiteness *as* property: "In protecting settled expectations based on white privilege," Harris notes, "American law has recognized a property interest in whiteness" (1997, 5). This has meant that throughout our legal history, the courts have recognized whiteness as a guarantor of rights over other things. On this, Harris reminds us that "the concept of property prevalent among most theorists, even prior to the twentieth century, is that property may 'consist of rights in "things" that are intangible, or whose existence is a matter of legal definition.' Property is thus said to be a right, not a thing, characterized as metaphysical, not physical" (17). Hence, in the courts, whiteness has been treated not as an aspect of identity but as a vested interest that accrues benefits to the bearer and provides legal entitlements that, if removed, are equal to dispossession. Harris's arguments move through cases beginning in the nineteenth century and ending with affirmative action, finding in each instance a constant use of whiteness as a vested interest that courts systematically protect.

If Glenn, Hong, Smith, Nelson, Shklar, and Harris are correct, then a central variant of political capital accumulation since the nation's formation must be linked to the ability of some people to write, control, and semanticize labor and labor law. Perhaps obviously, the interconvertibility (Bourdieu's term) of political capital gained through semanticization of labor and control of labor law is quite high: this is political capital that can quickly become economic capital. Legalizing slavery, indentured servitude, and the tactical appropriation of foreign labor (read: Mexican) through the Bracero program; defining women's labor as unprotectable; depicting unions as communist and anti-American; portraying public universal health care as socialism; and declaring undocumented immigrant labor rightless, the political capital extracted from the control of labor and labor law functions as the link that ties citizenship to the economy and problematizes the distinction between political agency and economic tyranny.

By virtue of being a Latino show that engaged with issues of citizenship, *Ugly Betty* became quickly entangled in the struggle over who gets to narrativize and give meaning to labor and labor law. This was evident in the reception of *Ugly Betty*, which activated a clear sense of ethnonational anxiety bound to contemporary nativist sentiment. Specifically, *Ugly Betty* received hate mail for the portrayal of Ignacio, and much to the dismay of Salma Hayek, one of the key Latinas/os responsible for producing the show, this hate mail was fundamentally racist. It is worth noting that the hate mail did not relate to the representation of queerness (which is central to the show's story lines) or black characters (which are also central to the show): the hate mail was about Ignacio and his status as an undocumented immigrant (Devlyn and Harlow 2007). This is a strong reminder that the way Latinidad was being constructed during George W. Bush's second term was heavily coded with labor and nationalistic anxieties, which typically fostered racist discourse against undocumented immigrants in general and Latinas/os in particular. This was the same epoch that saw the rise to popularity of the Minuteman Project in

Arizona, New Mexico, and Texas. This was also the time when the voices of Lou Dobbs (CNN), Glenn Beck (Fox), and Bill O'Reilly (Fox) began a relentless media campaign (Beck and O'Reilly were also quite important in the radio talk-show universe) targeting undocumented Latino immigrants and immigration law. Given the tone of politics at the time, their voices seemed unopposed, even though they aggressively engaged in normalizing hate against undocumented immigrants.

Reading transcript from Dobbs, Beck, or O'Reilly, it is impossible not to notice that ethnonational anxieties about ethnic and racial others (today, immigrant Latinas/os; then, black slaves and Native Americans) have been used by dominant media and political forces to augment hegemonic control over the lower classes. In the nineteenth century, these forces expanded the reach of hegemonic power by bringing a diverse set of ethnicities under the umbrella of whiteness. Whiteness was attractive partly because it had been defined as freedom, a notion that relied on the idea of free labor as opposed to slavery.

Today, a similar expansion of the notion of legal labor is having the effect of homogenizing the class challenges of a racially diverse populace through the construction of multiracial solidarities against undocumented immigrants. Unsurprisingly, a common theme on Dobbs's show is arguing that opposing "illegals" is not an act of racism, and he proves it by often including the voices of nonwhite nativists. For example, on April 26, 2006, during the weeks in which the huge immigration reform rallies were taking place, CNN's *Lou Dobbs Tonight* show included Marvin Stewart, a black member of the Minuteman Project, stating, "There are passionate people that love this nation. There are passionate black men like myself who have a love for this nation. There are passionate Hispanics—I've served with Asians on the borders, Los Compos (ph), Sierra Vista, Pacumba (ph), various other places, who have a passion for this nation." Later, Dobbs includes another segment with black voices: "Tonight, an increasing number of black Americans are coming to the realization that some illegal aliens are a threat to their economic well-being. A group called the Crispus Attucks Brigade held a rally in Los Angeles against illegal immigration yesterday, calling the illegal alien crisis the greatest threat to black people since slavery." Later, the show gives camera time to Ted Hayes, a member of the brigade: "We're not saying don't come. We want anybody to come to America, no matter color or religion or race. Just come legally to the country. And as black people, we feel we have a duty and responsibility to stand up against this illegal invasion, which is ultimately destroying our people." With Dobbs constructing the illegal threat as the greatest since slavery, the show is giving meaning to a new notion of "free labor" and definitions of inequality that substitute labor laws for immigration laws. In a labor system that systematically has twice as much black unemployment as white unemployment and that typically protects corporate over labor or union interests, shows such as Dobbs's are magnifying the impact of undocumented labor on black unemployment and, in the process, diminishing the impact of neoliberal labor policies that constantly attack equalizing law such as equal opportunity employment and affirmative action (EEO/AA), living wage, universal health care, and educational rights. Shows such as Dobbs's are also giving neoliberal shape to racialized political capital accumulation, popularizing alibis for corporatism and transracial but pro-neoliberal allegiances.

In this section, I have briefly presented a history of citizenship franchise that is filtered through the instrument of labor laws, and I have connected processes of exclusion at the birth of the nation with similar racial anxieties happening around *Ugly Betty* and during the second Bush administration. Although mainstream media was typically anti-immigrant and nativist in tone with regard to the show, *Ugly Betty* did enter the mainstream cultural markets and got to participate in giving meaning to citizenship, labor, and labor laws. The next section expands on this issue and pays particular attention to the narrative concessions the show had to make in order to make it to prime time.

Narrativizing Citizenship and Labor Laws

Inclusion in mainstream media is partly dependent on the ability of a text to connect with the political imaginary of millions of people. This imaginary gives meaning to the diverse politics of resource distribution that define the nation-state, making some processes politically proper (e.g., expelling "illegal" workers) while making others politically wrong (e.g., affirmative-action labor policies), antinational, and/or unfair. Labor is and has been central to the distribution of powers and resources in the nation-state, and it occupies a key role in many political imaginaries, impacting the relationship of the state with individuals, industry, and corporations. Although at any time a nation-state is home to multiple, fragmented, and even contradictory political imaginaries (e.g., labor unions; anti-affirmative-action beliefs; legal and illegal laborers), some political imaginaries have institutional expressions that are recorded as what

Pierre Bourdieu (1990) has called "doxa," or the unconscious beliefs and values that seem in harmony with the way a social field is organized. Who counts as a legal worker and who does not belong to this labor doxa. Defining the role of the state in hiring and firing is another element of labor doxa. Because a politics of distribution depends on legal frameworks to institutionalize practices, a doxic political imaginary is also a legal subjectivity that helps individuals make sense of themselves as political and legal subjects in relations of alterity to those whose political/legal identity is imagined as foreign or substantively different and hence unworthy of protection. As I argued in chapter 3, in the nativist political imaginary, the political unworthiness of undocumented immigrants relies on the discursive tactic of primarily defining them as "illegal" residents and "illegal" workers. In the past decade, the nativist political imaginary has increasingly become doxa in mainstream English-language media, which, among other things, has embraced the term *illegal* and has failed to provide speaking platforms to antinativist, pro-Latino voices.

By some measures, *Ugly Betty* is an exception to this doxa. The show includes one of the few positive fictional representations in mainstream English-language television of an undocumented Latino. The show, much like Ignacio, has a complex transnational history that spans several countries (Valdivia 2010, 33). It began in Colombia, passed through Mexico, and ended up in the United States, first as an imported narrative aired by Univision and, now, in its English version, as an immigrant story. A hugely successful telenovela in its original version (the Mexican version of *Ugly Betty—La Fea Mas Bella*—is a ratings success at Univision, typically taking several spots in the top-ten highest rated shows on Spanish-language television), *Yo Soy Betty la Fea* has become an international phenomenon, re-created several times in only a few years. Chiefly another retelling of the "Ugly Duckling" story, all the versions of *Yo Soy Betty la Fea* tell the story of a young, homely woman who wishes to pursue a career in fashion, where she is an outcast for her physical appearance (Rivero 2003). In the Latin American versions, Betty's wit, intelligence, and integrity help her succeed and gain her boss's heart.

The American version, *Ugly Betty*, is an unusual televisual text. It is performed, written, and produced partly by Latinas/os. However, just as Latinas/os are often coded as partly foreign regardless of whether they have lived in the United States for generations, this rare Latino show is heavily coded as immigrant for several reasons. Its script, parts of which have traveled across borders, has been modified by making Betty and her family immigrants who must endure not only the challenges brought by class (as in the Colombian version) but also the challenges brought by race, ethnicity, and nationality. Also, those who are in charge of bringing the show to non-Latino audiences identify themselves as immigrants, and they refer to the show as an immigrant story. Silvio Horta, one of the show's three key executive producers and the person most responsible for its American adaptation, is a Cuban American who, in his speech when receiving the 2007 Golden Globe for Best Television Series (Musical or Comedy), described the show as an "immigrant" effort. On the business side of things, Salma Hayek, a Mexican American international media star, has been one of the persons most responsible for convincing ABC to pick the series and continues her involvement as executive producer and guest star.

Because *Ugly Betty* is coded as immigrant, it manifests the tensions between the national and transnational, tensions that are more evident when considering the nationally bound legal systems that shape labor alongside the show's transnational textualization and international distribution. On the textual side, the tensions are more clearly shown through Ignacio's story line. On the political economy side, explored in the sections that follow, the tensions are found in the legal field's relation to media industries and their employment practices that exemplify the worrisome shape of the television industrial field.

Ignacio's story line is a strong reminder that citizenship and labor exist in the political imaginary as legal subjectivities constructed through interaction with institutions, peoples, and cultural texts. For a legal subjectivity to be possible, law necessitates culture and media to normalize it, to make it unavoidable, to give it a benign aura, and to publicize it (B. Edelman 1979, 9–10; Streeter 1996, 8). Yet media does more than teach citizens how to become law-abiding individuals. Alongside legal behavior and mental schemas, media publicizes systems that rely on impunity, accepted illegality, and unequal application of legal principles to different peoples. Because of media's complex function as the publicist of law, its role in the legal production of citizenship and labor is not a direct translation of law into culture but a preferred translation. Certainly, in television, characters do not have to abide by legal precedent or the egalitarian principles of law. Media's legal "work" can thus be simply hegemonic (or, in some instances, counterhegemonic) and invested equally in producing a system of legal obedience and one that naturalizes strategic forms of legal impunity, central to the operations of legal cultures. *Ugly Betty* shows several of these practices.

In the show, Ignacio is an undocumented immigrant who is depicted sympathetically. As mentioned earlier, he is constructed through ideas of masculinity not typically associated with Latino males, who are often framed by stereotypical machismo. Instead of being violent, sexist, and thoughtless, Ignacio is caring, wise, and fair. He is the primary caregiver to two adult daughters, who look up to him for tenderness, comfort, and advice. Often found in the kitchen, cooking for his daughters and his grandson, Ignacio has a soft masculinity that makes him the perfect, non-threatening representation of an undocumented immigrant. Through his dealings with his HMO, viewers learn that Ignacio is not only undocumented; he has also stolen a Social Security number. Consequently, he should be the ideal target of new immigration-enforcement measures championed by then Homeland Security secretary Michael Chertoff. Charging undocumented immigrants with identity theft was one of the latest measures proposed by nativist voices to worsen the legal status of undocumented people in the United States. Since 2006, these powerful voices have succeeded in convincing many news organizations, politicians, and lawmakers that being an undocumented immigrant is equal to being a petty thief who engages in fraud and even money laundering. This depiction of undocumented immigrants as threatening identity thieves, whose actions have been hyperbolically described by xenophobes as equal to having pointed a gun at their victims' heads, is opposed by *Ugly Betty*'s narrative and Ignacio's character, both of which are attempts to pose a public counterargument to unjust law. That this counterargument was almost unique in our mainstream media speaks to the lack of cultural citizenship experienced by Latinas/os and to the truly marginalized status of undocumented immigrants, whose voices outside Spanish-language media were and are practically silent.

It is important to remember that *Ugly Betty*'s credentials as a pro-Latino-immigrant show exist alongside its character as a mainstream English-language fictional show. Hence, the space for counterhegemonic textualization is small. It follows that although elements of the textualization of Ignacio are, indeed, positive, the discourses about law and immigration around Ignacio are much more than simply sympathetic notions about "illegal aliens." These discourses show ambivalences that undermine (or explain) *Ugly Betty*'s speech about citizenship and labor law. Some are the result of genre conventions ("dramedy"), which push the narrative toward comedic and farcical situations, precluding it from having clear-cut positions and proposals about law, citizenship, and labor justice (White

1991, 85–86). The clearest example of this genre limitation is the depiction of the U.S. Citizenship and Immigration Service (USCIS), the agency that after 9/11 was put in charge of dealing with immigration. Prior to 9/11, the Immigration and Naturalization Service agency (INS) was part of the Justice Department. Since June 2002, the USCIS is housed within the Department of Homeland Security, converting immigration from an issue of law into one of national security. The USCIS is represented through the character of Constance Grady (played by Octavia Spencer), a jovial, young, African American caseworker who tries to help Ignacio walk the path to citizenship. In the episode "I'm Coming Out" (aired on February 1, 2007), Ignacio learns that Grady has failed to turn in his paperwork, making his case impossible to win unless he marries her. Later, viewers learn that Grady has the habit of seducing her male clients in exchange for Permanent Resident Alien cards, the notorious green cards. In this plot twist that betrays the painful complexity of the immigration process, *Ugly Betty* is at its worst and does a disservice to its "immigrant text" status. Instead of working with the real comedic and tragic processes that immigrants must go through to get a green card, the writers choose a Hollywood cliché made famous by the popular 1990 film *Green Card* (dir. Peter Weir) and repeated since in other popular televisual texts such as *Will and Grace* (NBC, 1998–2006), in which Rosario (Shelley Morrison) must marry Jack (Sean Hayes) to stay in the country as a maid.

Immigration law is not the only type of law narrativized in *Ugly Betty*. In fact, labor law is referenced constantly. But most references to labor law are subtle and easily confused with social conventions. Because much of the show develops in Betty's workplace—the headquarters of a fashion magazine called *Mode*—it frequently references legalized processes such as hiring, firing, and contract law. As a workplace, *Mode* is hardly exemplary. The show depicts many behaviors that could be grounds for lawsuits and criminal prosecutions in real life but that never turn into such realistic legal consequences on the show. In the first couple of episodes ("Pilot" and "The Box and the Bunny"), Betty is forced to work under conditions that can be interpreted as illegal. In "Pilot," Daniel, who just inherited his way into the presidency of *Mode*, wants to get rid of Betty, who was hired by Daniel's father, Bradford Meade (Alan Dale), in an attempt to stymie his son's tendency to engage sexually with his assistants. Trying to force Betty to quit, Daniel abuses her, asking her to perform tasks totally outside her contracted obligations, such as going to Daniel's apartment at three a.m. and cleaning the soles of his shoes, and exposes her to his sexual behavior. These two things should provide the grounds for at least a labor complaint and likely a legal lawsuit on the grounds of sexual harassment, but they do not. The thought never crosses the plotline, which relies on the construction of a heroic narrative. Betty shall overcome, but what she will end up overcoming is illegal behavior that cannot be treated as illegal because it exists within a system of impunity. Her heroics only reproduce this system, which stipulates that Daniel's kind should be left to roam the labor and sexual markets unfettered by policies or restrictions. And Daniel does, repeatedly philandering with women who are his subordinates, including people who work at *Mode* (Amanda) and people looking to model in the magazine. The closest we come to seeing him in legal trouble is when he sleeps with a Russian model looking for a job. She turns out to be underage, and Daniel is forced into hiring her. Although Betty saves the day by finding the model's passport, which proves that she is not underage, the narrative never questions Daniel on the grounds of child abuse or statutory rape. The case of Amanda (played marvelously by Becki Newton) is just as astounding. Amanda sleeps with Daniel in the hope of getting Betty's job. Over the course of two seasons, she comes to understand that Daniel is only using her and commits to changing her unwise willingness to be sexually on call for Daniel. In the narrative, this is seen as growth. Meanwhile, Daniel has impunity, not only in the world of law but also in the world of the narrative, which seems committed to constructing him sympathetically as a "bad boy" whom viewers hope can be reformed. As demonstrated through the characters of Daniel, Amanda, Betty, and others, the experience of being American can be quite different for different people.

The legal lessons derived from popular culture can sometimes be surprising. In the case of *Ugly Betty*, they often are. We learn some of the ways in which the law can be and is used (who gets to be illegal? Ignacio; who breaks labor laws but remains legal? Daniel), but we also learn the valuable lesson that the law is not some rigid standard that applies equally to each occasion or to everyone. The law is alive, moldable, and ephemeral. Its substance is not in the words that we sometimes confuse with it (the Constitution, the Bill of Rights, or case law) but in the people who believe their right is to utter the laws, who feel authorized to interpret them, and whose franchise permits them to break them. As critical legal scholars have noted for decades now, the people through which the law exists, the ones who mediate it for the rest of society, tend to be of one kind and in close familiar or filial proximity to wealth and political capital. In *Ugly*

Betty, those who control *Mode* (Daniel and Bradford) embody the characteristics of the first citizens; they are the rulers of their kingdoms to the point of making obsolete some, if not most, state laws. They are the "who" and the "what" of citizenship.

Much in the same way that NBC's *CSI* has likely altered expectations about legal technology, mainstream popular texts such as *Ugly Betty* construct or reconstruct our expectations of our legal world and culture. Depending on the show's politics, which at times are as clear as the politics of *JAG* or *24* (both of which manifest pro-military, conservative, unilateralist politics), a televisual text references the legal world to produce specific political relations in the social world. *Ugly Betty* is a complex popular text that embodies the political ideas of immigrants and women yet plays, or has to play, to the assumed cultural and political expectations of millions of people in order to survive. So the process by which *Ugly Betty* references the law is a multilayered product of ABC's rating expectations, the way Nielsen has designed its measuring tools (which, according to Hispanic media, typically undercount Latinas/os), and the willingness of advertiser agencies to interpret the show's audience as a desirable one. None of these things are clear-cut. All rely on cultural understandings of citizenship (understood as a national, political, and social franchise), race/ ethnicity, and the law.

These textual ambivalences are integral to the show's ability to speak about citizenship and labor. By using comedy and farce, the text tones down its critical potential; instead of critique, viewers are invited to share a laugh at Ignacio's tribulations and empathize with Daniel, who deep down has a heart of gold. *Ugly Betty* speaks to immigration, politics, and labor but does so within the limitations of media markets, carefully avoiding a full counterhegemonic, heterodoxic stance. Because of this, the show's textual characteristics must be seen as a careful negotiation with contemporary nativist political imaginaries and cultures of production, in particular, labor and market cultures. Textualizing Ignacio's dealings with the USCIS through farce is a way of minimizing the threat that a benign narrative of illegality may pose to viewers. Producing this text as immigrant and as Latina/o challenges the way media, as a social field, is organized, but the challenge has to be and is contained by blanching Latinidad in the name of ratings. Cultures of production behave like any other social system, vacillating between normativity, internal cohesion, and change. Because of this doxic inertia that helps mainstream media reconstitute already powerful political imaginaries, mainstream media cultures participate in and co-create political cultures that reaffirm paths of political capital accumulation. In this political imaginary, the law has little bearing on Daniel but is all important to Ignacio. This insidious labor lesson is itself the product of labor. Through labor practices, which are given meaning through market-oriented discourses and a political imaginary of labor justice, media helps define participation and belonging, inclusion and exclusion, and gets to separate those who have zero political capital (the Ignacios of the world) from those who have all the political capital, who, in this fictional show and perhaps in reality, own the media and the means of production.

Rule 2: Anti-Latino Media Cultures

Ugly Betty participates in the privilege of narrativizing labor laws and does so in contradictory fashion, sometimes courageously presenting minoritarian views about undocumented immigrants but more often reproducing hegemonic notions on labor and citizenship that undermine the show's pro-immigrant character. This section continues showing the links between capitalism, law, and the state by briefly showing how media industries have participated in and influenced labor law and the discourses about labor, often to the detriment of Latinas/os. Labor laws continue producing differentiated citizenship experiences, and this is particularly true in media. Labor regulation in media industries is magnified by the economic, cultural, and political might of our media system, which has the unusual ability to influence government and society by constructing the cultural frameworks that, as I showed earlier, give meaning to political and legal behavior. Whoever controls our media system is also in partial control of mainstream political imaginaries, including the way we imagine just behavior in labor markets.

Media control cannot be exercised without government intervention. It requires a particular type of political capital. For instance, *Ugly Betty* airs on ABC, a television network that belongs to Disney, which, like other successful media corporations, has been successful at interacting with governmental and legal structures. According to Robert McChesney (2004) and Paul Starr (2004), media such as ABC have always existed within close proximity of political structures in at least two ways: First, they exist as industries tightly regulated by government, which monitors ownership patterns, holdings and mergers, technological infrastructure, market performance (competitiveness), and the media's relation to the public good. As McChesney states, "The U.S. media system—even its most 'free market' sectors—is the direct result of explicit government policies and in fact would not exist without those policies" (2004, 17). Second, media industries shape the democratic process by influencing the types of knowledge the citizenry has about the political and legal world, thus helping legitimize this knowledge or put it into question. McChesney and Starr help us understand that the relative harmony between the political and media worlds, their multiple connections and interdependences, have profound implications for the political health of the nation.

In the 1960s, it became evident that our political structures were sick. During that decade, the government set the basis for the regulation of labor in all industries, including media, on the principles of the Civil Rights Act of 1964. The Equal Employment Opportunity Commission (EEOC), created to monitor discrimination in the workplace, was part of the Civil Rights Act, and while it exemplified the act's achievements, it was also one of its biggest compromises. The EEOC's official history acknowledges that the agency was toothless from 1965 to 1971; as a testament to the influence of corporations and industry in federal policy, the EEOC was created on the condition that it would only "receive, investigate, and conciliate complaints" (EEOC 2007). The EEOC could not enact remedies until later in the 1970s. Other research shows that corporate influence on these government agencies has led to weak enforcement of labor law or inefficient ways of using legal sanctions (Bullock and Lamb 1984; Leonard 1985). Our social ills were partly due to media, as the Kerner Commission argued. According to the commission's final report, media news organizations contributed to the racial unrest by failing to convey the urgency of racial problems. This failure, the report continued, was based on the fact that television "is almost totally white in both appearance and attitude" (qtd. in Brooks, Daniels, and Hollifield 2003, 125). As Chon Noriega, among others, has observed, this conclusion placed employment and representation at the center of racial unrest, in a sense acknowledging the political and social power of media and the necessity to regulate it more closely (Noriega 2000, 29). During the following years, the media industries became regulated by different government agencies, chiefly the EEOC and the FCC, with the goal of remedying labor inequality (Brainard 2004, 45–46; América Rodriguez 1999, 62–63). Media also became the logical target of much civic activism. Noriega suggests a three-part historiography of this effort by Latino organizations. From 1968 to 1977, he notes, Latino media activists used the state's civil rights institutions to

demand labor and representational justice. Between 1974 and 1984, La-
tinas/os made direct demands on the television industry but relied on
public funding sources for production. Since 1981, Latino media activism
has taken a corporate logic and has demanded from the state and the industry "'consumer sovereignty' in commercial *and* public broadcasting."
In Noriega's view, during this time, activists have staked "a moral and economic claim to the Chicano citizen-consumer" (2000, 25).

Unfortunately, by and large, legal and activist efforts have failed. Latino numbers in English-language media industries remain dismal (Keller
1994; Mayer 2003; Noriega 2000; Ramirez Berg 2002; América Rodriguez
1999; Valdivia 2010, 39–46). Simply, Latinas/os have a hard time getting
access to mainstream media jobs, and though it is hard to get a clear picture of the complex labor markets that we call media industries, as Angharad Valdivia notes, some numbers clearly indicate the challenges that
Latino media workers face (2010, 39–46). In 2007, the National Association of Hispanic Journalists found that, in journalism, Latinas/os account
for 4 percent of personnel in print news and 6 percent of news staffers
on English-language television (Lopez Buck 2012). Bob Papper (2003, 21)
has found that Latinas/os account for only 1.5 percent of radio news staffers and, in television, for only 4.4 percent of news directors. The lack of
Latino personnel in news has a predictable effect on coverage. Federico
Subervi-Vélez's latest report on Latino representation in television news
media shows that stories about Latinas/os account for only 0.82 percent of
all stories on the major television networks and CNN (2005, 4). In mainstream, English-speaking television, Latinas/os accounted for 6.5 percent
of prime-time characters and 6 percent of all people listed in the opening
credits in 2003 (Children Now 2004). This is a significant improvement
from 1999, when Latino prime-time representation was around 2 percent,
but it is still unsatisfactory if we consider census figures in the United
States and, in particular, California. As the U.S. Census figures have indi-
cated for the past few years, Latinas/os have surpassed African Americans
as the most populous racial/ethnic minority in the nation and account
for more than 15.3 percent of the population in general and 35.5 percent
of the population of California, the state where most media is produced.
This lack of representation in media work is worrisome not only because
it represents banning Latinas/os from the enormous wealth that media
industries generate but, as important, because it has set the basis for culturally normalizing Latino disenfranchisement. Referring back to Richard
Delgado and Jean Stefancic (1998), the "Latino condition" is largely caused

by legal disenfranchisement in most significant spheres of life, including, I add, media employment.

Lack of Latino representation in media industries has been normalized partly because of hiring practices that tend to work under what organizational demographers call the "similarity-attraction paradigm" (people tend to hire and promote others like themselves), partly because post-Reaganism has succeeded at eroding EEO/AA provisions, and partly because organizations have never fully believed in the value of racial justice (see also Valdivia 2010, 49). In a social system such as media organizations, Nan Lin (2001) notes, some values are interpreted as commonsensical and are internalized by most members of the system. He calls them "persuasive" values. Other values are developed through "coercion," a "process by which fellow actors are forced to recognize the merit of a resource or face certain sanction or punishment" (30). Resources that become valued because of coercion (e.g., racial justice) are often not understood as holding intrinsic merit.[3] Given the history that media corporations have with the values of racial and sexual equality, it is safe to assume that these have been perceived mostly as coercive values.[4] Not surprisingly, researchers and civil rights state organizations have found that media corporations have tried, and too often succeeded in, cheating EEO/AA law, sidestepping their legal responsibilities, and lobbying against racial (and sexual) justice policies. Either by using the "twofer" (a woman of color whom a media corporation would report twice, as both a woman and a nonwhite employee), inflating their numbers of hires of color, isolating these hires from the advancement track, or placing them in highly visible but relatively powerless positions, media organizations have reacted to the values of racial and sexual justice in chauvinist but predictable ways (Wilson and Gutiérrez 1995; United States Commission on Civil Rights 1977, 93–97; Brooks, Daniels, and Hollifield 2003, 127). In doing so, they have normalized different ways of experiencing citizenship: one reserved for communities of people who, in their embodied selves, convey persuasive values and another one for those whose embodiment conveys coercive values.

Perhaps the biggest impact that corporations have had on legal remedies for racial discrimination in labor was semanticizing the ideas of racial justice within corporatist and managerial logics (L. Edelman 1992). This is the context for the current state of affairs: a media industry that four decades after the formation of the EEO/AA provisions still lacks racial and sexual equality (Brooks, Daniels, and Hollifield 2003, 123–146). Regarding EEO/AA, media and government have produced a state of deregulation. This does not mean that the idea of diversity is not current or popular in contemporary organizations but rather that diversity has been redefined in ways that weaken its applicability to the goal of racial and sexual justice.

For the past couple of decades, the work of Lauren Edelman has shown the ways in which civil rights legal prescriptions, including labor justice laws (e.g., EEO/AA), have been adopted by organizations, corporations, and the managerial class. She notes that EEO/AA law is particularly open to mediation by organizations because it is ambiguous, has weak enforcement, and emphasizes procedural over substantive effects. Title VII of the 1964 Civil Rights Act, for instance, makes it unlawful to discriminate but fails to define the term. EEO/AA law is weakly enforced because the EEOC's first goal is to conciliate between employer and employee; this process is lengthy and costly, and it has one of the lowest rates of success of any legal suit (plaintiffs win only 21 percent of cases). To make matters worse, the courts today emphasize process over substance. For instance, compliance with Title VII is widely interpreted as being based on whether employers followed hiring processes that encourage diversity rather than on actual hires. So if employers make a "good-faith effort" to achieve EEO goals, they are safe (L. Edelman 1992, 1536–1541). In Edelman's view, EEO/AA law is mediated by organizations in ways that minimize their effect on long-held cultural beliefs and managerial processes. The means by which organizations can do this is by creating offices, positions, and rules that visibly show the public and law enforcers that they are complying with the law.

Media organizations are not exceptions, as the amount of EEO/AA initiatives and postings show. Most media corporations now have diversity officers, diversity initiatives, and so on. Fox has an office of Diversity Development that proudly displays the racial variety of shows such as *House* (Omar Epps's photograph is on the front page), *24*, and the diversity jewel *K-Ville*, with Anthony Anderson's proud face legitimating these practices and goals.[5] The ABC Television Group has a program for developing talent that prominently displayed in its 2007 calendar a "Native American Actors Mixer" in January, as well as an "African American Heritage Ceremony" and a "Hispanic Symposium Multicultural Day" in February.[6] NBC has created what it calls "DiverseCity NBC," a webspace that showcases the diversity that already exists in NBC's programming and that also functions as a space that agents and casting executives can use to locate "unsigned talent."[7] Media leaders often argue that "diversity" is one of their key goals.

Fox Entertainment president Peter Liguori has stated, "We think, as a network, [diversity is] the moral thing to do. And it's the right business thing to do. When you look at the top 10, top 20 shows out there, they're diverse. For TV and certainly for Fox to be vibrant, relevant and authentic, we need to be reflective of the general population" (qtd. in Toledo 2007) In a similar vein, Anne Sweeney, president of the Disney-ABC Television Group, declared to *Variety*, "The more textured, the more real, the more authentic our writing and directing staffs are and our on-air talent, the more successful we'll be, because we are reflecting the real world around us, not just the bubble world" (Toledo 2007). Because many of these initiatives, with these stated goals, have been going on for some time, there is reason to believe that they are not having quite the desired effect, which supports what Edelman and her colleagues theorize: "Organizations create EEO/AA structures, then, largely as gestures to their legal environments; these structures are designed to secure legitimacy and minimize the threat of liability" (Edelman, Fuller, and Mara-Drita 2001, 1590).

Although these network initiatives are meant to bring these organizations into compliance with the EEO/AA legal environment, they exist within a discursive framework of diversity that no longer has as its goal racial and sexual justice, a value widely perceived as coercive. Instead, the new managerial discourse of diversity, which Edelman and her colleagues note has changed since the 1980s (Edelman, Fuller, and Mara-Drita 2001, 1589), recasts diversity as a legal prescription of a different sort. Typically, today's discourse of diversity has expanded to include diversity of all sorts, including diversity of thought, religion, lifestyle, dress, and the like (ibid., 1616). As important, diversity has become a matter of organizational success, a new managerial tactic that tries to create wealth for the organization (1618). In this discourse, different types of employees have different ways of thinking and working and different background knowledge, thus providing organizations with increasing ways of succeeding in a changing world and a new economy. Fox's office of Diversity Development justifies this initiative with precisely this language. Not surprisingly, the most frequent reason to embrace diversity in this managerial rhetoric is profit.

In this deregulated environment, a show such as *Ugly Betty* becomes evidence of the media industry's compliance with current legal expectations of diversity. Sylvia Franklin (2007), in perfect corporate media liberal lingo, follows this rationale when she writes for *Television Weekly* regarding *Ugly Betty*, "Diversity pays." She is referring to the ratings and critical success of *Ugly Betty* and other shows such as *Grey's Anatomy* and *Lost*, which also have diverse casts in front of and behind the camera. In today's media world, Franklin's definition, rooted in managerial rhetoric, has become the standard view of a diversity that can be embraced by profit-seeking organizations. As Charo Toledo (2007), *Variety*'s writer, declares, ABC's diverse lineup has made it a success with Latinas/os. Six of the top-ten highest rated shows among Latinas/os (age eighteen to forty-nine) are shown on ABC. Although perhaps privately these media leaders may indeed believe that opening media to Latinas/os is a matter of basic justice, in public speeches, they seem to consistently stick to the script and justify their own positive behaviors as profitable. Such discourse of diversity is also reproduced by media activists working closely with the industry. For instance, Alex Nogales is the president and CEO of the National Hispanic Media Coalition, a wonderful organization that brings together Latino media workers and helps them enter into the industry's social networks. Nogales, in receiving an award from Southwest Airlines, justified diversity in terms of profit. In his speech, he noted, "ABC is the biggest model for everyone to follow. . . . Diversifying led to their success in ratings with hit shows like *Ugly Betty* and *Grey's Anatomy*" (Ruano 2007, 52). *Ugly Betty* also presents itself as a text extremely conscious of the extended notion of diversity by including in its story line transsexual, gay, immigrant, undocumented, black, Latina/o, and other so-called ugly characters, all of which have been understood as diverse by viewers and/or critics.

According to Edelman and her colleagues, the managerial view of diversity has arisen "in response to the decline of political support for affirmative action and civil rights law" (Edelman, Fuller, and Mara-Drita 2001, 1626). As troublesome, there is evidence that this definition of diversity is now mirrored in legal communities and major legal decision such as the 2003 Supreme Court ruling on university admissions at the University of Michigan. The rationale in that case framed diversity as a resource valued in universities because it provides a benefit to the existing university population (Harvey 2007, 57). The Supreme Court here, in a move that betrays the principles of legal frameworks created during the civil rights era, disregards the standard of racial justice and substitutes it with a standard that benefits the majority.

Embracing *Ugly Betty*

Ugly Betty succeeds in the public sphere partly because it exemplifies a type of media ethics and positive corporate civic behavior that is becoming increasingly hegemonic at this time when the notion of diversity is linked to new profit opportunities (Aparicio 1998, 116). Here, ethics is complexly bound to good capitalism, which substitutes the nation-state as the primary grantor of citizenship rights. This is a perfect example of corporate liberalism, under which the definition of diversity morphs, and a term once rooted in the racial and sexual struggles of the civil rights movement becomes an ethnocentric term valued for the benefits it can provide to the national majority that identifies with our current racial patriarchy. In the media corporate world, diversity becomes a cross-cultural marketing strategy aimed at strengthening a media network's chances of victory in the ratings war. In mainstream politics and law, as our Supreme Court now believes, diversity should be valued only if it represents a net gain for the political majority, which in the current racial formation means net gains for the white, heterosexual, and patriarchal middle and upper classes. As a way of showing how *Ugly Betty* negotiated this media corporate value, in this section, I explore further how diversity itself became the corporate tactic to tackle ratings, signaling a moment in our political culture when the social space often referred to as the public sphere becomes, under this definition of diversity and these conditions of citizenship, neatly occupied by the values and ethical concerns of corporations.

Streeter (1996) argues that our broadcasting regulatory structure, led by the FCC, increasingly abides by the utilitarian, individualistic, and capitalist rules of corporate liberalism, and he suggests that the current legal field regulating media is under its spell. This is evident not only to scholars but also to Latino media activists who have adapted to this language. As Valdivia (2010, 42), Noriega (2000), and Dávila (2001, 2008) posit, many Latinas/os have understood that in order to share the privilege of media access, they have to stop using the argument that diversity is a stand-alone resource and utilize it, instead, in addition to or as a frame for corporatist logic. It is because of corporatist logic that *Ugly Betty* is able to enter ABC's lineup, and it is capitalism that authorizes this show to speak about citizenship and some of the laws that constitute it.

The most important corporate reasons for ABC to develop *Ugly Betty* have to do with the show's ability to plug into promising Latino textual forms and demographic potential. Regarding textuality, the show borrows from telenovelas. The telenovela, as a format (long series, with scripted endings) and a narrative style (melodrama, with over-the-top situations), has been made famous around the world by Latin American television, especially by Televisa in Mexico, Venevisa in Venezuela, and Globo in

Brazil. In Latin America and in the U.S. Spanish-language media market (e.g., Univision and Telemundo, Azteca America, and Galavision), tele-novelas are the prime time. Their success is sustained and international. Hoping to replicate this success, all American English-language television networks are developing telenovela-influenced series. The most advanced projects—and the ones that got airtime—are Fox's MyNetworkTV pro-grams *Desire* and *Fashion House* and ABC's *Ugly Betty* (Domestic drama 2006). Part of the appeal of telenovelas is related to narrative style and conventions, which have typically produced stories that have multigen-erational audiences. CBS senior vice president of daytime programs Bar-bara Bloom stated, these are programs that "I can watch with my 16-year-old daughter, and my mother" (Domestic drama 2006). The attraction of multigenerational audiences is not necessarily related to embracing "fam-ily values" or some kind of wholesome view of what television ought to be. The attraction of multigenerational shows is that this viewing prac-tice may slow down network viewership erosion due to age-based market fragmentation (Potter 2004). Since the introduction of cable in the 1970s, the networks' audiences have dwindled. Today, the four English-language networks (CBS, NBC, ABC, and Fox) average a 41 percent share during regular broadcast season and a 30 percent share during the summer (in 2007, the four networks averaged only a 27 percent share) (Consoli and Crupi 2007). Multigenerational shows may increase their audience share and revenue. The economic challenges faced by the networks due to losing viewers also forces them to rely more than ever on their ability to market their programming internationally and through different media. The tele-novela scores high in both standards. Telenovelas are products that can be sold internationally, as Globo, Venevisa, and Televisa have shown, and that can be repackaged in different formats, such as DVDs and video-on-demand (VOD) (Whitney 2007, 26). Already *Ugly Betty* has been success-ful internationally, ABC having no difficulty placing it in national markets as dissimilar as Germany, Britain, Dubai, and Spain. The show has also been selected to be delivered on VOD and DVD (Hopewell and de Pablos 2006; Jaafar 2007; Valdivia 2010, 33).

The format's attraction and the potential international success of tele-novelas are part of the backstory to the development of *Ugly Betty*. An-other part is the growing importance and wide recognition of the size of the Latino market and the mainstreaming of Latinidad. As Dávila (2000), Isabel Molina-Guzmán and Angharad Valdivia (2004, 206) have commented, Latinas/os are the "It" market. Partly this is so because of demography. As stated before, Latinas/os are the fastest growing minority in the nation; they have surpassed African Americans as the numerically most important minority, and, if census projections are correct, they will only become more important as time goes by. Latino wealth is also quickly increasing. Since 1990, Latino wealth has been compounding at a rate of 8.2 percent, almost doubling the wealth growth of non-Latinas/os (4.9 percent). Their buying power has grown from $220 billion in 1990, to $687 billion in 2004 and will grow to a projected $923 billion by 2009 (Humphreys 2006, 6). Because of this, marketers and advertisers who specialize in targeting Hispanics are thriving. As Dávila has shown, for more than five decades, professionals in the business of crafting markets have, sometimes painstakingly, given shape to a Hispanic market that can be described to advertisers in terms of ethnicity, language, international and national geographies (e.g., California and Texas or the growing Latino concentration in the South), and cultural specificity (2001, 24–38). Today, these marketers are harvesting the benefits of this groundwork.

The Hispanic market is not equal to the Latino communities it claims to represent. It is constructed through an array of archetypes, cultural stereotypes, and profit-driven exaggerations. For instance, Hispanic marketers have often suggested that "Hispanics" favor Spanish-language media, yet millions of middle- and upper-middle-class Latinas/os (who are one of the most marketable segments of the Latino community and many of whom have lived in the United States for generations) do not speak Spanish (Dávila 2001, 60–63). Highlighting the importance of Spanish, however, has allowed these marketers to sell their services and linguistic expertise: Hispanic marketers speak Spanish; most advertisers and mainstream marketers do not. Such a Spanish-centric view of the Hispanic market is eroding, and *Ugly Betty* is evidence of this. The show proves that cross-linguistic, transcultural marketing strategies are increasingly feasible. One of the target audiences for the show, according to ABC, is bilingual Latinas/os who are both viewers of *Betty la Fea* on Univision and *Ugly Betty* on ABC. As a nod to this audience, in the finale of season two of *Ugly Betty*, Betty, who travels to Mexico in order to try to fix her father's migration status, meets her look-alike cousin, played by Angélica Vale, the Mexican actress who plays Betty in Televisa's version of the telenovela (Ayala 2007). ABC's tactic seems successful if we consider that *Ugly Betty* attracts eight hundred thousand Latinas/os every week. This same bilingual Hispanic market is also attractive to Univision, which partnered with ABC to produce a Spanish-language adaptation of ABC's hit *Desperate Housewives* in 2008. (This remapping of Univision's audiences came only months after Univision was acquired by the Texas Pacific Group, Thomas H. Lee Partners, and Haim Saban, two equity firms and an Egyptian media mogul. See chapter 4).

But for the show to be successful, ABC needed to target more viewers than bilingual Latinas/os. The show needed to have crossover appeal, and ABC has not been disappointed. The first two seasons were quite successful, and though the show was canceled after four seasons, *Ugly Betty* is a relative hit in syndication, international sales, and its DVD repackaging.

Because today more advertisers believe in the strength of the Hispanic market, television, which typically has been inhospitable to Latinas/os, may see a gradual change. If discourse around *Ugly Betty* is any indication, these changes will be defined partly in terms of diversity. But this is not the diversity of the civil rights era; instead, this is a social and economic tactic aimed to attract new profits, to infiltrate new markets, and to secure success for mainstream media in a Latinized future. By pointing this out, I am not arguing that such a view of diversity cannot have a positive impact on Latino representation and employment in mainstream media. But I believe that the recasting of diversity as a self-serving economic tactic also damages Latinas/os for several reasons: it precludes Latinas/os from using the language of justice; it forces Latina/o narratives to become "universal" rather than particular; it reconstitutes current stratifications between citizens and communities; and it helps resemanticizes one of the few legally defined political gains of the civil rights era, the expectation of media and labor diversity. At the root of this newer notion of diversity is a tension between racial ethics (doing the right thing for racial/ethnic equality) and profit. Media makers almost invariably only espouse an ethics that can also be profitable and very rarely risk economic losses for a principle, however important this principle may be. The prioritization of profit over ethics has become normalized to the point that the inherent contradiction of having a principle that can only be embraced when it is economically convenient is never vocalized by media insiders or the press that reports on them.

Conclusion

Because *Ugly Betty* makes us laugh, it is perhaps easy to forget how unusual it is for Latinas/os to share in the privilege of broadcasting narratives in English-language media. It is equally easy to forget that mainstream media is, at all times, dominated by the views of citizens—and not just any citizens. The bulk of those who are working in media industries, at all levels, are white, male, upper middle class, and aware of it. As the numbers show, with their cold, factual poise, English-language media is in the hands of a community of embodied individuals that reconstitutes itself through labor and through the control of political discourses including, now, its increasing control over the discourse of racial justice. This reality is citizenship excess, as is the grotesque morphing of civil rights ideals from ethical and political principles meant to protect and help minorities into political principles applicable only if they help majorities. Something was lost in translation between civil rights law and corporate structures. Beginning in the 1980s, the Reagan era of neoliberal policies and the language of diversity management transformed the discourse of diversity from one connoting racial justice to one connoting profit. Following the logic of this discourse, media corporations have created many diversity initiatives, all with the goal of fitting the legal environment of compliance with EEO/AA prescriptions, but only in cases in which this compliance can be translated into economic success. Everybody loves *Ugly Betty*: Latinas/os, immigrants, and media professionals. It is the latest example that diversity can indeed be profitable and the latest opportunity for a mostly white structure to embrace mainstream racial protocols without giving up structural privileges.

According to Streeter and Dávila, the influence of corporate liberalism in our political system has given form to a type of citizenship discursively regimented by corporate logic. Consumer rights stand in for political rights. Beyond this, I believe that changes in the discourse of diversity are evidence of more complex interiorizations of corporate citizenship. In naturalizing the idea that diversity should produce profit and benefit the majority (*Ugly Betty*, the University of Michigan), we redefine the legal and political elements of our subjectivity, circumscribing ethics to capitalism. Because our experiences as citizens are manifestations of legal structures, and because the legal field is so entwined with corporate logic, our political values become equal to our ability to generate profit for the majority. This is a highly racially conservative and alienating political schema that forces individuals to define their political worth based on majoritarian values. Central to these values is the idea that broadcasting televisual texts should speak to the majority, thus sidelining the argument that to have a just society, the majority must substantially learn about the other. This idea is at play in the public discussions of *Ugly Betty* and other

Latino programming. Ferrera, extremely happy and proud of having won a Golden Globe, explained to the press that Betty's story is "universal." Horta has repeated this notion on several occasions (Garvin 2006). Nina Tassler, who oversaw the development of *Cane* (another Latino-focused program) at CBS, has similarly stated, "This series illustrates our overall philosophy about diversity. It's the quintessential American dream. In its specificity, it becomes universal. We have to tell universal stories, and this is an American family" (Braxton 2007). To be universal is to despecify race, class, and origin and to highlight majoritarian values, fantasies, and narratives. For whites, this is the norm. For nonwhites, this is cross-marketing.

6

Mediating Belonging, Inclusion, and Death

In chapter 5, I engaged with the problem of inclusion and explored it in relation to media industries and labor. As that chapter shows, the inclusion of noncitizen Latinas/os in English-language media is possible only if the fictional narrative rendering of Latinas/os is profitable. As I showed in other chapters, it is much harder for noncitizen Latinas/os to be represented positively in news and political speech. It is, in fact, quite extraordinary. The mainstreaming of nativism of the past two decades has meant that noncitizen Latinas/os can be part of news and political speech only as problems, as threats, and, of course, as foreigners (Ono and Sloop 2002; Santa Ana 2002). This chapter investigates some of the only cases in recent memory in which noncitizen Latinas/os became the positive focus of news media among conservative and moderate media and political speech. The chapter concerns soldiers killed in action during the Iraq War and examines closely the way these soldiers and their deaths were described by journalists and politicians. These descriptions, I show, paved the way for extraordinary changes to immigration law supported by both parties in Congress. Yet the discourse of politics and citizenship found in these descriptions and in the congressional debates that followed are sobering reminders of the trade-offs required of minorities if they are to be protagonists in narratives of nation.

The invasion of Iraq began the evening of March 20, 2003. Four of the first coalition soldiers to die in Iraq were noncitizens. Marine Lance Corporal José Gutiérrez (killed March 21, 2003, and reported as the first U.S. Army soldier killed) was a native of Guatemala; Marine Lance Corporal Jesús Suárez del Solar (March 27, 2003) and Corporal José Angel Garibay (March 28, 2003) were from Mexico; and Army Private First Class Diego Rincon (March 29, 2003) was from Colombia. Although U.S. public law existed that could eventually give these soldiers posthumous citizenship (8 USC Sec. 1440-1), new bills that would expedite or make automatic the naturalization processes were quickly written.[1] Attesting to the extraordinary times, the new bills were introduced only days after the Iraq invasion had begun, by politicians of the states where these young men had lived. For instance, eleven House representatives from Georgia, home to Diego Rincon, introduced House Resolution 1691 within days of Rincon's death. The same happened at the Senate level, where U.S. Senators Zell Miller (D-GA) and Saxby Chambliss (R-GA) advocated for bill S. 783 on April 3. Legislation giving citizenship to Gutiérrez, Suárez, Garibay, Rincon, and others killed in battle was both bipartisan and backed by enormous public support, including the support of the executive office. This is not surprising because public discussion hailed these Latinas/os as national heroes and civic examples and, thus, as deserving the honor of posthumous citizenship. The key elements of these bills were written into H.R. 1954, also known as the Armed Forces Naturalization Act of 2003.[2] Besides granting posthumous citizenship to armed forces personnel killed in battle, H.R. 1954 also reduced the qualifying time to apply for citizenship from three years to one year for those nonresidents serving in the military.

This chapter engages with political/juridical illiberalism by presenting and evaluating the political and legal processes surrounding the death of these Latino soldiers. It wrestles with the liberal principle of consent and investigates the political, legal, and discursive reasons for giving posthumous citizenship to the deceased soldiers. Then I use the framework of coloniality to examine how media presented the issue of consent in relationship to American history and armed forces practices. The armed forces are here presented as institutions that inherit the colonial practices of drafting noncitizens into armed conflicts. Because of this, the armed forces become instruments of illiberalism designed to extract desire, energy, and life from marginalized populations. The concluding section synthesizes findings and proposes that only through a framework of citizenship excess that engages mediation can these events be illuminated.

Governing with Citizenship and Consent

When I have given talks about the research presented in this chapter, I invariably get the question, "Why did these noncitizen Latinas/os enlist?" The question comes from a good place, the assumption that joining the armed forces is the most intimate ritual of national belonging. To most people, it is puzzling that noncitizens would do something that it is often described as an act of love for the nation. Because, most imagine, only love can explain the sacrifices of serving in the military. But our history shows otherwise: First, the majority of those who have risked their lives in war have done so because they have been drafted, and a significant portion of them have been noncitizens. Second, love for the nation is a traditional way of explaining social realities that would otherwise be unseemly. When drafted, individuals are obliged to kill or die for the nation. Calling it sacrifice or love for the nation is simply sweetening the harsh reality of subjection (Alonso 1994, 386). Third, though many people have indeed volunteered to serve, loving the nation is not the exclusive purview of citizens. I believe that coloniality can partly explain these three issues and help us understand first why these noncitizens enlisted and whether enlistment in the armed forces meant that they wished to become citizens.

Coloniality is a type of social and political analysis that places social facts such as legal decisions or historical events into the long frame of modernity (see chapter 2 and 3). Hence, coloniality forces us to do a sort of double-take on research objects, analyzing them against the diachronic backdrop of colonialism's remnants and against the synchronic pertinent contexts and processes of hegemony. A diachronic glance at noncitizen participation in the U.S. armed forces shows that citizenship has traditionally been a political technology used for the reproduction of the nation-state. As a political technology, citizenship connects immigrants to the armed forces for the simple reason that traditionally the U.S. government has used citizenship (including naturalization) as a political tool to fatten the military. During the Revolutionary War, five thousand blacks were fighting alongside the Revolutionary forces in the North, with the understanding that freedom from slavery was near (Zinn 2003, 89). During the Texas War, not only Irish immigrants but also Mexican nationals fought on the side of the seceding army (seceding from Mexico). Noncitizen African Americans and Latinas/os fought on both sides of the Civil War (Lopez 1998). Puerto Rico was ceded by Spain on December 10, 1898. Though not yet citizens, the first company of native-born Puerto Ricans was organized in 1899 to join the American Colonial Army. In 1917, during World War I, the needs of the U.S. Army were such that the draft went on targeting immigrant populations. As Nancy Gentile Ford (1997) has argued, in 1918, noncitizens accounted for some 18 percent of the U.S. Army (almost two hundred thousand troops). European nations protested the drafting of their citizens; to calm these nations, the U.S. government quickened the pace of naturalization. In all these cases, the noncitizens were fighting either because they were drafted (Puerto Ricans in World War I, Chinese Americans in the Civil War) or because they voluntarily enlisted to gain citizenship rights (blacks in the Revolutionary War, Irish and Mexicans in the Texas War).

Drafting noncitizens (or giving citizenship to people so that they can be drafted) can easily be argued to be coloniality in practice.[3] However, volunteering to join the army, as in the case of these soldiers, adds complexity to the issue because volunteering would seem to be a classic example of liberalism. If liberalism is understood as governance that gives primacy to personal freedom, the best examples of liberalism become those consensual relations between state and subject, such as voluntarism. But voluntarism and consent are not transparent social facts that demonstrate the free will of a subject and her or his willingness to participate in a state-building project. Voluntarism and consent need to be scrutinized, particularly when they are associated with noncitizen Latinas/os, immigrants whose juridical subjectivities have been shaped by transnationalism and marginalization (Pérez 2004, 138, 191, 199). Although clearly they were not coerced into volunteering, the question of why the Latino immigrants enlisted remains open. I propose that the first element of the answer relates to the type of technology of governance that citizenship is vis-à-vis Latino immigrant subjectivities.

As stated in previous chapters, citizenship is governance that relies on the interiorization of legal and political imaginaries. Toby Miller (1993) observes that contemporary societies characteristically use this interiorization, making citizenship an instrument of self-government. He adroitly writes, "Citizenship is an open technology, a means of transformation ready for definition and disposal in dispersed ways at dispersed sites. . . . It produces a 'disposition' on [citizens'] part not to accept the imposition of a particular form of government passively, but to embrace it actively as a collective expression of themselves" (12). Described in this way, besides being a set of political mechanisms affecting Latinas/os, citizenship is an internalized set of dispositions that legitimize and reconstitute broad social structures.

Because this internalized set of dispositions must legitimize, or at least make bearable, ongoing stratifications, they do different work on different communities. In general, Miller proposes, citizenship is a technology of governance that works via the perception of incompletion (1993, 12). That is, individuals contrast their lives with standards of citizenship and perceive a gap between themselves and the ideal. This gap signals incompletion and insufficiency and is the subjective motivation for self-improvement and the psychic foundation for the internalization of the law. This general mechanism is at play in immigrant subjectivities, and one of its particular manifestations is the desire to assimilate (when that desire is present) or, as I have argued elsewhere, to perform assimilation (Amaya 2007). The impetus is the ongoing marginalization of Latinas/os in the United States, which questions the civic worth of Latina/o values and lives, producing a large gap between the individual's self-image and civic ideals. Latina/o immigrants in particular are constantly bullied by legal and cultural norms to occupy subject positions from which the need and desire to assimilate seems logical (Pérez 2004, 48). Marginalized in popular culture, politics, and civic narratives (e.g., U.S. history), Latinas/os may find few incentives to construct public identities that defy assimilation. Citizenship ideals compel immigrant Latinas/os not only to confront their social devaluation but also to legitimize the legal and social prescriptions that predispose immigrants to embracing legal and social norms often deleterious to their well-being. As George Mariscal (1999) writes of his father and generations of Latinas/os, military service has been one such social norm that, he opines, has taken the lives and plundered the psyches of many in our communities.

Miller's idea of incompleteness gives us a clue as to why noncitizen Latinas/os enlisted, but the issue remains regarding whether their voluntary enlistment should be read as the desire to become U.S. citizens. At stake is whether posthumous citizenship was a way of granting a wish to the deceased Latinas/os or whether it was imposed citizenship. To explore this question, it is necessary to understand the relationship of naturalization to consent as a legal process and then to evaluate the noncitizens' behaviors in terms of the legal standard of naturalization.

Consent has been central to liberalism from its origins. Early liberalism, linked to the revolutionary decades of France and the United States, emphasized individual freedom (Isin and Wood 1999, viii) and engendered ideas of citizenship that included the individual's free association with the state (Schuck 1998, 20). In "advanced liberalism," citizenship continues to be associated with consent, but the consent of the state to protect the subject is understood as something that can be withdrawn and is thus conditional (ibid., 21). The ideal of consensus has been codified in naturalization law, which polices the process whereby individuals born outside the nation acquire citizenship willingly and only if they fulfill the requirements set by government (U.S. Citizenship and Immigration Services, USCIS, formerly the Immigration and Naturalization Services, INS). As is implied, naturalization is one of the most clearly contractual processes of the liberal state because the individual willing to be naturalized swears allegiance to the state and the Constitution and undergoes a long, difficult, and expensive (often in the thousands of dollars) legal process. In exchange, the state is to protect and grant rights and privileges to the individual (Tienda 2002, 588).

The legal procedures initiated by members of Congress after the deaths of Gutiérrez, Garibay, and Rincon had the goal of modifying immigration law and producing a simpler (even automatic) postmortem naturalization process for noncitizens killed in battle. With this in mind, Republican House Representative for Georgia John H. Isakson and others introduced bill H.R. 1691 on April 9, 2003. The bill's goal was "to expedite the granting of posthumous citizenship to members of the United States Armed Forces." News media positively reported the introduction of the bill in the House and its quick passage in both the Senate and House on the evening of April 10 (Chu 2003; Fagan 2003; Goldstein and Moreno 2003).[4] Other bills also were written to address similar issues. For instance, bill H.R. 1850, introduced on April 29 after the death of another Latino (Marine Staff Sergeant Riayan Tejeda) and referred to as the Fairness for America's Heroes Act, was designed to provide immigration benefits to the immediate surviving family (children, wife, parents).[5] H.R. 1685, introduced in the House on April 9, 2003, also aimed at granting posthumous citizenship and added an amendment to the Immigration and Nationality Act that provided citizenship rights for those military personnel killed by illness or in combat, as well as their families. In addition, it made this amendment retroactive to September 11, 2001.

Typically, citizenship is given to those (Latina/o) immigrants who have lived in the United States within the boundaries of legality and who have shown not only a respect for U.S. law but also an awareness of the economic and cultural imperatives governing this society as well as the ability to live by them (Glenn 2002, 144–190).[6] These imperatives are protected by American institutions such as the U.S. Citizenship and Immigration Service (USCIS) that have the goal of sustaining a cultural, legal, and economic national constancy or identity. USCIS states that one of the key objectives is to enhance "the educational opportunities in English, Civics, and History for all immigrants of all ages to assist their integration into U.S. society and foster participation in civic activities."[7] As a result, naturalization can be seen as a reward for previous actions and also as a leap of faith regarding the quality, legality, and productivity of the individual's future actions. To most people, these are reasonable provisions, for they try to protect the viability of a society reshaped by new members. At stake is the future of the nation, at least as is imagined by members of government and some interested publics.[8]

However, the cases at hand differ from these legal and theoretical uses of naturalization. The core of H.R. 1691 (as of 8 U.S.C. Sec. 1440-1) is Section 1.d, written as follows: "Documentation of Posthumous Citizenship. If the Director of the Bureau of Citizenship and Immigration Services approves the request referred to in subsection (c), the Director shall send to the next-of-kin of the person who is *granted citizenship*, a suitable document which states that *the United States considers the person to have been a citizen of the United States at the time of the person's death*" (emphasis added).[9] Two things have to be mentioned. First, this bill grants one very peculiar type of citizenship. It is posthumous, thus retroactive ("to have been a citizen of the United States at the time of the person's death"), but very real citizenship. It is posthumous and retroactive because the legal status of citizenship has to be given to a "person." The dead cannot enter into the contractual aspects of naturalization. Thus, citizenship needs to be given just before death occurs. It is a very real citizenship ("granted citizenship") because it occupies a legal location within the range of legal citizenships currently existing in the United States. This range includes two large categories—citizenship by birth and naturalized citizenship —and several important subcategories: felons and ex-felons often lose legal and political rights, including the rights to privacy, movement, and voting rights; minors belong to a category of citizenship with a limited set of legal, political, and civil rights (Bhabha 2003, 53–59); residents of Puerto Rico and the Virgin Islands have a complex set of rights and legal prescriptions tailored for their extraordinary situations (Malavet 2002, 390; Nieto-Phillips 1999, 65; Hoover 2004, 503). Also a tailored category, posthumous citizenship exists in a very peculiar state, one that precludes its bearers from enjoying any personal benefits but that allows them to extend some of the benefits of naturalization to their families, as in the cases analyzed here.

Granting posthumous citizenship to deceased legal residents because of their role in serving the nation may seem to be an exception to the contractual understanding of citizenship. However, it is not. The contractual aspect of citizenship was considered during the debates regarding these bills, particularly when the House and Senate forced deliberations on the type of benefits the families of the dead would enjoy.[10] These deliberations aimed to clarify the details of the naturalization to be given to the war casualties. In general, naturalization is a contract that includes clauses that make the naturalization process of the spouse and parents of the subject being naturalized, for instance, a priority to the USCIS. Simply put, it is easier to get naturalization if you are the parent or spouse of a naturalized citizen. If you are an unmarried, underage offspring of a naturalized citizen, your naturalization is even easier. On June 4, 2003, Congress debated whether these same benefits would be extended to the families and children of the dead soldiers. Although Congress eventually granted benefits to these families, the existence of the debates evidences the state's contractual understanding of *all* naturalization, even posthumous citizenship. Congress, in this case, represents the state and the nation, and Congress's actions legally signify consent. In sum, the state's consent to entering into the contract with these men and their families was important and was treated with legal thoroughness. Given that the subjects were dead, we know that the Latinas/os' consent was not treated legally; however, consent could have been ascertained based on other arguments. With this in mind, I ask, did actions of these noncitizens before their deaths amount to consent? And, if they did not, why is it that so many believed so?

Did They Consent?

Two arguments have to be considered here: First, an argument can be made that the Latinas/os' Oath of Enlistment, required to sign into the

army, constituted a type of consent that signaled that they were agreeing
to become citizens. A second argument can be made that the Latinas/os
stated that they wanted citizenship and thus the government is simply fulfilling their wishes or their stated wills (with the awareness that an "oral
will" is simply not legally binding). The basis for the first argument is that
the Oath of Enlistment conveys some important ideas of citizenship. The
current oath, written in Title 10 of the U.S. Code and amended on May 5,
1960, reads,

> I, _____, do solemnly swear that I will support and defend the Consti-
> tution of the United States against all enemies, foreign and domestic;
> that I will bear true faith and allegiance to the same; and that I will obey
> the orders of the President of the United States and the orders of the
> officers appointed over me, according to regulations and the Uniform
> Code of Military Justice. So help me God.

With this oath, the enlistee consensually embraces important elements of
citizenship, including civic duties such as supporting and defending the
Constitution and obeying the president and military officers. As important as these elements of civic conduct are, I argue, they are not equiva-
lent to a citizenship oath. The great majority of green-card holders consensually embrace elements of citizenship (they pay taxes, abide by the
law, participate in politics), but this does not mean they want to become
citizens. A large percentage of Latino immigrants never become citizens,
although they legally could (according to Schuck [1998, 168–169], by 1990,
56 percent of Latinas/os had failed to naturalize). Moreover, the Oath of
Enlistment does not require the enlistee to renounce allegiance to other
nations, states, or laws or to renounce a foreign citizenship. By contrast,
compare the Oath of Enlistment with the Naturalization Oath that military members have to read in order to become citizens. This Naturalization Oath begins with the following: "I hereby declare, on oath, that I absolutely and entirely renounce and abjure all allegiance and fidelity to any
foreign prince, potentate, state, or sovereignty, of whom or which I have
heretofore been a subject or citizen."[11] When read side by side, these two
oaths may resemble each other and signal a strong and willful relationship
to the army, but they do not signal the same relationship to the American nation. In the United States, naturalization is a dramatic change of
legal identity that means renouncing your past, your previous national allegiances, and the citizenship of your place of origin (Schuck 1998, 169).

Although the Oath of Enlistment cannot be considered a citizenship oath, it is possible that the soldiers had stated their wishes to become citizens and that the state was, in a sense, fulfilling their will. This is a harder issue to clarify. There is evidence that Rincon may have wanted to become a citizen, at least that is what his father told reporters (McMurray 2003). This may indeed be considered an expression of his will, and so perhaps in his case, posthumous citizenship should have been granted. However, there is nothing to suggest that the other soldiers wanted to become citizens. In fact, there are facts that negate the idea that these Latinas/os wanted to become citizens. First, in the cases analyzed here, all of these noncitizens (including Rincon) were green-card holders for more than five years (five years is the amount of time that individuals are required to hold green cards by the INS and USCIS before applying for citizenship) and thus had the option of applying for citizenship before their deaths. Rincon was five years old when his parents came from Colombia and settled in Georgia. Gutiérrez was fourteen when he arrived in California and twenty-two when he was killed. Garibay was only two months old when he arrived to the United States.[12] Suárez was fourteen and was killed at twenty.[13] What is more, his father, Fernando Suárez del Solar, had repeatedly stated that his son did not want to become a citizen and wished to remain a Mexican citizen. Posthumous citizenship was accepted in the case of Suárez by his next of kin, his wife, to access naturalization rights (Suarez's son was born on U.S. territory and thus was already a citizen by birth).

Although these soldiers' desire for citizenship was legally questionable, elected officials and others interpreted Gutiérrez's, Garibay's, Suarez's, and Rincon's actions as evidence of their wanting citizenship in order to justify their posthumous naturalization. Senators Miller and Cornyn, to name two strong supporters of the posthumous citizenship bills, believed that these soldiers' heroism was related to their wish to become citizens. Other individuals and politicians held similar beliefs, as is evidenced in the June 4, 2003, discussion in Congress.[14] For instance, Rincon's father repeated several times that Diego always wanted to become a citizen. Similarly, M. D. Harmon, writing in a news piece about all the immigrants who were killed, stated that these Marines "hoped to secure their citizenship by their service" (Harmon 2003; Washington Heights family 2003). Guillermo Martínez (2003, 76), writing for *Hispanic* magazine, also interpreted enlistment as evidence of these soldiers' desire to become citizens. This public discussion gave *meaning* to the soldiers' rationale for enlisting and fighting and interpreted their actions prior to their deaths as signaling that they wanted citizenship. Instead of consent, voluntary enlistment became evidence of desire to be citizens. This was a mistake. As shown earlier, there are no legal reasons to believe that enlisting in the army is equal to consenting to be naturalized (see the discussion on the Oath of Enlistment). Moreover, even if these interpretations were correct in some cases (maybe in Rincon's case), they cannot stand in for legal consent (an oral will is not a legal will). However, these interpretations clue us in to an ideology that reproduces existing racial and national fantasies about the military. In these fantasies, the military is an honorable liberal institution populated by volunteers wishing to serve the nation. What most of the interpretations of these soldiers' actions left out sheds light on what was left in: they failed to locate posthumous citizenship within the overall strategy by the state to secure ongoing voluntary enlistment by noncitizens.[15] Moreover, they failed to address the social, cultural, economic, and political reasons that make voluntary enlistment an important life choice for noncitizen Latinas/os in America.

The Armed Forces Naturalization Act of 2003 did more than grant posthumous citizenship to noncitizen Latino war casualties. It also allowed for the expedited naturalization of noncitizens serving in the military. Both modifications to immigration law are part of the overall strategy post-9/11 to secure military enlistment. The idea of expedited naturalization came from an initiative by President George W. Bush, who, on July 3, 2002, signed an executive order to this effect. This order allowed noncitizens serving in the armed forces to apply for citizenship more quickly. The waiting time (typically five years) was reduced to one year. This law has the goal, openly discussed by the enlistment services of the armed forces, of making the military more attractive to noncitizens at times when reaching enlistment goals is a challenge (the military seems less attractive since the Iraq invasion and occupation). According to the latest estimates, forty-two thousand noncitizens (roughly 2 percent of the armed forces) currently serve in different branches of the Army, Navy, Air Force and Civil Guard, (Gamboa 2003). Since July 3, 2002, more than ten thousand of these service members have applied for expedited citizenship. An irony and a deep contradiction that still prevails is that if they were to die in combat, these noncitizen soldiers would be awarded posthumous citizenship immediately.

There is evidence that expedited naturalization succeeded at bringing noncitizens to the armed forces. Sergeant First Class Rodolfo Abalos, who recruits for the armed forces, comments on the point: "That's another thing we can offer, especially to Asians who want to become citizens." Abalos, born in the Philippines, continues: "I tell them about how they can get their citizenship a lot faster joining the Army, compared to being a civilian and waiting for five years." Joseph Macaraeg, a Filipino resident who enlisted in 2003, hoped that his daughter would grow up as a citizen. In consonance with Abalos, Macaraeg said, "I'm always thinking about my daughter" (Kong 2003). Moreover, many Mexicans, hearing about President Bush's resolution, made inquiries to the American embassy in Mexico City regarding this quick method of acquiring citizenship. The embassy was forced to place a notice on its webpage stating that it was false that the United States was offering citizenship in exchange for enlistment (Ferriss 2003). All these legal redefinitions of immigration policy have allowed the armed forces to offer potential recruits an extra incentive to join up.

In spite of the clearly utilitarian way that naturalization has been used by the U.S. government to attract noncitizens, public discussions of the military continue to reproduce the suspicious notion that volunteers populate the armed forces. Voluntarism here is a reworking of the consensus principle at the level of the military, a notion central to the idea of the citizen-soldier and to the argument that soldiering is a type of civics. Leo Braudy (2003) has observed that, in a time of war, when the sovereignty of the nation is at stake, the ideal citizen often becomes discursively linked to the soldier, an ideal character that inhabits military narratives in which his civic qualities of heroism, sacrifice, and love for the nation are displayed.[16] However, for the idea of the citizen-soldier to work as a model of ethical behavior, it is required that we imagine the individual's actions as voluntary. Political liberalism, after all, sits atop humanist liberalism and its emphasis on individualism, freedom, and the power of the will to guide the self toward betterment.

Since 1973, the U.S. armed forces have relied on volunteers; because of this, the targeting of the poor and nonwhite communities can more easily be hidden from public scrutiny. *Voluntarism obscures the illiberal, racialized, and classed ways the American military works*; voluntarism veils the institutional practices that have secured the military's ability to attract personnel, such as the locations for recruitment offices in our middle- and lower-class neighborhoods (see Palaima 2004; Seeley 2004; Lovato 2005)[17] or the targeting of some populations or geographical areas over others (Crawley 2003). The Department of Defense recognizes the South, which is home to a huge minority population, as a great enlistment source and preferred target of recruiters and military advertisers (Sackett and Mavor 2004, 64). Enlistment, in short, is all about targeting some, not all.

In spite of the relevance of nationalism in media and politics, most Americans embrace discourses and practices of privilege that ignore enlistment practices and the unfair connection between enlistment, race, and class. Nathanial Fick enacted this privilege in July 20, 2004, by publishing an article in the *New York Times* in which he criticized the draft proposal. In it, he argues against the notion that racial minorities and the poor constitute the bulk of the volunteer army. Fick, a former Marine captain who served in Afghanistan and Iraq, proudly remarks that his soldiers came "from virtually every part of the socio-economic spectrum." Though he observes that blacks make up 19 percent of the armed forces, compared to 13 percent of the population, Latinas/os, he misinforms us, are underrepresented in the military. To support his argument, he points out that Latinas/os make up 11 percent of the armed forces, compared to 13.3 percent of the population. Regardless of the merits of Fick's arguments, his "socio-economic" analysis is faulty (I show why shortly) but publishable, partly because Fick has an educational and class background that allows him media access. He graduated from Dartmouth, one of the most selective and expensive liberal arts universities in the United States, and now he can exercise his privilege by having some control over the discourse of honor, citizenship, military service, and race.

Fick's is a common defense of voluntarism that in the same breath romanticizes the civic attributes of the citizen-soldier while highlighting the liberal value of choice. Although this position may be correct in imagining that choice is at play in the enlistment of people like Fick, to whom privilege lends choice, in America, choices are stratified. Because of this, the armed forces have mostly been the "choice" of poor whites, racial and ethnic minorities, and increasingly, noncitizens. Let us briefly consider data on Latinas/os in the military. Given the growth of the Latino population, the Department of Defense is becoming more interested in learning to target Latina/o recruits (Hattiangadi, Lee, and Quester 2004). This includes noncitizen Latinas/os, who, according to the 2000 census, numbered 10.2 million. Already Latinas/os account for 11 percent of the armed forces in general, but they compose 13.6 percent of the Marines (the most risky of the branches) and 17.7 percent of all personnel that handle weapons. Considering that Latinas/os amount only to 9.6 percent of the U.S. population with the educational and legal credentials to enlist (only citizens and green-card holders with high school diplomas can serve), it is clear that Latinas/os are overrepresented in the armed forces in general and hugely overrepresented in risk positions. In fact, since 2000, Latinas/os have exceeded the proportion of black recruits in the Marines (Hattiangadi, Lee, and Quester 2004, 19). This trend seems likely to continue if we consider that according to a report by the CNA Corporation (a nonprofit research organization used by the Department of Defense to investigate a variety of issues in the military), Latinas/os have the highest active-duty propensity of any racial group or ethnicity. That is, Latinas/os are more likely to see enlistment as attractive than others: "For example, male high school senior propensities were 44 percent for Hispanics, 36 percent for blacks, and 24 percent for whites. For male high school graduates who had not gone on to college, propensities were 21 percent for Hispanics, 18 percent for blacks, and 7 percent for whites" (ibid., 20). Those who were more likely to enlist cited money for education and job training as the two most important reasons to enlist. Aware of these motivations, recruiters aggressively target Latino communities, and the Army's advertising, in a concerted effort to maintain the number of military enlistees, does the same (Moniz 1999; Leyva 2003). Duty propensity numbers are hardly surprising considering the poverty levels among Latinas/os in comparison to the poverty levels among whites. According to the U.S. Census, in 2000, 22.8 percent of Latinas/os and 8 percent of whites lived under the poverty line. Although it is not my intention to make a sociological correlation between poverty and duty propensity, it is hard not to notice the following: duty propensity for Latino males who do not go to college is 21 percent. The poverty level among Latinas/os is 22.8 percent. Duty propensity for white males who do not go to college is 7 percent. The poverty level among whites is 8 percent. The similarity in both sets of numbers opens the possibility for arguing that duty propensity is directly proportional to poverty levels. Finally, green-card holders can serve in the military and currently account for 2.6 percent of the armed forces, numbering sixty-five hundred in the Marines (Hattiangadi, Lee, and Quester 2004, 16).

These data force us to consider the fact that the armed forces are structured in a racialized and classed fashion and that the notion of a volunteer army is, at best, a lazy idea, if not an outright fantasy. This notion fails to acknowledge the social, economic, and cultural pressures that the poor and nonwhites disproportionately face and that make palatable the risks of service. In light of this, it is important to reconsider the validity of the belief in the United States' volunteer army. The idea of voluntarism is a

cornerstone of illiberalism in America that fools most people into believing that we have an army of choice; it propagates the idea of the citizen-
soldier while hiding the racist and classist way in which such ideology
operates. As it stands, the "majority" is able to obscure the racialization
of military service, much in the same way that it has been able to make
granting of naturalization to dead Latinas/os seem perfectly logical. In
both cases, citizenship and naturalization are used as tools for governance
embedded in the ongoing project of securing the state.

The actions of these noncitizens before their deaths did not amount
to consent to becoming American citizens. This lack of consent, I argue,
should be relevant to Latinas/os because of our history in this nation as
colonial subjects and, later, as subjects of immigration forced by asym-
metrical capitalistic relations to exist between the nation's center and
its periphery. Questioning the uses of citizenship and naturalization regarding Latinas/os also forces us to understand the gap existing between
citizenship as an idealized political category deployed within liberalism
to justify the state and the historical applications of citizenship law and
its effects on Latina/o lives. Moreover, this gap is salient for Latinas/os
because it shapes what Raymond Rocco calls the "articulation between
[Latina/o] communities and the major institutions of power" (2002, 7), in
this case, the armed forces and Congress.

As important as is detailing the legal and political processes surrounding the granting of posthumous citizenship, these political and legal
events gained popular recognition and legitimacy because of the way they
were mediated. In the following section, I examine the news coverage of
these issues and find that majoritarian news media relied on problematic
characterizations of the soldiers' lives, a discursive tactic that illustrates
synchronic and diachronic evidence of coloniality in discourse.

Mediating War and Death

The reporting of the noncitizen Latino soldiers killed in Iraq coincided
with the beginning of the war, and their heavy mediation was a structural push for consensus. The deaths became politically profitable when
Congress introduced new bills that would grant the deceased soldiers
posthumous citizenship.[18] The press loved this move by Congress and reported extensively and positively on it, praising the quick passage of the
bills in both the Senate and the House. In less than three weeks (Gutiérrez was killed on March 21, and the bills were approved on April 10), the

deceased soldiers had become American heroes. In this section, I want first to analyze the mainstream coverage that helped define these events to the American people and second to analyze these congressional moves as performances of gender and nationalism. Both mainstream news coverage and the performance of Congress had a similar political and discursive basis, and together, these institutions worked toward securing support for the invasion of Iraq.

An analysis of news reports and speeches by politicians quickly reveals patterns worth mentioning that shed light on the type of political capital that the events could yield. Take Senator Miller, who stated, "These noncitizen soldiers have given the ultimate sacrifice to their adopted country, and we are free today because of their bravery and their loyalty" (qtd. in Fagan 2003). Or consider Vernardette Ramirez Broyles, who stated in the *Atlanta Journal-Constitution* (2003), "Many were moved to tears by Diego's earnest vitality, by his father's humble dignity and, most of all, by the fact that this young man gave his life for a country of which he had only dreamed of becoming a citizen." Besides giving their lives for the nation, these Latinas/os are examples of patriotism and citizenship. As Michael Buchelew (2003) wrote, "When I think of patriotism, I think of people who don't tell us how patriotic they are. They just do it without trying to shove it in our faces as some sort of bragging-rights contest. People such as Diego Rincon. . . . If everybody lived up to their brand of patriotism, I think the United States would be a better place." Similarly, Rick Harrivell (2003) described Rincon in patriotic terms: "You understood that being an American is a matter of the heart; and you [Rincon], our friend, our brother and our son, had an American's heart when you died. You died not in vain, but with courage and commitment and honor. As an American." Taken as a whole, the texts that appeared in the wake of these soldiers' deaths constructed a metanarrative of nationalism that communicated the following: these noncitizen Latinas/os have shown their "love" for their "adopted country" by "serving" the armed forces and "sacrificing" their lives for our "freedom" and for the "nation." Moreover, others should learn from these soldiers, for they have taught us the hard lesson that citizenship means service and sacrifice. Taken as a whole, these mediated texts were also invested in giving meaning to the deaths of these Latinas/os in ways that could preserve the nation and make American citizens the beneficiaries of the discourse surrounding their deaths.

Nationalism here works as a space of identification where personal narratives mediate identity and where biographies (as well as eulogies)

become perfect vehicles for enumerating the characteristics of the national and ideal citizen. Within this framework, the preferred narrative
used to describe U.S. subjects is not unusual; it replicates those narratives used to describe almost every killed soldier, regardless of national
origin, race, or gender. What is particular to the Latino cases is the fact
that the nationalistic narrative severely simplified the complexity of the
immigrant experience with regard to nation and the particularity of these
soldiers' lives, which unfolded both abroad and in America.

This simplification of social events and realities, a requirement of the
linguistic market, allows for the use of immigrant voices for radical purposes, such as support of the war. It is thus not surprising that two of the
most conservative voices that wrote about these Latinas/os used their stories to shame pro-peace American citizens. M. D. Harmon (*Portland Press
Herald*, April 7, 2003), after a long argument against those who opposed
the war, ends his piece as follows: "It is not strange that the first two casualties in Gulf War II were foreigners serving in the Marines who hoped to
secure their citizenship by their service. They have it now, and it is no less
honorable for being posthumous. Indeed, such men honor us. Perhaps we
will even begin to comprehend 'honor' again, as well." Ramirez Broyles
(2003) emphatically argued that Rincon "has put to shame many native-
born U.S. citizens," especially those who have opposed the war and used
their rights against the nation. Such uses of immigrant experiences contradict Latino reality. According to 2003 polls before the war, 51 percent of
foreign-born Latinas/os opposed the war in Iraq without the support of
the UN. By 2004, in California, 69 percent of Latinas/os opposed the war
(Field Research Corporation 2004).

Besides the radical uses of Latino experience, the simplification of
these soldiers' lives to a narrative of military heroics constituted a discursive space constructed at the expense of silencing critical aspects of
the immigrant experience. For instance, even in the instances when reporters and politicians addressed the lives of poverty and struggle that
these immigrants had to endure, this address reconstituted the fantasy of
America as an immigrant nation where everyone has a chance at fulfilling
the American dream.[19] The *San Diego Union-Tribune* published on the
Opinion page one such example:

> Consider Jose Gutierrez [*sic*], one of the Marines from San Diego who
> died in combat in the first days of the fighting. A 22-year-old lance cor-
> poral, Gutierrez was assigned to the 1st Marine Division headquartered

at Camp Pendleton. Like many others in San Diego's large Latino population, Gutierrez was penniless when he arrived here from Guatemala
as a teenager. For him, the military provided an opportunity for a better life—and an opportunity to serve his newfound country. The public
memorial service for him will be only one of several planned in Southern California to pay tribute to the sacrifices of local service personnel.
(War's bitter taste 2003)

The reader learns Gutiérrez's age, his origin, and his economic situation.
More important, the reader learns that the military was the institutional
vehicle for him to reach "a better life." Here, the military stands for the
American dream, allowing Gutiérrez to express his desire to achieve
the "dream" while "serving" his "newfound" country. Nowhere does the
reader learn that Gutiérrez grew up as an orphan, that he was raised in
several foster homes, and that it is more likely that his state of economic
and racial destitution forced him into the military, killing him at the age
of twenty-two.

Gutiérrez's brief biography is not unique, nor is the way the military
was depicted in these narratives as a savior institution. According to
Farah Stockman (*Boston Globe*, April 6, 2003), for Gutiérrez, "the military was a way to gain respect and to show gratitude to the United States."
Even Amy Goldstein and Sylvia Moreno (*Washington Post*, April 7, 2003),
who have the distinction of writing one of the most comprehensive pieces
on the matter, write of the soldiers, "As they explained it to their families,
the attraction is a blend of wanderlust, economic aspirations and adop-
tive patriotism. . . . This cadre of immigrants, now missing or dead, talked
of an indelible pride in the armed services, in the nation's elemental values." Though Goldstein and Moreno more critically analyze the economic
and patriotic factors that contribute to a decision to enlist and provide
lengthier biographies of the soldiers, they retain the basic metanarrative
of nationalism that flattens the diverse and complex immigrant experience into an ethnocentric fantasy in which the nation (the military here
serves metonymically as the nation) is the object of devotion, well deserving of the sacrifice of all its subjects.

Judging by the frequency of this ethnocentric fantasy (practically every
news item that presented a biography of one of the soldiers presented a
version of this ideological metanarrative), it rang true with many Americans. In this fantasy, Latino immigrants seek the armed forces for subjective reasons, to "gain respect and to show gratitude," or for "wanderlust,"

"patriotism," and "pride." Even when economic need is insinuated, it is framed as a subjective need or "aspiration."

To function, these narratives must strip away important parts of the soldiers' histories and fit biographical data to a nationalistic script. This script is burdened with an intrinsic paradox of nation: as Benedict Anderson (1991) suggests, while the nation is built on the idea of a horizontal community, society is not. In America, although the semantic structure of the nation has always pushed forward the idea of equality, foundational economic and political structures have deferred this reality from existing.

This paradox has definite textual characteristics that, I argue, shed light on the type of "ideal citizen" Latinas/os can play in the American narrative of nation today. According to Lauren Berlant, simplifying the understanding of citizenship has a structural function, which is to make citizenship usable for nationalism. Berlant's (1997) work provides a psychoanalytic and feminist approach to citizenship amenable to theorizing gender, sexual, and racial marginalities in the national semiotic landscape. She sees citizenship as a legal and cultural category that in the United States has been used to construct a national identity that can help the process of governance. Her scathing critique of contemporary America is based on the understanding that our "knowledge cultures," which include mass media, have constructed mythologies of citizenship in which the ideal citizen is often depicted as what she calls the "infantile citizen." This discursive and narrative construct, which Berlant finds in popular films such as *Mr. Smith Goes to Washington* and television shows such as *The Simpsons*, teaches the viewer to embrace a way of being civic that is potentially prejudicial to society. Berlant notices that this infantile citizen, devoid of history and opposed to critical engagement with reality, is a common figure of political writing in U.S. history:

> The infantile citizen of the United States has appeared in political writing about the nation at least since Tocqueville wrote, in *Democracy in America*, that while citizens should be encouraged to love the nation the way they do their families and their fathers, democracies can also produce a special form of tyranny that makes citizens like children, infantilized, passive, and overdependent on the "immense tutelary power" of the state. (1997, 27)

The infantile citizen is a popular representation of civics for it allows individuals to define their affective and intellectual relationship to the nation in terms of simplistic nationalism, mainstream social identity, and normalized behavior, much in the same way that the metanarrative of citizenship constructed the dead Latino soldiers as ideal patriotic citizens. Let us remember that most media described the deceased as Latino and American heroes who "sacrificed" their lives for their adopted nation. And similar to the way that most reporters and legislators admired these soldiers, Berlant notices that "adult citizens" nostalgically admire infantile citizenship, for it reminds them of a time when they were also "'unknowing' and believed in the capacity of the nation to be practically utopian" (1997, 29). While the reality of the nation may challenge any utopian vision of the present or of history, the infantile citizen is one who still believes, regardless of life experiences that should have taught him or her better. In the case of the Latino soldiers, these experiences include living as members of an economically challenged and culturally marginalized racial minority. Nevertheless, these immigrants are narrativized as embracing patriotism and naively trusting in the metanarratives of development, justice, and modernity advertised in political discourse and the national imaginary. The type of citizen produced by such narratives is no longer Latino or immigrant, for he or she is without history or a critical understanding of reality; the infantile citizen is moved only by emotion and intellectual simplicity.

Berlant identifies infantile citizenship in popular narratives; however, narratives about immigrants play a similar role in American society, for, as Berlant reminds us, they help constitute nationalism by providing an opportunity for mainstream America, in its classed, gendered, and racialized constitution, to gaze at a romantic rendition of the American myth. In this myth, immigrants come to the United States seeking and finding opportunities; this makes them love the nation and renders them willing to make the "ultimate sacrifice" for it. Commenting on similar uses of the immigrant experience for a nationalist agenda, Berlant writes, "immigrant discourse is a central technology for the reproduction of patriotic nationalism . . . because the immigrant is defined as *someone who desires America*" (1997, 195). As Berlant suggests, infantile citizenship also fosters consensus, because it is a model of citizenship that limits our critical engagement with reality and history, although this happens, in our case, at the expense of publicly discussing the immigrant experience as one of destitution.

I argue that the media's systematic simplifications and naive biographies of the soldiers' lives are renditions of the narrative of the infantile citizen, and this fact helps explain the interpretive and historiographical consensus reached thanks to their deployment. In the instances of discourse I have analyzed, the Latinas/os were treated like "ideal citizens" and as "adopted" children of the nation. Harrivell, quoted earlier, describes Rincon as "our brother" who "had an American's heart." New York City mayor Michael Bloomberg spoke of Marine Staff Sergeant Tejeda, a Dominican citizen who also died in Iraq, as giving his life "for his adopted nation" (Bloomberg, at funeral, praises marine sergeant 2003). Tejeda and the other noncitizens, construed as adopted children, become exemplars because of their behavior but also because they can help the nation "raise" the nation's real children. Ramirez Broyles (2003) brings up this more dramatic description of the American family when she writes that Rincon "has put to shame many native-born U.S. citizens. Like the spoiled offspring of parents who have given them too much and demanded too little in return, some Americans used their First Amendment rights to express contempt for our leaders and our country during the war in Iraq."

The infantilization of these Latinas/os explains the structuring of the narratives, biographies, and discourses regarding these soldiers. More explicitly, it explains why the life histories of the noncitizen soldiers were stripped of all critical content and were fitted into narratives of nationalism, in which an ethnocentric fantasy of the nation as the object of love and devotion was central. The sharing of this ethnocentric fantasy built a sphere of intimacy, an imagined community based on feeling, that was mediated by narratives of Latino immigrants as ideal objects to be gazed at and admired. Functioning as objects of admiration, the Latinas/os provided a service to the nation that far exceeded their military service and their sacrificial deaths. They became "heroes" in a narrative of patriotism and "others" that could be gazed at from afar; they are adopted children born out of displacement, whose destitution and uprooting must be hidden, just one more secret that the family must keep quiet in order to remain united.

To make matters worse, these particularly troubling mediations had the effect of legitimizing the nonconsensual naturalization of the soldiers. This effect painfully echoes the beginning of Latino history in the United States, which is characterized by the imposition of citizenship. The two most obvious cases, and the ones that underscore the legal or illegal status of most Latinas/os in America, are the histories of Mexicans and Puerto Ricans, who first became American citizens via U.S. imperial expansion.

Mexicans were "assimilated" into the American polis during the war of 1846–1848 after Mexico was forced to sign the Treaty of Guadalupe Hidalgo. This treaty also gave U.S. citizenship to everyone living in the territories of New Mexico, Nevada, Colorado, California, Arizona, and Texas.

Puerto Rico was annexed by the United States in 1898. Drawing on arguments about the racial and educational composition of Puerto Ricans, the U.S. government denied American citizenship to Puerto Ricans, giving them Puerto Rican citizenship in 1900. This did not mean that Puerto Rico was independent; it was more a reflection of the conflicting ideas that the U.S. government had regarding these new subjects (Nieto-Phillips 1999, 58–64). In 1909, President Theodore Roosevelt ran on a platform that included the proposal of giving Puerto Ricans American citizenship. This only spurred new debates about the racial and educational character of Puerto Ricans. Representative Atterson Walden Rucker of Colorado stated, "The English language was scarcely known in the island [in 1898], and . . . 87 percent of the million people could neither read nor write their own language; . . . and it can be furthermore fairly said that 60 percent of these native voters are colored people" (qtd. in Nieto-Phillips 1999, 63). Echoing debates regarding Mexicans in the Southwest, Congress assessed the right of Puerto Ricans to become citizens on the basis of race and culture. Citizenship was again denied. In 1917, President Woodrow Wilson and Congress made the decision to naturalize Puerto Ricans through the Jones Act, quickly drafting sixty thousand to fight on the European front. As many Puerto Ricans had feared, the citizenship they got was a second-class citizenship that did not allow them to participate in federal politics or to receive the economic benefits of statehood (Nieto-Phillips 1999, 64; De Genova and Ramos-Zayas 2003, 8).

The cases of Mexicans and Puerto Ricans shed light on the historical impact of citizenship law on Latina/o communities, particularly when related to naturalization and consent. Naturalization cannot be seen as simply a privilege or an honor. Consent is important, particularly for Latinas/os, many of whom choose not to become citizens, not to enter into the contract, even though they may qualify. What is more, when imposed, as the history of American imperialism shows, naturalization is a more complex process. It does not only signal the accessing of citizenship rights; in fact, in the cases reviewed, most political rights are not available to the naturalized citizen for a long time. Without irony, I must remark that the same was true for the Iraq War soldiers who received posthumous citizenship. Moreover, in the cases of Mexicans and Puerto Ricans, imposed naturalization was part of processes of territorial, economic, and labor appropriations by the racial, cultural, and class majorities. Again, without irony, I must remark the obvious. The U.S. government, as well as the great majority of Americans (the fraternity of raced and classed individuals), have appropriated not only the physical bodies of these noncitizens, their lives, but also their cultural memories, which are now recast in a national history structured by race, gender, and class in which Latino immigrants are often defined as opposite from the economic and cultural ideals of the ethno-racially white majority. Imposed naturalization is an illiberal practice of citizenship that, I argue, should be rejected by Latinas/os.[20]

The discourse that gives way to the equation "immigrant = infantile citizen" is rooted in the same system of coloniality that has engendered citizenship laws and enlistment practices. This discourse engenders and energizes ethnocentric fantasies that occlude actual legal and enlistment practices, which can then be reproduced generation after generation without political fallout. As I argued earlier, the Latino soldiers did not consent to citizenship, and the assumption of consent could only be supported by an ethnocentric fantasy.

The Discourse of Nationalism and Administration

The metanarratives of nationalism and the ethnocentric fantasy are bound together and produce truths that hail an imagined community of definite racial and political filiations. In this section, I address this community and the urgency of its actions, including instances of speech, which is social practice (Bourdieu 1991, 37), and governance, particularly legislative practices. Urgency of action, particularly in acts of institutions, hint at the particular type of performance that Congress may use to reconstitute its power. By urgency I mean to suggest an organization of priorities that give individuals immediate courses of action. Besides establishing priorities, urgency relates to self-definition because things become urgent when their absence is perceived to challenge self-understanding. In this case, Congress's performance of the discourses of nationalism and citizenship involved "looking at" Latinas/os; it was highly public; it was discussed in local and national media by highly ranked officials; and it had the goal of creating law. The central characters of this performance were members of Congress who, with little or no direct pressure from publics or activists, volunteered to sponsor bills that would change immigration law. This is historically extraordinary, as the rest of this book demonstrates. But these were extraordinary times, and Americans' self-understanding was challenged by these unusual events. That the first soldier killed in battle was Gutiérrez was perhaps a historical improbability, but it became a social fact and a news item. The actions that ensued after his death can be read as attempts to restabilize America's identity by following discursive and procedural tactics that had the effect of regaining the virility of American nationalism while reconstituting racial differences.

Leo Braudy has pointed out that the citizen and the soldier are mutually constituted historical constructs, particularly relevant during the republican revolutions of the eighteenth and nineteenth centuries but also meaningful today, as our cases show (2003, 246–255). The idea of the citizen-soldier proposed that military masculinity, which emphasized self-sacrifice and responsibility to the nation, could serve as a general model for citizenship. Beyond the transference of values from soldiering to civics, the citizen-soldier model also served as an early model for community. Much in the way soldiers established a fraternity based on common enemies and the necessity to survive, early citizenship was made possible by the need to form coalitions against designated racial others. Class differences between the wealthy aristocracy and the rest of the white population in eighteenth-century America, for instance, were "negotiated" so that the lower and middle white classes would help the aristocracy to police and subdue native and black communities and their ongoing insurrections. These negotiations were complex and required the constitution, on the one hand, of the discourses of racism and, on the other, of the structuring of ideas of whiteness, nationality, and citizenship that could serve as a basis for community.

Dana Nelson (1998) observes that establishing a fraternity of citizens during the eighteenth and nineteenth centuries was quite challenging. Individuals, in this case, white men, had to interact as citizens and as competitors and members of different classes. In spite of the antagonistic nature of these interactions, they constructed a community centered mostly on the abstract idea of nation. As extraordinary as nationalism's ability to unite individuals under the single aegis of the nation is, it is equally remarkable that this fraternity was built between commercial, political, and class competitors, as well as between ethnic others (Dutch, British, Scottish, etc.). These differences, Nelson posits, were sublimated in the category of "white manhood," which became coterminous in early America with citizenship. White manhood was a useful category for unity, for it abstracted men from their local specificities and bound them to a general identity that could foster capitalism. Other benefits accrued in whiteness. Because of its abstraction and placelessness, whiteness was the perfect invisible standpoint from which to wield "objectivity," "reason," and "justice," central elements in the idealized view of democracy. Whiteness, a placeless category of which members have no spontaneous awareness, became associated with valuefree, objective, and equitable rationality and government: the ideal Law. "When white, there is no sense of belonging to a specific group, so the group itself always remains outside the frame of reference, is never referred to as a group" (Nelson 1998, 10).

The abstract category of white manhood secured fraternity when its members turned their warring, legislative, and epistemological impulses toward others. By fighting racial others (chiefly natives, blacks, and Mexicans), controlling sexual others (through sciences such as gynecology and psychology), and producing institutions for administering and knowing others, the community of white men found kinship and belonging (Nelson 1998, 17). Nelson defines "altero-referentiality" as the process of looking at the Other in order to establish fraternity with people who occupy the same standpoint, in this case white men. Military (and terrorist) campaigns, popular culture, administration, and scientific enterprises (ethnology and gynecology) converged in the goal of government to produce a community of equals, with enough room for class, gender, and racial exploitation. Altero-referentiality is then a historical manifestation of a power schema invested in carving out locations from which it is possible to "truthfully" legitimate the stratification of races and sexes.

Although Nelson only briefly discusses recent examples of alteroreferentiality, there are good reasons to believe that her basic observations are applicable to our analysis, particularly when we consider the permanence of the racial and sexual systems that give meaning and structure to Congress. Briefly, I want to bring to your attention the elements of our case that are homologous to Nelson's insights and that can help bridge the distance between our case and her ideas: masculinity and race.

An easy lesson to be learned from the popularity of war genres in America is that the soldier is one of the preferred ways of imagining citizenship. Since the invasion of Afghanistan and Iraq, and thanks to our media system, this preference has become hegemonic and has reenergized the link between nationalism and masculinity. In times of war, the fantasy of nationalism relies on a process of narrative identification whereby the actions of soldiers are understood as actions of the community of citizens.

In the grammar of nation, the soldier becomes a synecdoche that stands for the fraternity of citizens, who fancy themselves heroic, patriotic, and courageous through the sinister identification with the soldier. In the cases we are examining, this synecdoche is complicated by the legal and ethnic status of the soldiers. Their nationality and race hinders easy identification unless the granting of posthumous citizenship is placed within the narrative. This narrative tactic was widely used and successful, for people were able to imagine these soldiers "Americans at heart" and true patriots. The other option is unsavory. In the American mythology of citizenship, it would be hard to acknowledge that these Mexicans, Salvadorians, Dominicans, and Puerto Ricans were standing for American citizens; this figure of speech, of course, is too close to the grammar of imperialism, which contradicts the regime of the nation. Beyond that, because the soldier also stands for masculine citizenship, this synecdoche carries gender connotations: what type of manliness can America have if those who are performing its masculinity are foreigners?

To make sense of these questions, I want to point out that masculinity is not a monolithic category. As R. W. Connell reminds us, masculinity exists in a system and a hierarchy that is composed, at the very least, of the following four typologies: hegemonic masculinity, which acts as a cultural ideal that exemplifies all the qualities required to preserve patriarchy; subordinating masculinity, exemplified by homosexual masculinities, which is low in the hierarchy and thus subjugated; complicit masculinity, which is the broadest category and comprises a multitude of styles of being masculine, all of which reconstitute hegemonic cultural ideals of the masculine; lastly, marginalized masculinity, which is exemplified by race and plays the role of reconstituting social hierarchies and of supporting hegemonic masculinities (Connell 1995, 76–81). Given the context of our discussion, it is easy to recognize that most of the Congresspeople and journalists who advocated the posthumous naturalization of the Latino soldiers were enacting complicit masculinities (as they have for the most part since the beginning of the war) that glorified the traits of hegemonic masculinity, presently associated with the military, violence, sacrifice, gun culture, imperialism, oppression, body toughness, and unilateralism. Patriarchy, closely bound here to racial supremacy and imperial design, depends on this glorification, which happened to have Latino noncitizens at its center.

What makes complicit the writings and words of politicians and journalists is the way a racial patriarchy is reconstituted through textuality and institutional actions. For instance, reporting on Rincon's burial, Nora Achrati, a woman and the performer of complicit masculinity, writes in the *Atlanta Journal-Constitution* (April 11, 2003), "[Rincon's] brother, Fabian, told the 500 mourners packed into the Conyers Seventh-day Adventist Church that the suicide bomber was a 'coward' who should 'burn in hell for what he did.'" At a time of high emotion and pain, Achrati chooses to use Fabian Rincon's gendered description of the enemy ("coward") to inform readers of the hierarchy of masculinity that she values, and with the religious inflection, she also communicates the hierarchy of peoples that she values. Although this example may be subtle, practically every report and political speech on these men highlighted their affiliation to hegemonic masculinity by way of their military behavior, their honorable lives, their sacrifice, their willingness to sacrifice, and their toughness.

But do not think that because Latinas/os were used to reconstitute hegemonic masculinity these men were invited into the hegemonic winners' circle. They were "tools" that conveyed nationalistic values, while sustaining racial and economic hierarchies. Valerie Alvord, writing for *USA Today* (April 9, 2003) exemplifies this when she writes,

> Some of the families of these servicemen killed in the war in Iraq want them buried as citizens, which they can become if their families apply for it. "My son is dead, and I'm broken inside," says Jorge Rincon of Conyers, Ga. His son, Army Pfc. Diego Rincon, came to the USA from Colombia as a youngster. He was killed March 29 in a suicide bombing attack. His funeral is Thursday.
>
> "The only thing that keeps me going now is to make sure that he's buried as an American," says Rincon. "That will be my dream come true." Other families feel the same and are taking advantage of a presidential order last year that allows relatives of slain troops to apply for posthumous citizenship. The gesture carries no additional financial benefits for surviving relatives.

Notice Alvord's quick dismissal of Rincon's father's state of despair ("I'm broken inside") in exchange for the ethnocentric fantasy in which citizenship for his slain son is the father's "dream." She continues this bizarre representation of absolute pain (through the lens of infantile citizenship) by suggesting that other families have the same dream, a dream that comes without social and economic benefits. It is an altruistic dream that places the immigrants as naive givers and not as structurally dispossessed. In addition, Alvord portrays these Latino families as looking forward to "taking advantage" of a government decree, thereby shifting attention away from the pain these families are enduring and away from the fact that, to many people including myself, the government seems responsible for taking advantage of social and class disparities to enlist these men and place them in the line of fire. Later Alvord writes, "Patriotism is sustaining Jorge Rincon." Again, in a reversal, the institutional cause for Rincon's death is portrayed as savior and source of consolatory feelings. In this, as in other writings, hegemonic masculinity (e.g., patriotism, the presidency, the army, the nation's values) is a powerful benefactor, and the Latino soldiers and their immigrant families benefit from masculinity's gracious generosity.

In addition to the textual actions that rendered visible a system of masculinities, other evidence hints at the centrality of masculinity in the events that followed the Latinas/os' deaths. I see the frenzied discursive and legislative activity of the media and Congress as an attempt to maintain what Nelson calls America's National Manhood. Consider the way politicians performed their duties in this instance: they publicly led; they quickly brought justice; they aggressively created laws; they caringly protected the weak (immigrants); they effectively administered; they governed. Each instance marks a reassertion of Congress's power to make objective meaning out of "history" and to assert control over peoples and signification. An exercise of manly governance, Congress's actions, with the help of the media, were also able to construct masculine-citizen fraternity by hailing a racialized community of citizens and inviting them to look, to gaze at these noncitizens' actions. Considering that black and foreign-born Latino populations opposed the war (Field Research Corporation 2003), I see the hail of Congress as a hail to whiteness, its base of support, and a hail for self-identification and imperialistic self-adulation. Notice the curious phrasing of the praise of Latino soldier Tejeda by Steve Farquason (USCIS): "We're honored to be able to recognize the sacrifice of your son and tell you how proud you should be of him" (Santos 2003). Harmon (2003) also wrote about Rincon, Gutiérrez, and Garibay, "Such men honor us." Narcissistically, the linguistic tropes used by these speakers perform a reversal where not only does the granting of posthumous citizenship honor the soldiers, but the soldiers' sacrifice also honors the fraternity of citizens. Placed against the background of the ethnocentric fantasy discussed earlier, this traditional way of talking about soldiers becomes an instance of reversal that must be understood within the fantasy of nationalism and whiteness. This is not far from the fantasies of slaveholders who imagined that the fact that slaves sang meant that they were happy. Notice that the fantasy does not work without the belief that the Latinas/os enlisted for love of the nation.

If the posthumous naturalization of Latino soldiers served to give manliness back to the nation, to remedy the crisis of American masculinity, and to create a fraternity of citizens, the racial connotations of these cases solidify the idea that altero-referentiality was at play. On the legislative side, you have a community composed of mostly white males producing legislation for nonwhites. Though the House currently has a small minority of nonwhite and nonmale representatives (roughly 15 percent), the Senate has traditionally been a white domain. Only five African Americans, five Latinas/os, five Asian Americans, and three Native Americans have ever served in the Senate's two-century-plus history. Currently, the Senate has only two Latinas/os (who were not yet elected when these events happened), one black member (who was not yet elected when these events happened), and fourteen women (U.S. Senate 2012). The practically monoracial (and monosexual) composition of this legislative enclave contrasts with the multiracial composition of the armed forces, in which whites are slightly underrepresented in combat positions and blacks and Latinas/os are, logically, overrepresented.[21] The contrast between the racial composition of these institutions reproduces the American racial hierarchy, with whites (the Senate, the executive branch, and the Supreme Court) at the top and in control of the discourses associated with race and citizenship. From this perspective, the politicians' quick praise of the valor of Garibay, Rincon, and Gutiérrez become racialized administrative actions designed to control by rewarding sacrifice without questioning current racial hierarchies of citizenship and military service.

The way in which legislative and media communities came together to honor these dead soldiers by giving them citizenship can be seen as altero-referential processes when analyzed in relationship to publicity, administration, and control. For, as heartwarming as it is to hear the praise that such important citizens gave to these immigrants, it is important to recognize the role that Congress and the mainstream media played in validating the invasion of Iraq and reproducing American militarism. Such bellicose patriotism re-creates the army's need for more military personnel and compels army recruiters to actively seek the enlistment of noncitizens, poor whites, and racial minorities.

Consent and Voluntarism Revisited

Citizenship's consistent role in American politics is governance. Citizenship has been a central part of the legal and rhetorical arsenal used by hegemonic racial, economic, and political classes to reconstitute the grounds of their domestic and foreign dominance. The granting of posthumous citizenship to noncitizen Latinas/os killed during combat in Iraq reveals the hegemonic cultural impetus to use citizenship as governance. On the one hand, this impetus elides the fact that naturalization was given without the individuals' consent, and on the other, it serves to obscure, yet again, the way in which the armed forces are structured as a racialized and classed institution. Both practices contradict liberal ideas of governance. Nonconsensual naturalization goes against the notion that, in a liberal state, naturalization is a contract that secures the legitimization of the relationship of governor and subject. The rhetoric surrounding these cases also demonstrates that military practices presented to the American people as liberal (the idea of the "volunteer" army) actually rely on persistent economic, cultural, and educational stratifications.

The power of liberalism as a political theory (or system) depends on how governments under its rubric distribute rights and responsibilities. Ideally, these rights and responsibilities ought to be equal for all citizens. Not surprisingly, liberalism can be a radical and powerful force against social injustices. As it exists in American society, it can also be the basis for further oppression and inequality. The U.S. volunteer army illustrates the contradictions of liberalism. Sought out by Latinas/os as an avenue toward education, prosperity, and social respect, the U.S. armed forces do require a certain amount of enlistee consent. But the armed forces also falsely legitimize liberalism by propagating the fantasy that, because the U.S. military is composed of volunteers, it *equally* doles out the civic responsibility to defend the nation. The impossible contradiction behind the ideal of the liberal, voluntary army is that enlistment can be at once self-serving (in the Latino cases, politicians and news people believed that the soldiers sought citizenship) and civic minded (the Latinas/os "loved" the nation). The Latino soldiers who return to the nation as citizens and heroes in body bags symbolize the limits of liberalism in America; they demonstrate how the articulation of ethnicity and militarism are made possible by the contradictions of liberalism.

In light of the history of race and militarism in America, I have argued here that giving posthumous citizenship to these Latinas/os is another way of giving legal form to illiberalism. For, as a category for the living, with consent, citizenship is a portfolio of rights and an invitation to fraternity; as a category for the dead, citizenship is reduced to a cultural frame for memory, an invitation to self-centeredness. I say this because our traditional narratives of heroism have a racial inertia that will likely erase these Latinas/os from memory, much in the same way that it erased the patriotic service of noncitizen Native Americans, Chinese, Mexicans, Puerto Ricans, blacks, and Filipinos. Briefly, Congress and mainstream news praised these soldiers' service, and with this praise, they added support to the invasion of Iraq and recentered militarism in immigrant life. The seventy-fifth annual League of United Latin American Citizens (LULAC) national convention was held in San Antonio, Texas, from July 6 to 11, 2004. In a surreal fashion, like any other year, the convention was teeming with armed forces members, representing all branches of the military, in full recruiting mode.

Conclusion: The Ethics of Nation

Be assured, fellow citizens, that in a democracy it is the laws
that guard the person of the citizen and the constitution of the
state, whereas the despot and the oligarch find their protection
in suspicion and in armed guards. Men, therefore, who administer an oligarchy, or any government based upon inequality,
must be on their guard against those who attempt revolution by
the law of force; but you, who have a government based upon
equality and law, must guard against those whose words violate
the laws or whose lives have defied them; for then only will you
be strong, when you cherish the laws, and when the revolutionary attempts of lawless men shall have ceased.
—Aeschines, *Against Timarchus*, 346 BC

Timarchus was unfortunate. He, with Demosthenes, had accused Aeschines of treason but underestimated Aeschines's viciousness. In one of
the most famous speeches by an Athenian citizen, Aeschines destroyed
Timarchus's character and proved that Timarchus's youthful indiscre-
tions had broken the law and thus that Timarchus no longer had legal
standing. He was sentenced to *atimia*, a sort of political excommunication
common in classical Athens that foreclosed Timarchus's ability to ever
defend himself. Some historians believe he hanged himself immediately.
But what happened, in a sense, does not matter, for Timarchus's voice was
never again found in the public record. Ironically, Demosthenes, another
equally skillful orator, later showed Aeschines to be a traitor, but this was
too late for Timarchus. So, if in the epigraph Aeschines sounds like a
poster child for democracy and the rule of law, his contextualized speech
helps me illustrate how a legal oligarchy uses the law as effectively as others use the sword and how having a public voice is quite similar to having

citizenship standing. The epigraph also shows that, in a democracy, the discourse of law sharpens the state's mighty sword.

Starting this conclusion with an example from Athens is not meant simply to find similarities between the present and the past but to reiterate, as I have done from the beginning of this book, that citizenship excess is at the very roots of our contemporary political imaginary. In the name of democracy and equality, powerful Athenians wielded citizenship as a weapon designed to defend a contingently defined polis. Some of this weapon's most exacting attributes were meant to silence a person, as in Timarchus, or a community, as in the plethora of residents of Athens who did not have legal standing or voice. Although Aeschines's victory was temporary, he left a profound imprint on the liberal democratic imaginary. He taught us that to be a citizen is to have a voice that can be heard without prejudice, and that this voice can only exist in the precious little space that the law decides.

So much is assumed when we talk about the public sphere, so much that we forget that it is not the voice's relation to sound or reason's relation to intellect that determines the ability to deliberate. Prior to deliberation is the law and, in the contemporary mediated public sphere, policy. These two highly prescriptive systems channel social forces and normalize practices that have two significant effects on Latinas/os. First, law and policy help determine what aspects of reality will be part of the legal and political apparatus and which will be part of the market. Spanish illustrates this point. Although Spanish becomes part of legal and policy codifications in complex ways, increasingly, the regulation of Spanish in media policy, bilingual education, and political systems (English-only prescriptions in law and policy) shows how the English-speaking majority uses law and policy to limit the political capacity of Spanish as a language (media ownership policies), even if some of its economic capacities are given free rein. Although Latinas/os are not the only Spanish-speaking U.S. residents, limiting the political capacity of Spanish disproportionately affects Latinas/os.

Second, law and policy impact Latinas/os when they become part of culture and normalize ideas about ethics, reciprocity, and mutuality that have the potential to weaken the ground on which Latinas/os function. When discussing *Ugly Betty*, I showed how this fictional text represents law and policy issues through the culture and normalizes ideas about legality and illegality that negatively affect disenfranchised groups, including Latinas/os and women. It is comedy when Ignacio, Betty's father, interacts with the immigration system and fails to normalize his undocumented status. And it is comedy when, within the fictional world of the magazine where Betty works, labor laws are broken to the advantage of the men and of the wealthy (see chapter 5). Fictional media texts transform systems of legality (immigration) and impunity (labor laws) into normality, setting the basis for intersubjectivity, informally teaching what in the law should be obeyed and what should be dismissed. Other media practices are equally insidious in the way they connect law and policy to cultural expectations. As the Hutto issue illustrates (chapter 3), the journalistic practice of avoiding the use of human rights law terminology within the United States had an impact on immigrants and refugees. Reporters regularly made human rights violations a matter of ethics, disabling the strongest framework for improving the conditions of detention of undocumented families. These majoritarian journalistic practices seem to indicate that human rights violations do not happen in the United States. But they do, and they go unpunished.

The dual impact of law and policy ultimately impacts the type and quality of participation Latinas/os will have in the two segments of the public sphere key to their future. These two segments of the public sphere, organized around Spanish and around English, are the primary spaces for broad democratic deliberation, yet, for different reasons and due to specific institutional characteristics, neither works in the way it should work.

Although the impact of law and policy in the public sphere is particularly important to democratic life, it is only one aspect of citizenship excess. The processes of political capital accumulation and erasure that define this impact are central to hegemony in general, granting a relatively small community of citizens undue influence over law, justice, media, and politics. In the post-9/11 United States, this privileged community often congregated around nativist and ethnonationalist principles, which provided the legal and rhetorical basis for constructing a political culture of us versus them. Their voices were, simply, anti-immigrant and anti-Latina/o, and accordingly, they invested political capital in the suppression, coercion, control, and disciplining of immigrants and Latinas/os. Whatever success nativists and ethnonationalists have had in the past decades is due to media, which amplifies their voices beyond their numeric power and regardless of their rational import. Here, as always, media is a central pillar in the architecture of the liberal state, giving life to the political discourses that animate liberal governmentality. To risk tautology, media mediates and hence constitutes. For this reason, the cultural genetics of media, to continue the life-granting metaphor, becomes part of a political culture eager to respond to the traditional yet nasty allure of ethno-racial patriarchy.

Political capital accumulation and erasure lead to a perversion of power, citizenship excess, that has helped produce legal and political oligarchies ever since Aeschines's time. The citizen, who has a political voice and legal standing, is given historical, political, and legal form through ascription and alterity, and the citizen of excess has exploited this privilege. The citizen has plundered the economic and political worth of the other within and outside the nation, codifying his or her privilege deep into the legal and cultural heart of the state.

Ascription has rendered visible, legible, and legal certain individual and community characteristics and occluded other ones. In the past, ascription in citizenship made race and sex highly visible and gave legal value to both. Today, ascription also makes highly visible nationality and language, characteristics that greatly affect Latinas/os, their voices, and their experiences in politics, law, and media. As in the past, ascription today is grafted onto law and policy, shaping the way cultural and political resources are distributed to Latinas/os. In media, ascription energizes nativist language and politics and is embedded in deregulatory media policies without regard for the role media plays as a cultural space fundamental to the political well-being of Latinas/os. As a result, FCC media-ownership rules have participated in the conglomeration of Spanish-language media, now mostly under the control of Univision and Telemundo, and in the selling of Univision and Telemundo without regard for the political well-being of Latinas/os. Today, the great majority of Latino media is owned by non-Latinas/os, a situation that is likely to affect the types of media practices that characterize it. It is just as likely that, as Kristin Moran (2007) has anticipated, Latino media will continue its commitment to corporatism, unfazed by the neoliberal regulatory system.

Citizenship excess is given form through *alterity*, in direct relation, response, and attention to the other. As a result, citizenship excess points to a nation-centric ethics that depends on the other for its concretion. Through processes of alterity, citizenship excess participates in the creation of symbolic hierarchies between self and others, giving preeminent value to self-serving discourses, narratives, and histories that normalize specific politics of resource distribution. Resource distribution refers here to material distribution implicit in labor laws and broadcast-ownership rules and also to the distribution of more ephemeral resources such as social prestige. Alterity, hence, is more than a cultural or ethical process. Alterity has a political economy that harnesses the power of law, cultural capital, and economic resources to build, for instance, media platforms welcoming of some and closed off to others. Because of labor laws and ownership rules, Latinas/os, as is evident in the current Spanish- and English-language media landscape, are mostly unwelcome. Control is always elsewhere and always complexly shaped by political economy.

The nation-centric ethics of alterity depends on hierarchical differences between self and other, and cultural processes that allocate social prestige or social shaming become integral to the political economy of alterity. In the contemporary United States, prestige is distributed along ethnic, national, and linguistic lines. Either because Spanish-language media stars are typically ignored by mainstream English-language media or because academics do not or cannot research Spanish-language media or because Latino soldiers cannot become national heroes in their own terms, the huge Latina/o community has only a few symbolically powerful spokespeople who are known and respected outside the Latino community (for instance, Bill Richardson, Antonio Villaraigosa, Edward James Olmos, and, now, Sonia Sotomayor). The scant number of Latino national figures legitimizes anti-Latino national voices set on shaming the Latino community through the figure of the "illegal" and determined to ignore the value of Latino cultural markers such as Spanish.

In this political and media world of ascription and alterity, there is limited room for change and progress and practically no room for radical transformations. The rules of hegemony, if you wish, apply, making the system stable, self-regulating, and relatively impervious to external forces or dramatic internal changes. It is a political and media world imagined through the dystopian figure of the citizen, the troubling practices of citizenship excess, and the nation-state's monopoly of power. It is, in other words, the political world of coloniality, which since the first modernity in the sixteenth century has been expanding its reach and influence across the globe. Enrique Dussel (1996) notes that the remarkable developments of the first modernity, which include capitalism, technological innovation, and, eventually, liberalism, depended on the political and economic exploitation of Amerindia, which provided the material and human resources necessary for European power to overtake competing civilizations such as Muslim, Indian, and Chinese politico-military forces. Therefore, at the root of the contemporary world-system of Eurocentrism (Dussel's term), there lies exploitation and the epistemic narrowing down of the world to the rational dualism that allowed for the efficient management of things and people (Dussel 1996, 132).

Reimagining the nation-state through the framework of coloniality is an antidote to the utopianism that gets in the way of properly assessing the political, economic, and media challenges of Latinas/os in the United States. The bulk of this book has been dedicated to challenging utopian visions of the nation-state, citizenship, and liberalism, particularly as these relate to limited definitions of the public sphere (part 1) and the belief that liberal processes of cultural and media inclusion can significantly alter the hegemony of ethno-racial patriarchy (part 2).

The lessons found in coloniality should alert us to the suspect nature of those basic political artifacts of modernity that are part of emancipatory discourses, such as liberalism, citizenship, the public sphere, and the legal apparatus. With every chapter, I have shown that the practices of citizenship excess are not an epiphenomenon of racist and xenophobic practices and beliefs, which contaminate the otherwise emancipatory nature of U.S. liberalism and liberal governmentality. Rather, I have argued that citizenship excess is as central a cog in our political imaginary as wealth accumulation is in our economic imaginary. Much as one cannot explain capitalism without engaging with the problem of excess of wealth, one cannot understand our political world without engaging the political capital accumulation that citizenship excess organizes, makes possible, and legitimizes. That our political imaginary has roots both in Athens and in colonialism only adds substance to my arguments.

For Latino media studies, this means querying the connections between citizenship excess, emancipatory citizenship, ethnicity, and the national episteme. But it also means criticizing the a priori belief that the future of Latinas/os is dependent on their successful participation in the public sphere, civil society, and formal political structures. This foundational belief must be questioned, not abandoned: it must be understood much as feminists have tried to understand what it means to participate in patriarchy or as advocates against poverty have tried to understand what it means to participate in capitalism.

I use these examples because they have helped me see how undertheorized citizenship has been and how blindly ideological is our relation to citizenship's emancipatory potential. The pursuit of the reformist goal of integrating women into already existing systems of law, politics, economics, and culture is referred to as liberal feminism. But another brand of feminism, called radical feminism, has also tried to query the very categories of gender, sex, and power at the base of our liberal patriarchy. More conventional studies of citizenship tend to treat traditional political power similarly to the way liberal feminists treat gender and theorize patriarchy. Such studies hold fast to the idea that an expansion of traditional political power will result in a decrease in the ill effects of racial patriarchy. Just as radical feminism has tried to get outside these systems and understand the root causes of oppression in order to question patriarchal domination, this book has tried to get outside of liberalism and understand the root causes of the contemporary relationship between ideas of citizenship and the media. My goal is similar to radical feminism in that I want to query the roots of ethnicized political oppression, and for this reason, I also find it necessary to question political foundations and use coloniality to this end.

The use of coloniality is expanding in cultural analysis, but the original group of Mignolo, Quijano, Dussel, and Mendieta share a set of concerns and theoretical propositions worth reiterating.[1] All of their projects try to denaturalize the epistemic cage of modernity and Eurocentrism from the standpoint of the colonialized other. Their projects, however, do not squarely fit into postcolonial theory, for they tend to share some mistrust of the epistemological roots of postcolonialism, which they understand as an extension of theoretical modernism (Mignolo 2007, 452). More clearly neo-Marxian, these thinkers engage with questions of history, politics, and culture skeptical of philosophies lacking a political economic dimension. In their views, modernism, capitalism, racism, Eurocentrism, and the nation-state share a common origin: the invasion of the Americas (e.g., Quijano 2000; Dussel 2002, 234).

There is a sense in the work of these thinkers (as in much work inspired by what is beyond Western academies) that the prison house of language, to use Martin Heidegger's beautiful metaphor, uses the building codes of the national episteme. Hence, the unavoidable need to name what is beyond traditional epistemology, ethics, and experience is proportional to the need to express what is beyond, before, and around the nation. Mignolo, a bit self-conscious about the neologisms and anachronisms that he invites us to use in order to reflect on what he terms "border thinking" (or, even better, "border gnoseology"), writes, "It is not always the case that jargon is unnecessary, and often uncommon words show us the invisible. In any event, plurotopic hermeneutics," the term he is apologizing for, "was necessary to indicate that colonial semiosis 'takes place' in between conflicts of knowledges and structures of power" (2000, 16).

Instead of "emancipation," Dussel uses "liberation," a term preferred by decolonizing movements of the 1960s and 1970s. Instead of "universalism," he uses "pluriversalism," a term that engages difference as an ethical value and a social, political goal.[2]

The necessity of new language is evident in the case of Hutto, in which the very idea of justice seems fused to the idea of citizen rights. Rights are legal semiosis. Their meanings become disarticulated in cases of alienage, war, and social crises. The *Flores* settlement, the legal precedent that the ACLU and the University of Texas School of Law calculated would have the best chance of improving the children's conditions, was enough to create a degree of accountability on behalf of ICE and CCA, but it was incapable of exacting legal decisions that would, for instance, make the ICE and CCA legally culpable. Moreover, it is precisely because human rights have historically been weakened by war and social crises that Western states pushed for international law and international institutions. The Universal Declaration of Human Rights, the International Covenant on Civil and Political Rights, and the Convention on the Rights of the Child are all the result of these efforts to produce international frameworks for justice, and all should have been applied to Hutto. But human rights are policed by weak institutions. The nation, especially a nation such as the United States, wins anytime there is a conflict between national and human rights. What does it mean that a nation is more powerful than humanity? Can there be an ethical imperative without the ability to command? Can you command without an army, a police force, or strong institutions? Are these institutions at all possible without a media fostering internationalism?

Gnoseology, plurotopic hermeneutics, pluriversality, and even *liberation* (as is used by Dussel), all neologisms found in the work of these Latin American scholars, are terms meant to participate in a theoretical field constructed, as Arjun Appadurai (1996) argues, at a moment of disjuncture. The main causes for this disjuncture are migration and electronic media, which have co-participated in a qualitative change regarding the role of the imagination in social organization. Migration has altered, perhaps permanently, the ethno-racial formation of nation-states, forcing us to imagine our futures, our pasts, and our presents with an array of affective structures that energize the opposite processes of cosmopolitanism and ethnic strife. The political activisms of those who protested Hutto represent the former; the xenophobic basis of the detention practices and their legal contexts represent the latter. Here, cosmopolitanism is partly the result of electronic media and its increasingly global circulation, which has repositioned deterritorialized culture as a central player in the organization of our affective structures, preparing communities to live with the phantasmagoric and real presence of the other.

The disjunctures brought about by immigration are not unique to the United States. They are now common to most western European nations, Canada, Australia, and Japan, to name a few. Like the United States, nations with European ethno-racial identities (which include Canada and Australia) have given increased space to nativist political forces and have allowed legal expressions of xenophobia to taint the otherwise liberal and even leftist juridical agendas that characterize these nations. As in the United States, new immigrants to these European nations are the targets of nativist agendas that constitute them as essentially different legal subjects from western Europeans. From prohibitions on traditional religious wear in France to harsh internment practices of refugees and immigrants that defy common interpretations of human rights law in Italy (often referred to as "expulsion centers"), immigrants from Africa, the Middle East, and East Asia are subject to extraordinary political speech and practices from increasingly popular nativist political parties.

Undoubtedly, the West is under threat, and its politics are retrenching. I began this book with the example of Arizona under Governor Jan Brewer. This example is intimately linked to the first case that I analyzed extensively, the 2006 pro-immigration reform marches, the social advertising campaign headed by Spanish-language radio, and what I have called the partial defeat of the reform marches. Governor Brewer's new law is, if anything, a moment of political inertia, a continuation of the political and cultural excesses that characterized the United States after Reagan, excesses that accelerated after 9/11. By 2010, the first decade of the twenty-first century had become the temporal stage for the recentering of nativism and the systematic scapegoating of undocumented Latinas/os, who were often blamed for the largest economic crisis since the Great Depression. Latinas/os in general were collateral damage in a war that began on conservative radio, Fox News, and increasingly state and federal legislatures. Just as they were during the Great Depression, Latinas/os were pushed away, deported en masse, detained unjustly, and subject to civil rights violations. The majoritarian public sphere normalized the anti-Latino rhetoric that began at the margins and, by decade's end, participated in reproducing the public agenda set by nativists. According to this agenda, the issue of undocumented immigrants ought to be debated in terms of the major and/or minor harms these immigrants inflict on the nation-state and the community of nationals.

But the nativist agenda is not the end of history, nor will nativists forever succeed. Timarchus is not alone. The thousands of Latino activists who organized the 2006 marches are not gone; the millions of Latinas/os and non-Latinas/os craving change have not changed their minds. As the Cuban Silvio Rodríguez once sang, "La era está pariendo un corazón. No puede más, se muere de dolor" ("The era is giving birth to a new heart. It cannot stand it anymore, it's dying of pain"). These are the birthing pains of a new United States transformed by the Latino trans-nation.

1. In this book, I use *excess* in the Marxian, not psychoanalytic or poststructuralist, sense. While in psychoanalysis and poststructuralism, *excess* means the unruly and potentially progressive undisciplined aspects of reality or language, here I use *excess* as the accumulation of surplus political value. In this tradition, excess leads to abuses of power.

2. For an elaboration of ethno-racialization of Latinas/os, see Aparicio (1994) and Molina-Guzmán (2010, 4–7). For a fascinating example of its complexity, see Frances Negrón-Muntaner (2002).

3. I am particularly indebted to the following: Rodolfo Acuña, Tomás Almaguer, Linda Bosniak, Wendy Brown, Nicholas De Genova, Enrique Dussel, Lisa Flores, Ian Haney-López, Cheryl Harris, Bonnie Honig, Engin Isin, Walter Mignolo, Toby Miller, David Montejano, Armando Navarro, Chon Noriega, Michael Omi, Aihwa Ong, Anibal Quijano, América Rodriguez, George Sanchez, Otto Santa Ana, Rogers Smith, Howard Winant, and Aristide Zolberg. Others play a very important role, in particular in the developing of cases, but these scholars are this book's theoretical and historical DNA.

4. I use the term *Latinas/os* to designate populations with ethnic or historical roots in Latin America and the Caribbean (Romero and Habell-Pallán 2002). I am aware that the category itself is unstable and racially and ethnically complex and that it includes communities that seem to have little in common. It designates families with centuries-old roots in the U.S. territories, particularly in the Southwest, as well as immigrants who have just arrived. It includes colonial subjects such as Puerto Ricans and Mexicans, Cuban political refugees, part of the Latin American intellectual elites who have found themselves immigrants in the metropoles, and what some scholars call "economic refugees," a large category of immigrants forced north for economic reasons. Differences notwithstanding, most of these communities have been ethnicized and racialized similarly by racial formations that construct them as foreign (regardless of their citizenship status) and as ethnic and racial others (De Genova and Ramos-Zayas 2003, 2; Mayer 2004; Oboler 2006, 11; Pérez 2004; Rivero 2005, 129–131). Lastly, it is worth remarking that the culture of Latinas/os with Mexican ancestry looms large over other immigrants and Latino citizens and that this culture is also quasi-hegemonic. This produces tensions. For instance, in reference

to Puerto Ricans living in the United States, Gina Pérez (2004) refers to the pressure to assimilate to Mexican markers of Latinidad as the forced Mexicanization of Puerto Ricans (177).

5. I expand on nativism in chapters 2 and 3. I expand on ethnonationalism in chapter 4.

6. I am deeply indebted to Raymond Williams's (1977) ideas on Marxism and profoundly aware that Marx's concerns took him from the field of politics to the field of economics. Like others, I find myself filtering the world through an array of theories all inspired by Marx, including Marxian approaches to the sociology of culture and Marxian aesthetics. Unlike Marx, I stay within politics but note that the field of politics can be explained by referencing some basic economic rules, which I list later in the introduction. In addition, there are two clearly Marxist elements in this book. The first has to do with the recognition that the juridical and the political are bound and form a field where elites roam (see Marx, in R. Williams 1977, 75–78). The second element concerns Marx's notion of the superstructure, which Williams notes is constituted in institutions, forms of consciousness, and political and cultural practices (1977, 77). Although I do not use the term *superstructure*, I am inspired by it. This chapter, in fact, is organized to highlight the three elements of the superstructure noted by Williams.

7. The Tea Party began as a right-wing fringe to the Republican Party after the Republican defeats of 2008. It is based on the political values of radical populism, nativism, and neoliberalism. In 2010, the Tea Party succeeded at electing ultraright candidates to the House and Senate and helped the Republican Party retake control of the House.

8. For an elaboration on Bourdieu and political capital accumulation, see chapter 1.

9. See similar observations on African American challenges in Oliver and Shapiro (2006).

10. From here on, I use Pierre Bourdieu's term *field of power* to speak about the political market.

11. Law exists in two discrete markets: the judicial and the political. But there are no other two markets that share more members, and, for the purposes of this book, the difference between the judicial and political market is negligible. See R. Williams (1977, 75–82).

12. See note 11.

13. The most recent and significant example is the 2010 Supreme Court ruling in *Citizens United v. Federal Election Commission*. The Supreme Court removed the ban on "electioneering communications" for incorporated organizations and unions. This ban prohibited corporations from using general treasury funds to make direct contributions to political candidates or independent expenditures that expressly advocate the election or defeat of a specific candidate.

14. I use *liberal* and *republican* in the way political scientists use them. In political theory, liberalism is a type of government that has the central goal of engendering individual freedoms and equal rights. Republicanism is a type of government controlled by the citizens and, thus, is the basis for democracy. The United States is typically historicized and theorized as a political organization based both on liberal and republican ideals.

15. On this I am not alone. Nicole Waligora-Davis (2011) does the significant work of refiguring the effects of race on African Americans by theorizing a racial location based on ethno-territoriality. Her work wisely privileges the terminology of *refugee*, *asylum seeker*, and *alien* to help us reimagine African American history from the position of space or, better, lack of space. Simply, centuries after arrival, African Americans are yet to find sanctuary in this nation, "a site in which the sanctity of human life is preserved" (xiii). Similar to Waligora-Davis in my commitment to reimagining race from the position of space and legal imaginaries, but less expectant that the nation can become sanctuary for Latina/os, my theory of citizenship excess avoids the language of yearning.

16. This issue was already relevant in Marx's time. He discusses it in his famous writing "On the Jewish Question," where he supports the evolution of an abstract, as opposed to religious or, I might add, ascriptionist, state (Marx 1975, 211–241).

17. For theories of the new racism, see Bonilla-Silva (2001, 193), Oliver and Shapiro (2006, 19), and Wilson (1996, 219).

18. For a detailed elaboration on subjectivity and self, see P. Smith (1988, xxiii–xiv) and Miller (1993).

19. There are significant differences in the way different communities relate to citizenship. The clearest cases are differences between Mexicans, who are often linked to foreignness and illegality, and Puerto Ricans, who have been U.S. citizens but colonial subjects for a century (De Genova and Ramos-Zayas 2003).

20. To read on issues of whiteness in the Puerto Rican context, see Negrón-Muntaner (2002, 47–53).

21. It is worth noting that legal historian José Cabranes never found evidence that World War I had anything to do with the Jones Act or that the plan existed to extend citizenship to Puerto Ricans so that they could serve (1979, 15). Yet they did serve, and they were drafted. But Cabranes is correct in pointing out that citizenship was not required for Puerto Ricans to be drafted by the U.S. armed forces and that the first Puerto Rican regiment had been drafted in 1899.

22. Aziz Rana (2010) has noted that Rogers Smith's work, while a significant improvement to the traditional account of American liberalism, tends to isolate democracy and its institutions from the critique of ascriptivism. The result is a theorization of the way the traditions of liberalism and republicanism are indebted to ascriptionism that does not recognize the way exclusionism energized U.S. democratic institutions. Rana, thus, proposes a history of

democratic institutions that makes evident their exclusionary roots. My work borrows from Smith but follows Rana's concern with institutions and their colonial history.

23. See note 7.

24. Coloniality is part of law, but it is also part of culture. Arguably, the performance work of Guillermo Gómez-Peña, the poetry work of Gloria Anzaldúa, and the musical work of Rubén Blades (Ana Rodríguez 2002) are examples of uses of culture that attempt to destabilize coloniality.

25. Devon W. Carbado (2005) offers ideas similar to Smith's. He argues that racial naturalization constitutes American citizenship because it is the legal a priori by which Americans become cognizable to law and to others.

NOTES TO CHAPTER 1

1. According to the 2010 census, there are fifty million Latinas/os and thirty-eight million Spanish speakers in the United States. The overlap between both populations is huge but hard to quantify. The census releases numbers on Spanish in relation to the ethnic category of Hispanic, and though we know that Spanish is the most learned language in universities, I have not found a reliable source listing the total numbers of Spanish speakers who are not Latinas/os. What we do know, thanks to the census, is that, 76 percent of Latinas/os five years and older speak Spanish at home, and thus it is possible to argue that the Latino public sphere is very similar to SLM. It is not, however, my intention to somehow erase the millions of non-Latinas/os who also speak Spanish.

2. Mendieta is at his strongest when pointing out the characteristics of publicity of Latino public intellectuals and at his weakest when engaging the specific cultural structures that Latino public intellectuals need in order to speak. See also comments on the subject by Paula Moya (2003), Jacqueline Martinez (2003), and Jane Juffer (2003).

3. See also Linda Bosniak's contribution to the conversation (2006, 23–28). Though she does not use the term *methodological nationalism*, her ideas are consistent with those of Chernilo and Wimmer and Schiller.

4. An example of this discursive monopoly is "political capital accumulation," a notion central to this chapter. Inspired by several of Marx's concerns, including the power harnessed by capital accumulation and the relationship of media production, labor, law and politics, political capital accumulation is an imperfect tool of analysis because of its relentless bias for the national, which becomes the implicit exchange market giving currency to political capital.

5. Governmentality offers several opportunities for theorizing culture in general and media in particular. In the past, I have theorized it under the banner of technologies of self (Amaya 2010). Laurie Ouellette and James Hay (2008) use it in a similar manner to theorize production and consumption practices as they link to theories of self-management. Instead of linking the macro to the

micro with theories of self-management and self-governance, in this book I use the macro elements of Foucault's theories and concentrate on his ideas of the pastoral and securitization.

6. These issues are also investigated under the umbrella term *cultural citizenship*. For an exploration of Latino cultural citizenship, see Flores and Benmayor (1997).

7. Criticizing Marx, Dussel (1994) places the first capitalism and the first modernity in Pacific Asia, specifically China.

NOTES TO CHAPTER 2

1. The history of nativism against Latinas/os starts off with white settler migration to the Southwest and the takeover of large swaths of Mexican territory. In the 1840s and 1850s, as Tomás Almaguer has noted (1994), it was manifested through the idea of white supremacy. Other historians, such as Richard Peterson (1975) and Leonard Pitt (1966), refer to these decades of white supremacy as nativism, but I am with Almaguer in that it took some decades for white supremacy to acquire the element of "rights by birth," including the right to imagine and heavily regulate national membership, with which nativism is associated.

2. For a closer look at how practices of enumeration served nativist goals, see Inda (2006, 74–93).

3. Thanks to Representative Tancredo, the act included one provision prohibiting grants to federal, state, or local government agencies that enact a "sanctuary city policy." See the text of the act at http://thomas.loc.gov/cgi-bin/query/z?c109:H.R.4437.RFS.

4. This includes important Latino figures such as Richard Rodriguez, who takes this position when he assumes that people migrate to the United States to assimilate and partake of liberal citizenship imagined as a legally neutral category (2002, 128–129).

5. Juridical subjectivity and its link to citizenship is relevant throughout history. Almaguer (1994) has described how land dispossession in California after the U.S. annexation of the territory was carried out partly through the legal cultures of the time. Although the Treaty of Guadalupe Hidalgo protected the property rights of Mexicans, long litigations placed the Mexican ruling classes at the hands of the lawyer class and the court system. Even if a claim was decided in favor of the Mexican owner, he would often have to pay lawyers with the land itself (65–68).

6. See also the work of Robert McChesney (1993, 2004), Paul Starr (2004). For a look at how the FCC and media policy are involved in global issues of politics, see Michael Curtin (1993).

7. Grace Hong (2006) develops a related way of linking citizenship to the juridical. She theorizes the centrality of property in defining citizenship and argues

that American definitions of individualism are bound to property ownership (3–30). Property, I add, is a legal category, and so the primary principle of American individualism and, Marx would note, capitalism is based on law, the juridical and legal cultures.

NOTES TO CHAPTER 3

1. The connections between immigrant populations are often profound, and these include ways of theorizing the state. Here, I am indebted to the work of Grace Hong (2006) and Lisa Lowe (1996), who have theorized, historicized, and criticized U.S. citizenship from the Asian American perspective, often referencing the treatment of Japanese Americans during World War II.

2. The ORR is an organization with very divided goals. Its mission statement fails to mention alien children, and the organization seems ill prepared to tackle the legal and administrative challenges of caring for alien children, particularly as the ORR sits relatively powerless between the legal guidelines set by international law on the care and custody of migrant children and the pressures imposed on them by the political realities of the DHS. Going through the central goals and objectives of the ORR, one quickly notices how the care and custody of unaccompanied children is not what the organization is meant to do. The bulk of the organization, as expressed on its website, is concerned with the multitude of challenges involved in the care of refugees and victims of human trafficking. See http://www.acf.hhs.gov/index.html.

3. U.S. House of Representatives, Committee on Appropriations, Department of Homeland Security appropriations bill, 2006, H.R. Rep. No. 109-300 (2005), 38.

4. Brown (1993) helps us understand how processes such as the increase in size and complexity of the judicial system and neoliberal economic policies are today credited with expanded legal and educational rights and are de facto credited with producing the conditions of social well-being through the proper management of people and the economy. In this type of liberalism, which Streeter (1996) called corporate liberalism and others call neoliberalism, the problems caused by economic stratification and obsessive capitalism (Brown mentions "alienation, commodification, exploitation, displacement," and others) move to the background and become depoliticized. But the problems persist, and Brown argues, their effects are displaced to identity politics claims for justice, which now bear "all the weight of the sufferings caused by capitalism in addition to that bound to the explicitly politicized marking" (395). Brown's argument moves to explain the strong attachments people have to their politicized identities, to their own exclusion, in terms of ressentiment and even revenge. This is less useful to my project because in her assessment of contemporary liberalism and identity politics, Brown is much better at exacting the vices of a liberal psyche (is identity politics not engulfing us all?) than at

locating the array of affects particular to identity politics. However, her insights into the depoliticization of capitalism are quite useful here, as is her insistence that contemporary justice claims are increasingly based on identity.

5. The most important requirements found in the *Flores* settlement include the following:
   - Separation of minors from unrelated adults;
   - Preference for release of unaccompanied minors to the care of parents, legal guardians, other relatives, or foster homes or other facilities whenever possible;
   - Detention of minors in licensed programs that comply with all relevant child welfare laws and regulations;
   - Provision of suitable accommodations, food service, clothing and personal care items;
   - Affirmation of children's right to wear their own clothes;
   - Provision of routine medical and dental care, family planning services and emergency medical care; administration of prescription medicine and accommodations for dietary restrictions; provision of mental health interventions as appropriate;
   - One individual counseling session each week with a trained social worker and group counseling sessions at least twice each week;
   - Provision of educational services appropriate to a child's level of development and communications skills;
   - Recreation and leisure time including daily outdoor activity and one hour of large muscle activity each day;
   - Prohibition of corporal punishment, humiliation, mental abuse and punitive interference with such daily functions as eating and sleeping; disciplinary actions may not adversely impact a child's health, physical or psychological well-being or deny a child regular meals, sufficient sleep, exercise, medical care, the right to correspondence or legal assistance;
   - Expeditious processing of apprehended minors and timely provision of notice of their rights and the availability of free legal services; and
   - Visitation privileges which encourage visitors and respect the child's privacy. (Women's Commission 2007, 7–8)

6. These issues have been present in much political philosophy and critical legal scholarship. Besides Wendy Brown, here I follow Enrique Dussel (2006), who uses a Marxist argumentation to theorize the fundamental rights of the state (including the right of coercion) and the disequilibrium to legal systems caused by counterhegemonic movements that use the logic of rights to argue their political positions.

7. Clearly, states do not need to behave as liberal states to claim legitimacy through liberalism or some of liberalism's central tenets. In my previous book, I found that practitioners of cultural politics in Cuba often resorted to the

language of liberalism (e.g., freedom, emancipation, self-determination) to justify themselves.

8. For a work that tracks down the historical roots of the idea of rights as property, from Hobbes and Locke to the present, see Zuckert (1994, 275–289).

9. Before continuing, I have to qualify my use of Walzer. His work is at times maddeningly nation-centric and, when it comes to talking about immigration, oddly parochial. For instance, Walzer assumes that immigrants are mostly trying to benefit from the material options of more advanced societies; yet he fails to see that advanced capitalisms, including our own, are mostly benefiting from the cheap labor of immigrants. This oversight makes him understand the social ethical dilemma of nations such as the United States as one centrally concerned with how to treat the disadvantaged other who has no choice but to leave her or his country (Schmidt Camacho 2008, 2). Seeing the issue of immigration in a different way (e.g., considering that immigrants arrive partly because they are expected) would force Walzer to rephrase the question of ethics as one of domination.

10. These results come from three databases: LexisNexis, Ethnic Newswatch, and the Vanderbilt Television News Archive.

NOTES TO CHAPTER 4

1. SLM is not equal to Latinas/os. Hence, the SLM-ELM difference is not equal to the Latino-majority difference. See chapter 2 on the difference between Spanish speakers and Latinas/os.

2. Starting in 1927, radio and, later, television, have been regulated by, among others, the Federal Radio Commission (FRC), which became the Federal Communications Commission (FCC) in 1934.

3. I am referring here to Spanish-language television in the mainland United States. For a history of Spanish-language television in Puerto Rico, see Rivero (2005).

4. Being part of English-language news organizations carries ethno-racial responsibilities. Navarrete and, for instance, Richard Rodriguez (2002, 114–115) are assimilationist because that is the way they ought to perform their professionalism.

5. My position (and Levy's), however, is not the only one. Anthony Appiah (2005) and Martha Nussbaum (1997), among others, have argued for the value of general political and cultural goals that can override the parochial grounds of ethnonationalisms. Both Appiah and Nussbaum refer to these in terms of identity and argue that identity is often the grounds for conflict (Appiah) and lack of global empathy (Nussbaum). Appiah and Nussbaum, like me, are trying to theorize social ethics with the goal of maximizing the chances for justice and egalitarianism. On this, we agree. However, Appiah's general goal of producing the conditions for a better liberalism and Nussbaum's goal of understanding the possibility for world citizenship leave to the side the difficult issue of whose

identity is overidentified with liberalism and cosmopolitanism and who, in practical terms, is required to forgo their identities, including languages, in order to achieve the ends proposed in these theoretical projects. Moreover, from my socio-historical location, I see no value in liberalism and cosmopolitanism if these ethical frameworks cannot protect Latinas/os from being forced into ethnic homogenization with majoritarian cultures. So my challenge is to use some of ethnonationalism for broad ethical projects such as liberalism and cosmopolitanism—hence the ongoing value, in my view, of Will Kymlicka's radical multiculturalism.

6. Counting Mexicans in the Southwest territory is no easy task. The U.S. government did not have an official category for Hispanics, Mexicans, or Latinas/os, or for Native Americans, for most of our existence as a nation-state; in 1930, Latinas/os were quantified by the census as a race (Almaguer 1994, 46). Only in 1970 did the census include the category of Hispanic (Gibson and Jung 2006, 9–10). By scavenging through other documents, estimates can be put together. The best estimate to my knowledge is the one produced by Brian Gratton and Myron Gutmann (2000).

7. Because census practices are related to taxation, Native Americans, who were not taxed, were not counted. See also Rose (1999, 215).

8. Comprehensive Immigration Reform Act of 2006, S.Amdt. 4064 to S. 2611, 109th Cong., 2nd sess. (2006).

9. For arguments on the complexities of transnationalism and Latina/o culture, see Ana Rodríguez (2002), Romero and Habell-Pallán (2002, 4), Valdivia (2008), and Molina-Guzmán (2010, 14).

10. Burns 2007. I do not have reason to doubt Saban's good intentions toward Latinas/os, but I question whether he can be consistently accountable to the political needs of Spanish speakers.

NOTES TO CHAPTER 5

1. On May 4, 2009, the U.S. Supreme Court overturned the law that declared the use of someone else's Social Security number an automatic aggravated identity theft and a felony that increased jail time by two years (Savage 2009).

2. The racial category of whiteness was first used by European settlers trying to differentiate themselves from Native Americans and, later, slaves. Historians debate whether whiteness was a strong factor differentiating white from black workers prior to 1800. What seems clear is that black revolts in the eighteenth century and the increasing political use of the term *slavery* to justify the fight for independence from Britain solidified the racial opposition of whites and blacks, clearly delineating white workers from black slaves. See Roediger (2007, 19–36) and Hong (2006, 2–25).

3. To further understand how media industries work as cultural, racial, and sexual echo chambers, see Caldwell (2008) and Mayer (2011).

4. Most industries and organizations have reacted similarly to media industries.

For resistance to the EEOC and affirmative action, see the work of James Coleman (1984) and Christopher Stone (1975).

5. The source was the website for Fox's office of diversity at http://www.fox.com/diversity/ (accessed July 2009).

6. The source was ABC's Talent Development site at http://www.abctalentdevelopment.com (accessed July 2009).

7. See DiverseCity NBC at http://www.diversecitynbc.com/.

NOTES TO CHAPTER 6

1. As it is, 8 U.S.C. Sec. 1440-1 grants a very limited version of citizenship that prohibits granting any benefits to survivors and limits filing privileges to next of kin.

2. This bill became an act on June 16, 2003.

3. For a discussion on how more recent drafting practices are illiberal and have affected Latinas/os, see Jorge Mariscal (1999) and Ramon Gutierrez (2007).

4. H.R. 1691, 108th Cong., 1st sess. (2003). See also its Senate counterpart, S. 783 ES, 108th Cong., 1st sess. (2003).

5. Fairness for America's Heroes Act of 2003, H.R. 1850, 108th Cong., 1st sess. (2003); Riayan Tejeda Memorial Act of 2003, H.R. 2887, 108th Cong., 1st sess. (2003).

6. For a very practical take on the matter, see the U.S. Citizens and Immigration Services website. In the section titled "Office of Citizenship," the institution defines one of its roles as the training of legal residents on citizenship requirements. The goal is outlined as follows: "Reviving and emphasizing the common civic identity and shared values that are essential to citizenship." USCIS, "Office of Citizenship," February 7, 2004, http://www.uscis.gov/graphics/citizenship/index.htm.

7. Ibid.

8. For a look at the evolution of these ideals, see Schuck (1998, 12–81). For an examination of how naturalization law used whiteness as a legal standard, see Haney-López (1996, 3).

9. It is important to emphasize that the phrasing of this bill is common among these types of legislation. For instance, H.R. 150, which became public law on March 7, 1990, amended the Immigration and Nationality Act with a similar goal in mind, although it also included provisions to grant citizenship to aliens (8 U.S.C. Sec. 1440-1). The term *alien* may also refer to nonlegal residents or nonresidents of the United States. The term *legal noncitizen*, which was used in the 2003 bills, refers only to green-card holders. As it is written, the bill stipulated that according to the state, an alien who died while "serving on active duty with the US Armed Forces during certain periods of hostilities [was] to be considered a citizen of the United States at the time of the alien's death." Posthumous Citizenship for Active Duty Service Act of 1989, H.R. 150, 101th Cong., 1st sess. (2003).

10. See the speech by the Honorable Walter B. Jones of North Carolina in the House of Representatives on April 11, 2003. In this speech, Jones introduces the Fallen Heroes Immigrant Spouse Act, which aimed to extend rights to spouses of the fallen soldiers. See also the congressional record of the discussions on the Armed Forces Naturalization Act of 2003, H.R. 1954 (discussion that took place in the House on June 4, 2003).

11. Here is the full text of the oath:

I hereby declare, on oath, that I absolutely and entirely renounce and abjure all allegiance and fidelity to any foreign prince, potentate, state, or sovereignty, of whom or which I have heretofore been a subject or citizen; that I will support and defend the Constitution and the laws of the United States of America against all enemies, foreign and domestic; that I will bear true faith and allegiance to the same; that I will bear arms on behalf of the United States when required by the law; that I will perform noncombatant service in the Armed Forces of the United States when required by the law; that I will perform work of national importance under civilian direction when required by the law; and that I take this obligation freely, without any mental reservation or purpose of evasion; so help me God.

"The Military Member's Guide to Citizenship Application: Oath of Allegiance," About.com, http://usmilitary.about.com/library/milinfo/citizenship/blcitizen-4 .htm.

12. For some biographical information on the three soldiers, see *Fallen Heroes of Operation Iraqi Freedom*, a website-memorial to the soldiers fallen in combat: http://www.fallenheroesmemorial.com/oif/.

13. Interview by the author with Fernando Suárez del Solar, father of the victim, in September 2005, Austin, Texas. The family migrated from Tijuana, Mexico, in 1997.

14. For instance, Texas Rep. Sheila Jackson-Lee emphatically declared during the discussion of the bill, "This Nation continues to be a Nation built upon immigrants and their desire to be part of this great democracy." She also refers to Martha Espinosa, one of José Gutiérrez's foster parents, who stated that Gutiérrez once told her, "I was born the day I arrived in this country." Washington Rep. Doc Hastings also declared, "Mr. Speaker, these patriotic men and women have willingly volunteered to carry out one of the most solemn duties any nation can ask of its citizens, the defense of freedom. In doing so, I believe that they have truly earned the opportunity to become citizens of the country that they serve to protect. . . . As my colleagues know, some of our troops who died in Iraq wearing the uniform of the United States gave their lives before they were truly entitled to call themselves Americans." Both sets of statements are part of the House of Representative discussion, on June 4, 2003, regarding the Armed Forces Naturalization Act of 2003, H.R. 1954.

15. Notable exceptions include journalists such as David Conde (2003), David Halbfinger and Steven Holmes (2003), and Kristal Zook (2003).

16. The idea of the "citizen-soldier" as a political category of governance linked to idealized forms of citizenship is well documented. See Chambers (1987) and Cress (1982). For scholarship dealing with contemporary issues, including the issue of recruitment, see Moskos (2002) and Snyder (2003).

17. See also the publications in the Project on Youth and Non-Military Operations (YANO), directed by George Mariscal, http://www.projectyano.org/.

18. This bill became an act on June 16, 2003, as H.R. 1954 EH, 108th Cong., 1st sess. (June 16, 2003).

19. The importance of fantasy in the constitution of national identities has been argued by Michael McGee (1975, 239) and elaborated within the context of the construction of nationalism by M. Lane Bruner (2005, 311).

20. My position is the following: posthumous citizenship should be avoided in all cases involving noncitizens killed in combat. However, Congress should pass immigration law that would allow the families of the deceased soldiers to acquire the benefits of citizenship if so desired.

21. According to census figures, whites make up roughly 69 percent of the United States population but only account for about 58 percent of the armed forces. Numbers are taken from C. Johnson (1999, 24).

NOTES TO THE CONCLUSION

1. See for instance Ileana Rodríguez (2009), Darrel Enck-Wanzer (2011), and Hermann Herlinghaus (2009).

2. This is one of Dussel's most clearly Marxist gestures, for in criticizing emancipation, he follows Marx's advice found in "On the Jewish Question" (1975, 215).

REFERENCES

Achrati, Nora. 2003. War in the Gulf: Homefront: Memorials: Ranger buried at Arlington. *Atlanta Journal-Constitution*, April 11, 12A.

Achugar, Mariana. 2008. Counter-hegemonic language practices and ideologies: Creating a new space and value for Spanish in Southwest Texas. *Spanish in Context* 5 (1): 1–19.

Acuña, Rodolfo. 1988. *Occupied America: A history of Chicanos*. 3rd ed. New York: Harper and Row.

Agamben, Giorgio. 2005. *State of exception*. Chicago: University of Chicago Press.

Akers Chacón, Justin, and Mike Davis. 2006. *No one is illegal: Fighting violence and state repression on the U.S.-Mexico border*. Chicago: Haymarket Books.

Albarran, Alan B., and Brian Hutton. 2009. *A history of Spanish-language radio in the United States*. Denton: Arbitron and University of North Texas, Center for Spanish Language Media.

Alexandre, Laurien, and Henrik Rehbinder. 2008. Watching the 2000 presidential campaign on Univisión and Telemundo. In *The mass media and Latino politics: Studies of U.S. media content, campaign strategies and survey research: 1984–2004*, edited by Federico A. Subervi-Vélez. New York: Routledge.

Almaguer, Tomás. 1994. *Racial fault lines: The historical origins of white supremacy in California*. Berkeley: University of California Press.

Alonso, Ana María. 1994. The politics of space, time and substance: State formation, nationalism and ethnicity. *Annual Review of Anthropology* 23:379–405.

Alvord, Valerie. 2003. Non-citizens fight and die for adopted country. *USA Today*, April 9, 10A.

Amaya, Hector. 2007. Latino immigrants in the American discourse of citizenship and nationalism during the Iraqi War. *Critical Discourse Studies* 4 (3): 237–256.

———. 2010. Citizenship, diversity, law and *Ugly Betty*. *Media, Culture and Society* 32 (5): 801–817.

Anderson, Benedict R. 1991. *Imagined communities: Reflections on the origin and spread of nationalism*. Rev. and extended ed. London: Verso.

Aparicio, Frances R. 1994. On multiculturalism and privilege: A Latina perspective. *American Quarterly* 46 (4): 575–588.

———. 1998. *Listening to salsa: Gender, Latin popular music, and Puerto Rican cultures*. Hanover, NH: University Press of New England.

Aparicio, Frances R. 2003. Jennifer as Selena: Rethinking Latinidad in media and popular culture. *Latino Studies* 1 (1): 90–105.

Aparicio, Frances R., and Susana Chávez-Silverman, eds. 1997. *Tropicalizations: Transcultural representations of Latinidad.* Reencounters with colonialism—new perspectives on the Americas. Hanover, NH: Dartmouth College, University Press of New England.

Appadurai, Arjun. 1996. *Modernity at large: Cultural dimensions of globalization.* Public worlds 1. Minneapolis: University of Minnesota Press.

Appiah, Anthony. 2005. *The ethics of identity.* Princeton: Princeton University Press.

Archibold, Randal. 2010. Arizona's effort to bolster local immigration authority divides law enforcement. *New York Times,* April 21.

Aufderheide, Patricia. 1990. After the fairness doctrine: Controversial broadcast programming and the public interest. *Journal of Communication* 47:47–72.

Ayala, N. 2007. "Betty" finds herself in Mexico: A wink to the Hispanic market played out on ABC's *Ugly Betty* finale. *Marketing y Medios,* May 10.

Bacon, David. 2008. *Illegal people: How globalization creates migration and criminalizes immigrants.* Boston: Beacon.

Baker, C. Edwin. 1998. The media that citizens need. *University of Pennsylvania Law Review* 147:317–408.

Balibar, Etienne. 1991. The nation form: History and ideology. In *Race, nation, class: Ambiguous identities,* by Etienne Balibar and Immanuel Wallerstein. London: Verso.

Balibar, Etienne, and Immanuel Maurice Wallerstein. 1991. *Race, nation, class: Ambiguous identities.* London: Verso.

Baum, Dan. 2006. Arriba! A Latino radio scold gets out the vote. *New Yorker,* October 23.

Baynes, Leonard. 2009. *Changing media landscape and minority ownership disparity analysis.* Federal Communications Commission.

Beltrán, Mary. 2009. *Latina/o stars in U.S. eyes: The making and meanings of film and TV stardom.* Urbana: University of Illinois Press.

Benamou, Catherine L. 2007. *It's all true: Orson Welles's pan-American odyssey.* Berkeley: University of California Press.

Benhabib, Seyla. 1992. Models of public space: Hannah Arendt, the liberal tradition, and Jürgen Habermas. In *Habermas and the public sphere,* edited by C. J. Calhoun. Boston: MIT Press.

Benjamin, Walter. (1921) 1996. Critique of violence. In *Selected writings, Volume 1,* edited by Marcus Bullock and Michael W. Jennings. Cambridge: Harvard University Press.

Bennett, Tony. 1998. *Culture: A reformer's science.* London: Sage.

Bennett, W. Lance, Victor Pickard, David P. Iozzi, Carl L. Schroeder, Taso Lagos, and C. Evans Caswell. 2004. Managing the public sphere: Journalistic construction of the great globalization debate. *Journal of Communication* 54 (3): 437–455.

Benson, Rodney. 2006. News media as a "journalistic field": What Bourdieu adds to new institutionalism, and vice versa. *Political Communication* 23 (2): 187–202.

Berlant, Lauren. 1997. *The queen of America goes to Washington city: Essays on sex and citizenship*. Durham: Duke University Press.

———. 2002. The subject of true feeling: Pain, privacy, and politics. In *Left legalism/ left critique*, edited by Wendy Brown and Janet Halley. Durham: Duke University Press.

Bhabha, Jacqueline. 2003. The citizenship deficit: On being a citizen child. *Development* 46 (3): 53–59.

Bloomberg, at funeral, praises marine sergeant. 2003. *The Record* (Bergen County, NJ), April 22, A8.

Bonilla-Silva, Eduardo. 2001. *White supremacy and racism in the post-civil rights era*. Boulder, CO: Rienner.

Bosniak, Linda. 2006. *The citizen and the alien: Dilemmas of contemporary membership*. Princeton: Princeton University Press.

Bourdieu, Pierre. 1984. *Distinction: A social critique of the judgement of taste*. Cambridge: Harvard University Press.

———. 1986. The forms of capital. In *The handbook of theory and research for the sociology of education*, edited by J. G. Richardson. New York: Greenwood.

———. 1990. *The logic of practice*. Cambridge, UK: Polity.

———. 1991. *Language and symbolic power*. Edited by John B. Thompson. Cambridge: Harvard University Press.

———. 1993. *The field of cultural production: Essays on art and literature*. Edited by Randal Johnson. New York: Columbia University Press.

———. 1996. *The rules of art: Genesis and structure of the literary field*. Cambridge, UK: Polity.

Brainard, Lori. 2004. *Television: The limits of deregulation*. Boulder, CO: Rienner.

Braudy, Leo. 2003. *From chivalry to terrorism: War and the changing nature of masculinity*. New York: Knopf.

Braxton, Greg. 2007. White still a primary color: Black, Latino and Asian groups feel multicultural momentum at the networks has been lost. *Los Angeles Times,* June 6, 1E.

Brickhouse, Anna. 2008. Scholarship and the state: Robert Greenhow and transnational American studies 1848/2008. *American Literary History* 20 (4): 695–722.

Brooks, Dwight, George Daniels, and C. Ann Hollifield. 2003. Television in living color: Racial diversity in the local commercial television industry. *Howard Journal of Communication* 14:123–146.

Brown, Wendy. 1993. Wounded attachments. *Political Theory* 21 (3): 390–410.

———. 2004. Suffering the paradoxes of rights. In *Left legalism/left critique*, edited by Wendy Brown and Janet Halley. Durham: Duke University Press.

Brown, Wendy, and Janet Halley, eds. 2002. *Left legalism/left critique*. Durham: Duke University Press.

Bruner, M. Lane. 2005. Rhetorical theory and the critique of national identity construction. *National Identities* 7:309–327.

Buchelew, Michael. 2003. Letter to the editor. Saturday talk. *Atlanta Journal-Constitution*, May 31, 13.

Bullock, Charles S., and Charles M. Lamb, eds. 1984. *Implementation of civil rights policy*. Monterey, CA: Brooks/Coleman.

Burchell, Graham. 1991. Peculiar interests: Civil society and governing "the system of natural liberty." In *The Foucault effect: Studies in governmentality, with two lectures by and an interview with Michel Foucault*, edited by Graham Burchell, Colin Gordon, and Peter Miller. Chicago: University of Chicago Press.

Burchell, Graham, Colin Gordon, and Peter Miller, eds. 1991. *The Foucault effect: Studies in governmentality, with two lectures by and an interview with Michel Foucault*. Chicago: University of Chicago Press.

Bureau of Immigration and Customs Enforcement, U.S. Department of Homeland Security. 2003. *Endgame: Office of Detention and Removal strategic plan, 2003–2012: Detention and removal strategy for a secure homeland*. Available at http://www.fas.org/irp/agency/dhs/endgame.pdf.

Burns, Eric. Univision's voter registration drive stirs GOP concerns. *Fox News Watch*, May 12.

Cabranes, José A. 1979. *Citizenship and the American empire: Notes on the legislative history of the United States citizenship of Puerto Ricans*. New Haven: Yale University Press.

Calabrese, Andrew, and Jean-Claude Burgelman. 1999. Introduction to *Communication, citizenship, and social policy: Rethinking the limits of the welfare state*, edited by Andrew Calabrese and Jean-Claude Burgelman. New York: Oxford University Press.

Caldwell, John Thornton. 2008. *Production culture: Industrial reflexivity and critical practice in film and television*. Console-ing passions. Durham: Duke University Press.

Carbado, Devon W. 2005. Racial naturalization. *American Quarterly* 57 (3): 633–658.

Casey, Kimberley L. 2008. Defining political capital: A reconsideration of Bourdieu's interconvertibility theory. Paper presented at the Illinois State University Conference for Students of Political Science.

Casillas, Dolores Inés. 2006. Sounds of belonging: A cultural history of Spanish-language radio in the United States, 1922–2004. Ph.D. diss., American Culture, University of Michigan.

Castillo, Juan. 2006. March decries prison packed with children. *Austin American-Statesman*, December 15, A1.

———. 2007a. Frustration, embarrassment led to detention center. *Austin American-Statesman*, March 25, A10.

———. 2007b. Immigrant detention center education expands. Cox News Service, January 23.

———. 2010. Interview by the author. University of Virginia, Charlottesville.

Castoriadis, Cornelius. 1987. *The imaginary institution of society*. Cambridge: MIT Press.

Chambers, John W., II. 1987. *To raise an army: The draft comes to modern America*. New York: Free Press.

Chavez, Leo R. 1998. *Shadowed lives: Undocumented immigrants in American society*. Case studies in cultural anthropology. Fort Worth, TX: Harcourt Brace.

———. 2008. *The Latino threat: Constructing immigrants, citizens, and the nation*. Stanford: Stanford University Press.

Cheah, Pheng, and Elizabeth Grosz. 1996. The body of the law: Notes toward a theory of corporeal justice. In *Thinking through the body of the law*, edited by Pheng Cheah, David Fraser, and Judith Grbich. New York: NYU Press.

Chernilo, Daniel. 2007. *A social theory of the nation-state: The political forms of modernity beyond methodological nationalism*. New York: Routledge.

Children Now. 2004. *Fall colors: Prime time diversity report, 2003–2004*. http://www.childrennow.org/uploads/documents/fall_colors_2003.pdf.

Chu, Louise. 2003. Mourners remember Colombian born soldier killed in Iraq. Associated Press, April 10.

Coleman, James. 1984. Introducing social structure into economic analysis. *American Economic Review* 74 (2): 84–88.

Conde, David. 2003. Counting living, dead Latinas/os as war ends. *La Voz*, April 23.

Connell, R. W. 1995. *Masculinities*. Berkeley: University of California Press.

Connor, Walker. 1994. *Ethnonationalism: The quest for understanding*. Princeton: Princeton University Press.

Consoli, John, and Anthony Crupi. 2007. Broadcast's summer ratings swoon as cable blooms. *Mediaweek*, August 6.

Corbett, Krystilyn. 1996. The rise of private property rights in the broadcast spectrum. *Duke Law Journal* 46 (3): 611–650.

Corrections Corporation of America. 2007. Corrections Corporation of America announces 2006 fourth quarter and full-year financial results. Press release. February 15. Nashville, TN.

Crawford, James. 1992. Introduction to *Language loyalties: A source book on the official English controversy*, edited by James Crawford, 1–8. Chicago: University of Chicago Press.

Crawley, James. 2003. Navy hopes TV ad attracts black enlistees: Spot touts skills to use in civilian life. *San Diego Union-Tribune*, August 3.

Cress, Lawrence. 1982. *Citizens in arms: The army and the militia in American society to the War of 1812*. Chapel Hill: University of North Carolina Press.

Curtin, Michael. 1993. Beyond the vast wasteland: The policy discourse of global television and the politics of American empire. *Journal of Broadcasting and Electronic Media* 37 (2): 127–145.

Dahlgren, Peter. 1995. *Television and the public sphere: Citizenship, democracy, and the media*. The media, culture & society series. Thousand Oaks, CA: Sage.

Daniels, Lindsay. 2011. Engaging the Latino electorate. In *Research report*. National Council of La Raza.

Daniels, Roger. 2004. *Guarding the golden door: American immigration policy and immigrants since 1882*. New York: Hill and Wang.

Dávila, Arlene M. 2000. Talking back: Hispanic media and U.S. Latinidad. *Centro Journal* 12 (1): 36–47.

———. 2001. *Latinos, Inc.: The marketing and making of a people*. Berkeley: University of California Press.

———. 2008. *Latino spin: Public image and the whitewashing of race*. New York: NYU Press.

De Genova, Nicholas. 2005. *Working the boundaries: Race, space, and "illegality" in Mexican Chicago*. Durham: Duke University Press.

De Genova, Nicholas, and Ana Y. Ramos-Zayas. 2003. *Latino crossings: Mexicans, Puerto Ricans, and the politics of race and citizenship*. New York: Routledge.

Delgado, Richard, and Jean Stefancic, eds. 1988. *The Latino/a condition: A critical reader*. New York: NYU Press.

De Schutter, Helder. 2007. Language policy and political philosophy: On the emerging linguistic justice debate. *Language Problems and Language Planning* 31:1–23.

DeSipio, Louis. 2003. *Bilingual television viewers and the language choices they make*. Claremont, CA: Tomás Rivera Policy Institute.

Devlyn, D., and J. Harlow. 2007. Salma Hayek is changing the way Hollywood views the Latin world: The Mex factor. *Herald-Sun* (Durham, NC), May 23.

Domestic drama: Hugely popular internationally, telenovelas' cat fights and contretemps are trying to find a primetime niche on English-language TV. 2006. *Media Week*, September.

Dougherty, Tim. 2003. Merger gets green light: The Federal Communications Commission votes along party lines to sanction Univision's merger with Hispanic Broadcasting Corp. *Hispanic Business*, November, 72.

Dudziak, Mary L. and Leti Volpp. 2005. Introduction: Legal borderlands: Law and the construction of American borders. *American Quarterly* 57 (3): 593–610.

Dussel, Enrique. 1994. *El encubrimiento del otro: Hacia el origen del mito de la modernidad*. 3rd ed. Quito, Ecuador: Ediciones ABYA-YALA.

———. 1995. *The invention of the Americas: Eclipse of "the other" and the myth of modernity*. Translated by Michael D. Barber. New York: Continuum.

———. 1996. *The underside of modernity: Apel, Ricoeur, Rorty, Taylor, and the philosophy of liberation*. Translated and edited by Eduardo Mendieta. Atlantic Highlands, NJ: Humanities.

———. 2002. World-system and "trans"-modernity. *Nepantla: Views from the South* 3 (2): 221–246.

———. 2006. *20 proposiciones de política de la liberación*. Colección Letra viva. La Paz, Bolivia: Editorial Tercera Piel.

Edelman, Bernard. 1979. *Ownership of the image: Elements for a Marxist theory of law*. London: Routledge and Kegan Paul.

Edelman, Lauren B. 1992. Legal ambiguity and symbolic structures: Organizational mediation of civil rights law. *American Journal of Sociology* 97:1531–1576.

Edelman, Lauren B., Sally Riggs Fuller, and Iona Mara-Drita. 2001. Diversity rhetoric and the managerialization of law. *American Journal of Sociology* 106 (6): 1589–1641.

EEOC. 2007. 1965–1971: A "toothless tiger" helps shape the law and educate the public. EEOC website. http://www.eeoc.gov/eeoc/history/35th/1965-71/index .html.

Elliott, Anthony. 2001. The reinvention of citizenship. In *Culture and citizenship*, edited by Nick Stevenson. London: Sage.

Enck-Wanzer, Darrel. 2011. Race, coloniality, and geo-body politics: The garden as Latin@ vernacular discourse. *Environmental Communication: A Journal of Nature and Culture* 5 (3): 363–371.

Eule, Julian N. 1990. Promoting speaker diversity: Austin and Metro Broadcasting. *Supreme Court Review* 1990:105–132.

Fagan, A. 2003. Bills link service, citizenship: Aim is to speed process for green-card holders in military. *Washington Times*, April 11, 10.

Félix, Adrián, Carmen González, and Ricardo Ramírez. 2008. Political protest, ethnic media, and Latino naturalization. *American Behavioral Scientist* 58:618–634.

Ferriss, Susan. 2003. War in the Gulf: Mexico misinformation: Seeking visa. *Atlanta Journal-Constitution*, March 29.

Field Research Corporation. 2004. *The Field Poll*. Release 2113, May 25. http://field .com/fieldpollonline/subscribers/RLS2113.pdf.

Flores, Lisa A. 2003. Constructing rhetorical borders: Peons, illegal aliens, and competing narratives of immigration. *Critical Studies in Media Communication* 20 (4): 362–387.

Flores, Richard. 2000. The Alamo: Myth, public history, and the politics of inclusion. *Radical History Review* 77:91–103.

Flores, William V., and Rina Benmayor. 1997. Introduction: Constructing cultural citizenship. In *Latino cultural citizenship: Claiming identity, space, and rights*, edited by William V. Flores and Rina Benmayor. Boston: Beacon.

Ford, Nancy G. 1997. "Mindful of the traditions of his race": Dual identity and foreign-born soldiers in the First World War American army. *Journal of American Ethnic History* 16 (2) :35–59.

Forty megahertz and a mule: Ensuring minority ownership of the electromagnetic spectrum. 1995. *Harvard Law Review* 108 (5): 1145–1162.

Foucault, Michel. 1991. Governmentality. In *The Foucault effect: Studies in governmentality, with two lectures by and an interview with Michel Foucault*, edited by Graham Burchell, Colin Gordon, and Peter Miller. Chicago: University of Chicago Press.

———. 2007. *Security, territory, population: Lectures at the Collège de France, 1977–1978*. Edited by Michel Senellart. Translated by Graham Burchell. New York: Palgrave Macmillan.

Franklin, Benjamin. (1753) 1992. The German language in Pennsylvania. In *Language loyalties: A source book on the official English controversy*, edited by James Crawford, 18–19. Chicago: University of Chicago Press.

Franklin, Sylvia. 2007. Actors do the right thing. *Television Week*, February 5, 19.

Fraser, Nancy. 1990. Rethinking the public sphere: A contribution to the critique of actually existing democracy. *Social Text* 25:56–80.

———. 2007. Transnationalizing the public sphere: On the legitimacy and efficacy of public opinion in a post-Westphalian world. European Institute for Progressive Cultural Policies. http://eipcp.net/transversal/0605/fraser/en.

Fregoso, Rosa Linda. 2003. *MeXicana encounters: The making of social identities on the borderlands*. American crossroads 12. Berkeley: University of California Press.

Gamboa, Suzanne. 2003. House approves measure to provide expedited citizenship for non-citizens in military. Associated Press state and local wire, November 7.

———. 2007. Groups seek shutdown of Texas center for immigrant families. Associated Press Washington Wire, February 22.

García, Juan Ramon. 1980. *Operation Wetback: The mass deportation of Mexican undocumented workers in 1954*. Westport, CT: Greenwood.

Garnham, Nicholas. 1992. The media and the public sphere. In *Habermas and the public sphere*, edited by C. J. Calhoun. Cambridge: MIT Press.

Garvin, Glenn 2006. *Ugly Betty* producer grows into his role. *Miami Herald*, September 28.

Geron, Kim. 2005. *Latino political power*. Latinos, exploring diversity and change. Boulder, CO: Rienner.

Gibson, Campbell, and Kay Jung. 2006. Historical census population statistics on the foreign-born population of the United States: 1850 to 2000. In *Population division*. Washington, DC: U.S. Census Bureau.

Glenn, Evelyn Nakano. 2002. *Unequal freedom: How race and gender shaped American citizenship and labor*. Cambridge: Harvard University Press.

Goldstein, Amy, and Sandra Moreno. 2003. For immigrants, a special sacrifice: War takes its toll on foreign-born in armed forces. *Washington Post*, April 7, 17.

Gómez, Laura E. 2007. *Manifest destinies: The making of the Mexican American race*. New York: NYU Press.

González, Daniel. 2006. Radio host sparks immigrant fervor. *Arizona Republic*, January 17, http://www.azcentral.com/arizonarepublic/news/articles/0117elias17.html.

Gordon, Colin. 1991. Governmental rationality: An introduction. In *The Foucault effect: Studies in governmentality, with two lectures by and an interview with Michel Foucault*, edited by Graham Burchell, Colin Gordon, and Peter Miller. Chicago: University of Chicago Press.

Grasfoguel, Ramón, and Chloe Georas. 2000. "Coloniality of power" and racial dynamics: Notes toward a reinterpretation of Latino Caribbeans in New York City. *Identities* 7 (1): 85–125.

Gratton, Brian, and Myron P. Gutmann. 2000. Hispanics in the United States, 1850–1990. *Historical Methods* 33 (3): 137–153.

Gray, Herman. 2010. Culture, masculinity, and the time after race. In *Toward a sociology of the trace*, edited by Herman Gray and Macarena Gómez-Barris. Minneapolis: University of Minnesota Press.

Gutiérrez, David G. 1999. Migration, emergent ethnicity, and the "third space": The shifting politics of nationalism in greater Mexico. *Journal of American History* 86:481–517.

Gutiérrez, Félix. 1977. Spanish-language media in America: Background, resources, history. *Journalism History* 4 (2): 34–41.

———. 1985. The increase in Spanish-language media in California from 1970 to 1975: An index of the growing use of Spanish. *International Journal of Sociology of Language* 53:115–125.

Gutierrez, Ramon. 2007. Reflecting on 1972. *Aztlán* 32 (1): 183–190.

Habermas, Jürgen. 1989. *The structural transformation of the public sphere: An inquiry into a category of bourgeois society*. Studies in contemporary German social thought. Cambridge: MIT Press.

Halbfinger, David, and Steven Holmes. 2003. A nation at war: The troops: Military mirrors a working class America. *New York Times*, March 30.

Haney-López, Ian. 1996. *White by law: The legal construction of race*. Critical America. New York: NYU Press.

———. 2006. *White by law: the legal construction of race*. Rev. and updated 10th anniversary ed. Critical America. New York: NYU Press.

Harmon, M. D. 2003. The U.S. flags are coming back out—this time to stay? A lot of young folks are teaching us something vital every night on the news. *Portland Press Herald*, April 7, 9.

Harris, Angela P. 2000. Equality trouble: Sameness and difference in twentieth-century race law. *California Law Review* 88 (6): 1923–2015.

Harris, Cheryl I. 1997. Whiteness as property. In *The judicial isolation of the "racially" oppressed*, edited by E. Nathaniel Gates. New York: Garland.

Harrivell, Rick. 2003. Letter to the editor. *Atlanta Journal-Constitution*, April 20.

Harvey, David. 2007. A preference for equality: Seeking the benefits of diversity outside the educational context. *BYU Journal of Public Law* 21 (1): 55–82.

Hattiangadi, Anita U., Gary Lee, and Aline Quester. 2004. *Recruiting Hispanics: The Marine Corps experience, final report*. Alexandria, VA: CNA.

Hendricks, Tyche, and Joe Garofoli. 2006. Spanish-language radio DJs tone down call for action on May 1. *San Francisco Chronicle*, April 26.

Herlinghaus, Hermann. 2009. *Violence without guilt: Ethical narratives from the Global South*. New York: Palgrave Macmillan.

Herman, Edward S., and Noam Chomsky. 1988. *Manufacturing consent: The political economy of the mass media*. New York: Pantheon Books.

Hickman, Christine B. 2003. The devil and the "one-drop" rule. In *Mixed race America and the law: A reader*. edited by Kevin R. Johnson. New York: NYU Press.

Hong, Grace Kyungwon. 2006. *The ruptures of American capital: Women of color feminism and the culture of immigrant labor*. Minneapolis: University of Minnesota Press.

Honig, Bonnie. 2001. *Democracy and the foreigner*. Princeton: Princeton University Press.

Hoover, Donald. 2004. The Virgin Islands under American rule. *Foreign Affairs* 4 (3): 503–506.

Hopewell, John, and Emiliano de Pablos. 2006. U.S. skeins top Spain's wish list. *Variety*, December 15–31, 14.

Horwitz, Robert. 1997. Broadcast reform revisited: Reverend Everett C. Parker and the "Standing" case. *Communications Review* 2 (3): 311–348.

Humphrey, Katie. 2006. Taylor prison will add jobs as it takes in immigration detainees. *Austin American-Statesman*, January 26, B1.

Humphreys, Joseph. 2006. The multicultural economy 2006. *GBEC* (Selig Center for Economic for Economic Growth) 66 (3): 1–15.

Immigration: Let them stay but get tough. 2006. *Time* 167 (15) (April 10): 28–43.

Inda, Jonathan Xavier. 2006. *Targeting immigrants: Government, technology, and ethics*. Malden, MA: Blackwell.

Instituto Cervantes. 2011. Spanish report, June 2010. 1–42.

Isin, Engin F. 2002. *Being political: Genealogies of citizenship*. Minneapolis: University of Minnesota Press.

Isin, Engin F., and Patricia K. Wood. 1999. *Citizenship and identity*. Thousand Oaks, CA: Sage.

Jaafar, Ali. 2007. Imports dominate, but domestics swell. *Variety*, April 16–22, 20.

Jackson State University, Department of History. 2010. *Giving a voice to a shared past: Public education and (de)segregation in Mississippi, 1868–2000*. http://www .jsums.edu/history/Voices/Voices_From_A_Shared_Past_-_Unit_Overview .html.

Jacobson, Robin Dale. 2008. *The new nativism: Proposition 187 and the debate over immigration*. Minneapolis: University of Minnesota Press.

Johnson, Charles. 1999. The study of military recruit attitudes conducive to unit cohesion and survey of military leader opinions on recruit training and gender-related issues. In *Congressional Commission on Military Training on Gender-Related Issues: Final Report: Findings and Recommendations*, vol. 3, *Research Projects, Reports, and Studies*, 5–366. http://www.dtic.mil/dtfs/doc_research/ p18_16v1.pdf.

Johnson, Kevin R., ed. 2003. *Mixed race America and the law: A reader*. Critical America. New York: NYU Press.

———. 2008. A handicapped, not "sleeping," giant: The devastating impact of the initiative process on Latina/o and immigrant communities. *California Law Review* 96:1259–1297.

Juffer, Jane. 2003. In search of the Latino public sphere: Everywhere and nowhere. *Nepantla: Views from the South* 4 (2): 263–268.

Kagan, Elena. 1993. Regulation of hate speech and pornography after *R.A.V. University of Chicago Law Review* 873:873–902.

Kanstroom, Dan. 2007. *Deportation nation: Outsiders in American history*. Cambridge: Harvard University Press.

Kauppi, Niilo. 2003. Bourdieu's political sociology and the politics of European integration. *Theory and Society* 32 (5–6): 775–789.

Keller, Gary D., ed. 1985. *Chicano cinema: Research, reviews, and resources*. Binghamton, NY: Bilingual Review/Press.

———. 1994. *Hispanics and United States film: An overview and handbook*. Tempe, AZ: Bilingual Review/Press.

Kent, Robert B., and Maura E. Huntz. 1996. Spanish-language newspapers in the United States. *Geographical Review* 86 (3): 446–456.

Kong, Deborah. 2003. Casualty lists highlight thousands of non-citizens serving in the military. Associated Press state and local wire, April 3.

Kymlicka, Will. 1995. *Multicultural citizenship: A liberal theory of minority rights*. Oxford political theory. New York: Oxford University Press.

Kymlicka, Will, and Alan Patten, eds. 2003. *Language rights and political theory*. Oxford: Oxford University Press.

Leonard, Jonathan S. 1985. What promises are worth: The impact of affirmative action goals. *Journal of Human Resources* 20:3–20.

Levy, Jacob T. 2000. *The multiculturalism of fear*. Oxford: Oxford University Press.

Leyva Martinez, Ivette. 2003. US Hispanics see army as route to American dream. *Hispanic Market*.

Lin, Nan. 2001. *Social capital: A theory of social structure and action*. Cambridge: Cambridge University Press.

Lipschutz, Ronnie D., and James K. Rowe. 2005. *Globalization, governmentality and global politics: Regulation for the rest of us?* New York: Routledge.

Lopez, David A. 1998. Saving Private Aztlan: Preserving the history of Latino service in wartime. Unpublished paper in author's files.

Lopez Buck, Anna. 2012. Decrease of Latino journalists continues at U.S. dailies. National Association of Hispanic Journalists website, April 4. http://nahj.org/2012/04/04/decrease-of-latino-journalists-continues-at-u-s-dailies/.

Lovato, Roberto. 2005. The war for Latinos. *Nation*, October 3.

Lowe, Lisa. 1996. *Immigrant acts: On Asian American cultural politics*. Durham: Duke University Press.

MacDonald, Victoria-María. 2004. *Latino education in the United States: A narrated history from 1513–2000*. New York: Palgrave Macmillan.

Madison, James. 1997. *James Madison's "Advice to my country."* Edited by David B. Mattern. Charlottesville: University Press of Virginia.

Malavet, Pedro. 2002. Reparations theory and postcolonial Puerto Rico: Some preliminary thoughts. *Berkeley La Raza Law Journal* 13 (2): 387–424.

Mariscal, George. 1999. *Aztlán and Viet Nam: Chicano and Chicana experiences of the war*. Berkeley: University of California Press.

Marshall, T. H. 1973. Citizenship and social class. In *Class, citizenship and social developments*. Westport, CT: Greenwood.

Martinez, George. 1994. Legal indeterminacy, judicial discretion, and the Mexican-American litigation experience, 1930–1980. *UC Davis Law Review* 27:555.

———. 2000. Mexican Americans and whiteness. In *Critical race theory: The cutting edge*, edited by Richard Delgado and Jean Stefancic. Philadelphia: Temple University Press.

Martínez, Guillermo. 2003. Equal rights for Latino heroes: US citizenship benefits should extend to families. *Hispanic*, May, 76.

Martinez, Jacqueline. 2003. On the possibility of the Latino postcolonial intellectual. *Nepantla: Views from the South* 4 (2): 253–256.

Marx, Karl. 1975. On the Jewish question (1843). In *Early writings*. The Marx library. New York: Vintage Books.

Mayer, Vicki. 2003. *Producing dreams, consuming youth: Mexican Americans and mass media*. New Brunswick: Rutgers University Press.

———. 2004. Please pass the pan: Retheorizing the map of panlatinidad in communication research. *Communication Review* 7:113–124.

———. 2011. *Below the line: Producers and production studies in the new television economy*. Durham, NC: Duke University Press.

McCarthy, Thomas. 2004. Kantian constructivism and reconstructivism: Rawls and Habermas in dialogue. *Ethics* 105:44–63.

McChesney, Robert Waterman. 1993. *Telecommunications, mass media, and democracy: The battle for the control of U.S. broadcasting, 1928–1935*. New York: Oxford University Press.

———. 2004. *The problem of the media: U.S. communication politics in the twenty-first century*. New York: Monthly Review Press.

McGee, Michael C. 1975. In search of "the people": A rhetorical alternative. *Quarterly Journal of Speech* 61:235–249.

McMurray, Jeffrey. 2003. Georgia soldier's story inspires law granting posthumous citizenship. Associated Press state and local wire, November 12.

McMurria, John. 2009. Regulation and the law: A critical cultural citizenship approach. In *Media industries: History, theory, and method*, edited by Jennifer Holt and Alisa Perren. Malden, MA: Wiley-Blackwell.

Mendieta, Eduardo. 2003. What can Latinas/os learn from Cornel West? The Latino postcolonial intellectual in the age of the exhaustion of public spheres. *Nepantla: Views from the South* 4 (2): 213–233.

Mezey, Naomi. 2003. Erasure and recognition: The census, race and the national imagination. *Northwestern University Law Review* 97 (4): 1701–1768.

Mignolo, Walter. 2000. *Local histories/global designs: Coloniality, subaltern knowledges, and border thinking*. Princeton: Princeton University Press.

———. 2005. *The idea of Latin America*. Malden, MA: Blackwell.

———. 2007. The rhetoric of modernity, the logic of coloniality and the grammar of de-coloniality. *Cultural Studies* 21 (2–3): 449–514.

Miller, James. 2000. *The passion of Michel Foucault.* Cambridge, MA: Harvard University Press.

Miller, Toby. 1993. *The well-tempered self: Citizenship, culture, and the postmodern subject.* Baltimore: Johns Hopkins University Press.

———. 1998. *Technologies of truth: Cultural citizenship and the popular media.* Minneapolis: University of Minnesota Press.

———. 2007. *Cultural citizenship: Cosmopolitanism, consumerism, and television in a neoliberal age.* Philadelphia: Temple University Press.

Molina-Guzmán, Isabel. 2010. *Dangerous curves: Latina bodies in the media.* Critical cultural communication. New York: NYU Press.

Molina-Guzmán, Isabel, and Angharad N. Valdivia. 2004. Brain, brow, and booty: Latino iconicity in U.S. popular culture. *Communication Review* 7 (2): 205–221.

Moniz, Dave. 1999. Thinning military must learn to recruit in Espanol. *Christian Science Monitor,* August 6.

Montejano, David. 1987. *Anglos and Mexicans in the making of Texas, 1836–1986.* Austin: University of Texas Press.

Morales, Ed. 2006. The media is the *mensaje. Nation,* May 15, 6–8.

Moran, Kristin C. 2007. The growth of Spanish-language and Latino-themed television programs for children in the United States. *Journal of Children and Media* 1 (3): 294–300.

Moskos, Charles. 2002. Reviving the citizen-soldier. *Public Interest* 147 (Spring): 76–86.

Moya, Paula M. L. 2003. With us or without us: The development of a Latino public sphere. *Nepantla: Views from the South* 4 (2): 245–252.

Napoli, Philip. 2001. *Foundations of communications policy: Principles and process in the regulation of electronic media.* Cresskill, NY: Hampton.

———. 2005. Audience measurement and media policy: Audience economics, the diversity principle, and the local people meter. *Communication Law and Policy* 10 (4) (Autumn): 349–382.

Navarrete, Ruben. 2009. Latinos are assimilating in the USA. CNNPolitics.com, October 16. http://www.cnn.com/2009/POLITICS/10/15/navarrette.latino.in.america/index.html#cnnSTCText.

Navarro, Armando. 2005. *Mexicano political experience in occupied Aztlán: Struggles and change.* Walnut Creek, CA: AltaMira.

———. 2009. *The immigration crisis: Nativism, armed vigilantism, and the rise of a countervailing movement.* Lanham, MD: AltaMira.

Negrón-Muntaner, Frances. 2002. Barbie's hair: Selling out Puerto Rican identity in the global market. In *Latino popular culture,* edited by Michelle Habell-Pallán and Mary Romero. New York: NYU Press.

Nelson, Dana D. 1998. *National manhood: Capitalist citizenship and the imagined fraternity of white men.* Durham: Duke University Press.

Ness, Immanuel. 2007. Forging a migration policy for capital: Labor shortages and guest workers. *New Political Science* 29 (4): 429–452.

Ngai, Mae M. 2004. *Impossible subjects: Illegal aliens and the making of modern America*. Princeton: Princeton University Press.

Nieto-Phillips, John. 1999. Citizenship and empire: Race, language, and self-government in New Mexico and Puerto Rico, 1898–1917. *Centro Journal* 11 (1): 51–74.

Noriega, Chon A., ed. 1992. *Chicanos and film: Essays on Chicano representation and resistance*. New York: Garland.

———. 2000. *Shot in America: Television, the state, and the rise of Chicano cinema*. Minneapolis: University of Minnesota Press.

Nugent, Christopher. 2006. Whose children are these? Towards ensuring the best interests and empowerment of unaccompanied alien children. *Public Interest Law Journal* 15:219–235.

Nuñez, Luis V. 2006. *Spanish language media after the Univision-Hispanic Broadcasting*. New York: Novinka Books.

Nussbaum, Martha Craven. 1997. *Cultivating humanity: A classical defense of reform in liberal education*. Cambridge: Harvard University Press.

Oboler, Suzanne. 2006. *Latinos and citizenship: The dilemma of belonging*. New York: Palgrave Macmillan.

O'Grady, Candice. 2009. Hate speech, media activism and the First Amendment: Putting a spotlight on dehumanizing language. *FAIR: Fairness & Accuracy in Reporting*, May. http://www.fair.org/index.php?page=3776.

Olivas, Michael A. 2006. *"Colored men" and "hombres aquí": Hernández v. Texas and the emergence of Mexican-American lawyering*. Houston: Arte Público.

Oliver, Melvin L., and Thomas M. Shapiro. 2006. *Black wealth, white wealth: A new perspective on racial inequality*. 10th anniversary ed. New York: Routledge.

Omi, Michael, and Howard Winant. 1986. *Racial formation in the United States: From the 1960s to the 1980s*. New York: Routledge and Kegan Paul.

———. 1994. *Racial formation in the United States: From the 1960s to the 1990s*. 2d ed. New York: Routledge.

Ono, Kent A., and John M. Sloop. 2002. *Shifting borders: Rhetoric, immigration, and California's Proposition 187*. Philadelphia: Temple University Press.

Ouellette, Laurie, and James Hay. 2008. *Better living through reality TV: Television and post-welfare citizenship*. Malden, MA: Blackwell.

Palaima, Thomas. 2004. Military recruiters know their targets well. *Austin American-Statesman*, December 15.

Panganiban, Rik. 2007. Grantee profile: Study explores radio as a mobilization tool in Latino communities. Social Science Research Council.

Papper, Bob. 2003. Women and minorities: One step forward and two steps back. *Communicator*, July–August, 20–25.

Patten, Alan, and Will Kymlicka. 2003. Introduction: Language rights and political theory: Context, issues, and approaches. In *Language rights and political theory*, edited by Will Kymlicka and Alan Patten. Oxford: Oxford University Press.

Pérez, Gina M. 2004. *The near northwest side story: Migration, displacement, and Puerto Rican families*. Berkeley: University of California Press.

Perlman, Allison. 2007. Feminists in the wasteland: The National Organization for Women and television reform. *Feminist Media Studies* 7 (4): 413–431.

Petersen, Jennifer. 2011. *Murder, the media, and the politics of public feelings: Remembering Matthew Shepard and James Byrd Jr*. Bloomington: Indiana University Press.

Peterson, Richard H. 1975. *Manifest destiny in the mines: A cultural interpretation of anti-Mexican nativism in California, 1848–1853*. San Francisco: R and E Research.

Pitt, Leonard. 1966. *The decline of the Californios: A social history of the Spanish-speaking Californians, 1846–1890*. Berkeley: University of California Press.

Potter, Deborah. 2004. The end of sweeps? *American Journalism Review* 26 (2): 64.

Power in numbers: Hispanics, long under-represented as voters, are becoming political kingmakers. 2010. *Economist*, January 7. http://www.economist.com/node/15213228.

Preston, Julia. 2007. In increments, Senate revisits immigration bill. *New York Times*, August 3, A1.

Quijano, Anibal. 2000. Coloniality of power, Eurocentrism, and Latin America. *Nepantla: Views from the South* 1 (3): 533–580.

———. 2007. Coloniality and modernity/rationality. *Cultural Studies* 21 (2–3): 168–178.

Quijano, Anibal, and Immanuel Wallerstein. 1992. Americanity as a concept, or the Americas in the modern world-system. *International Social Science Journal* 134: 549–557.

Ramírez Berg, Charles. 2002. *Latino images in film stereotypes, subversion, resistance*. Austin: University of Texas Press.

Ramirez Broyles, Vernardette. 2003. Grateful nation pays off debt to immigrant. *Atlanta Journal-Constitution*, May 18, 13A.

Ramos, George. 1986. Owners seeking to settle Spanish TV outlets fight. *Los Angeles Times*, February 28. http://articles.latimes.com/1986-02-28/local/me-12833_1_spanish-international-network.

Rana, Aziz. 2010. *The two faces of American freedom*. Cambridge: Harvard University Press.

Rantanen, Terhi. 2005. *The media and globalization*. London: Sage.

Remarks by Secretary of Homeland Security Michael Chertoff, ICE Acting Director of Detention and Removal John Torres and CBP Border Patrol Chief David Aguilar on Secure Border Initiative. 2006. States News Service, August 23.

Rivero, Yeidy. 2003. The performance and reception of televisual "ugliness" in *Yo Soy Betty la Fea*. *Feminist Media Studies* 3 (1): 65–81.

———. 2005. *Tuning out blackness: Race and nation in the history of Puerto Rican television*. Durham: Duke University Press.

Rocco, Raymond. 2002. Transforming citizenship: Membership, strategies of containment, and the public sphere in Latino communities. *Latino Studies* 2:4–25.

Rodriguez, América. 1999. *Making Latino news: Race, language, class.* Thousand Oaks, CA: Sage.

Rodríguez, Ana Patricia. 2002. Encrucijadas: Rubén Blades at the transnational crossroads. In *Latino popular culture*, edited by Michelle Habell-Pallán and Mary Romero. New York: NYU Press.

Rodríguez, Clara E. 1997. *Latin looks: Images of Latinas and Latinos in the U.S. media.* Boulder, CO: Westview.

———. 2004. *Heroes, lovers, and others: The story of Latinos in Hollywood.* Washington, DC: Smithsonian Books, 2004.

Rodríguez, Ileana. 2009. *Liberalism at its limits: Crime and terror in the Latin American cultural text.* Illuminations—cultural formations of the Americas. Pittsburgh: University of Pittsburgh Press.

Rodriguez, Richard. 2002. *Brown: The last discovery of America.* New York: Viking.

Roediger, David R. 2007. *The wages of whiteness: Race and the making of the American working class.* New York: Verso.

Román, Ediberto. 2006. *The other American colonies: An international and constitutional law examination of the United States' nineteenth and twentieth century island conquests.* Durham, NC: Carolina Academic Press.

Romero, Mary, and Michelle Habell-Pallán. 2002. Introduction to *Latino popular culture*, edited by Michelle Habell-Pallán and Mary Romero. New York: NYU Press.

Roque Ramirez, Horacio. 2008. Memory and mourning: Living oral history with queer Latino and Latinas in San Francisco. In *Oral history and public memories*, edited by Paula Hamilton and Linda Shopes. Philadelphia: Temple University Press.

Rose, Ian M. 1995. Barring foreigners from our airwaves: An anachronistic pothole on the global information highway. *Columbia Law Review* 95 (5) (June): 1188–1231.

Rose, Nikolas S. 1999. *Powers of freedom: Reframing political thought.* Cambridge: Cambridge University Press.

Rowland, Willard D. 1997. The meaning of "the public interest" in communications policy, part I: Its origins in state and federal regulation. *Communication Law and Policy* 2:309–328.

Ruano, Edna. 2007. Advocating change: Leadership landing presented by Southwestern Airlines. *Latino Leaders* 8 (5): 52–54.

Rubio-Marín, Ruth. 2003. Language rights: Exploring the competing rationales. In *Language rights and political theory*, edited by Will Kymlicka and Alan Patten. New York: Oxford University Press.

Ruskola, Teemy. 2005. Canton is not Boston: The invention of American imperial sovereignty. *American Quarterly* 57 (3): 859–889.

Sackett, Paul R., and Anne S. Mavor. 2004. *Evaluating military advertising and recruiting: Theory and methodology.* Washington, DC: National Academies Press.

Sanchez, George J. 1993. *Becoming Mexican American: Ethnicity, culture, and identity in Chicano Los Angeles, 1900–1945.* New York: Oxford University Press.

Sandoval, Catherine J. K. 2005–2006. Antitrust law on the borderland of language and market definition: Is there a separate Spanish-language radio market? A case study of the merger of Univision and Hispanic Broadcasting Corporation. *University of San Francisco Law Review* 40:381–450.

Santa Ana, Otto. 2002. *Brown tide rising: Metaphors of Latinos in contemporary American public discourse.* Austin: University of Texas Press.

Santos, Fernanda. 2003. Slain marine hero finally named U.S. citizen. *New York Daily News,* July 17, 16.

Savage, David G. 2009. Supreme Court rules against government in immigration identity-theft case. *Los Angeles Times,* May 5.

Schmidt Camacho, Alicia R. 2008. *Migrant imaginaries: Latino cultural politics in the U.S.-Mexico borderlands.* Nation of newcomers. New York: NYU Press.

Schuck, Peter H. 1998. *Citizens, strangers, and in-betweens: Essays on immigration and citizenship.* New perspectives on law, culture, and society. Boulder, CO: Westview.

Schudson, Michael. 2002. The news media as political institutions. *Annual Review of Political Sciences* 5:249–269.

Seeley, John. 2004. Operation opt out: As military recruiters work the high schools, teachers and students urge a reality check. *L.A. City Beat,* October 24.

Shklar, Judith N. 1991. *American citizenship: The quest for inclusion.* The Tanner lectures on human values. Cambridge: Harvard University Press.

Shore, Elena. 2006. What is the role of Hispanic media in immigrant activism? *Social Policy* 36:8–9.

Simone, Maria, and Jan Fernback. 2006. Invisible hands or public spheres? Theoretical foundations for U.S. broadcast policy. *Communication Law and Policy* 11:287–313.

Smith, Anthony. 1983. Nationalism and social theory. *British Journal of Sociology* 34:19–38.

Smith, Paul. 1988. *Discerning the subject.* Minneapolis: University of Minnesota Press.

Smith, Rogers M. 1997. *Civic ideals: Conflicting visions of citizenship in U.S. history.* New Haven: Yale University Press.

Snyder, Claire. 2003. The citizen-soldier tradition and gender integration of the U.S. military. *Armed Forces and Society* 29 (2): 185–205.

Soltero, Carlos R. 2006. *Latinos and American law: Landmark Supreme Court cases.* Austin: University of Texas Press.

Starr, Paul. 2004. *The creation of the media: Political origins of modern communications.* New York: Basic Books.

Stevenson, Nick. 2001. Culture and citizenship: An introduction. In *Culture and Citizenship*, edited by Nick Stevenson. Thousand Oaks, CA: Sage.

Stockman, Farah. 2003. They leave lost hopes, but a duty fulfilled. *Boston Globe*, April 6, A1

Stone, Christopher D. 1975. *Where the law ends: The social control of corporate behavior*. New York: Harper and Row.

Streeter, Thomas. 1996. *Selling the air: A critique of the policy of commercial broadcasting in the United States*. Chicago: University of Chicago Press.

Subervi-Vélez, Federico A. 2005. *Network brownout report 2005: The portrayal of Latinos and Latino issues on network television news, 2004, with a retrospect to 1995: Quantitative and qualitative analysis of the coverage*. Austin, TX: NAHJ.

———, ed. 2008. *The mass media and Latino politics: Studies of U.S. media content, campaign strategies and survey research, 1984–2004*. LEA's communication series. New York: Routledge.

Subervi-Vélez, Federico A., Michael Salwen, Jennie Haulser, and Astrid Romero. 1988. The mass media and Hispanic politics during the 1988 presidential primaries. Paper presented at the Sixth Annual Intercultural Conference on Latin America and the Caribbean, Miami, 1989.

Talbot, Margaret. 2008. The lost children: What do tougher detention policies mean for illegal immigrant families? *New Yorker*, March 3.

Taylor, Paul, and Richard Fry. 2007. *Hispanics and the 2008 election: A swing vote?* Washington, DC: Pew Hispanic Center.

Tienda, Marta. 2002. Demography and the social contract. *Demography* 39 (4): 587–616.

Toledo, Charo. 2007. Alphabet spells hope for diverse America. *Daily Variety*, July 27, A1.

United States Commission on Civil Rights. 1977. *Window dressing on the set: Women and minorities in television*. Washington, DC: United States Commission on Civil Rights.

U.S. Senate. 2012. Minorities in the Senate. http://www.senate.gov/reference/reference_index_subjects/Minorities_vrd.htm.

Valdivia, Angharad N. 2000. *A Latina in the land of Hollywood and other essays on media culture*. Tucson: University of Arizona Press.

———. 2008. Transnational media, hybrid bodies and culture: Borders and the Latina transnation. Paper presented at the National Communication Association Conference, San Diego.

———. 2010. *Latina/os and the media*. Media and minorities. Cambridge, UK: Polity.

Vanden Heuvel, Katrina. 2006. Talk about a smear merchant! Katrina Vanden Heuvel's blog, *Nation*, April 3. http://www.thenation.com/blog/talk-about-smear-merchant.

Van Jacob, Scott, and Robin Vose. 2010. A report on Catalan language publishing. *Publishing Research Quarterly* 26 (2): 129–143.

van Zoonen, Liesbet. 2005. *Entertaining the citizen: When politics and popular culture converge.* Lanham, MD: Rowman and Littlefield.

Viego, Antonio. 2007. *Dead subjects: Toward a politics of loss in Latino studies.* Durham: Duke University Press.

Waligora-Davis, Nicole. 2011. *Sanctuary: African Americans and empire.* New York: Oxford University Press.

Wallerstein, Immanuel. 1974. The rise and future demise of the world capitalist system: Concepts for comparative analysis. *Comparative Studies in Society and History* 16 (4): 387–415.

Walzer, Michael. 1983. *Spheres of justice: A defense of pluralism and equality.* New York: Basic Books.

———. 1992. *What it means to be an American.* New York: Marsilio.

War's bitter taste: San Diego's ties to military evident in Iraq. 2003. *San Diego Union-Tribune*, March 27, B14.

Washington Heights family mourns Marine. 2003. Associated Press, April 14.

Weinberg, Jonathan. 1993. Broadcasting and speech. *California Law Review* 81 (5): 1101–1206.

White, Mimi. 1991. What's the difference? Frank's place in television. *Wide Angle* 13 (3–4): 82–93.

Whitney, Daisy. 2007. ABC-Cox deal paves way for series on VOD: Hits to be available on-demand in test, but no fast-forwarding allowed. *Television Week*, May 14, 26.

Wilkinson, Kent. 2009. Spanish language media in the United States. In *The Handbook of Spanish language media*, edited by Alan B. Albarran. New York: Routledge.

Williams, Patricia J. 1991. *The alchemy of race and rights.* Cambridge: Harvard University Press.

Williams, Raymond. 1977. *Marxism and literature.* Marxist introductions. Oxford: Oxford University Press.

Wilson, Carter A. 1996. *Racism: From slavery to advanced capitalism.* Thousand Oaks, CA: Sage.

Wilson, Clint, and Félix Gutiérrez 1995. *Race, multiculturalism and the media: From mass to class communication.* London: Sage.

Wimmer, Andreas, and Nina Glick Schiller. 2002. Methodological nationalism and beyond: Nation-state building, migration and the social sciences. *Global Networks* 2 (4): 301–334.

Winant, Howard. 2004. *The new politics of race: Globalism, difference, justice.* Minneapolis: University of Minnesota Press.

Women's Commission for Refugee Women and Children, Lutheran Immigration and Refugee Service. 2007. *Locking up family values: The detention of immigrant families.* New York: Lutheran Immigration and Refugee Service.

Zinn, Howard. 2003. *A people's history of the United States, 1492–present.* New York: Perennial Classics.

Zolberg, Aristide R. 2006. *A nation by design: Immigration policy in the fashioning of America*. New York: Russell Sage Foundation.

Zook, Kristal B. 2003. Neglecting women of color in combat. *San Diego Union-Tribune*, July 3.

Zuckert, Michael P. 1994. *Natural rights and the new republicanism*. Princeton: Princeton University Press.

Hector Amaya is an associate professor of media studies at the University of Virginia who specializes in North American transnationalism, including Mexico, Cuba, and the United States. He writes on the cultural production of political identities and the complex manner in which cultural flows and immigration are transforming the nation-state.